DETECTIVE FICTION AND LITERATURE

Also by Martin Priestman

COWPER'S *TASK*: Structure and Influence
PEASANTS AND COUNTRYMEN IN LITERATURE (*editor with
Kathleen Parkinson*)

Detective Fiction and Literature

The Figure on the Carpet

MARTIN PRIESTMAN

Senior Lecturer in English
Roehampton Institute of Higher Education

St. Martin's Press   New York

© Martin Priestman 1991

First published in the United States of America in 1991

Printed in Great Britain

ISBN 0–312–05306–1

Library of Congress Cataloging-in-Publication Data
Priestman, Martin, 1949–
    Detective fiction and literature: the figure on the carpet /
    Martin Priestman.
          p.   cm.
    Includes bibliographical references and index.
    ISBN 0 – 312 – 05306 – 1
    1. Detective and mystery stories — History and criticism. 2. Crime
in literature. I. Title.
PN3448.D4P75 1990
809.3′872—dc20
                                                        90–42639
                                                            CIP

For Ben and Anna

Contents

Preface

To look at a star by glances – to view it in a sidelong way . . . – is to have the best appreciation of its lustre. . . . By undue profundity we perplex and enfeeble thought; and it is possible to make even Venus herself vanish from the firmament by a scrutiny too sustained, too concentrated, or too direct.

Edgar Allan Poe, 'The Murders in the Rue Morgue'

Such a perception, it seems to me, is in its very structure dependent on chance and anonymity, on the vague glance in passing, as from the windows of a bus, when the mind is intent on some more immediate preoccupation: its very essence is to be inessential.

F. R. Jameson, 'On Raymond Chandler'[1]

Criticism of detective fiction seems to obey the law which these two quotations identify as operating within it: that the sidelong glance often reveals more than the 'scrutiny too sustained, too concentrated, or too direct'. Scrupulous studies of the genre, in terms of its historical development, its inalienable rules, or even of the reasons for its popularity, can result in the kind of snow-blindness that its heroes decry in the police. On the other hand, it is often when it is being made use of in relation to other kinds of evidence, in other kinds of quest, that its importance emerges most distinctively.

Much recent serious study of the genre assumes the relevance of three major types of adjacent inquiry: the Marxist, the Freudian and the narratological. The Marxist inquiry perhaps began, before the genre had emerged exactly as such, with Marx's own scrutiny of the noble redeemer-hero of Eugène Sue's *The Mysteries of Paris*. Bertolt Brecht, Walter Benjamin and Michel Foucault continued to find the detective genre a vital source of evidence about social constructions, as, in their less rigorous way, did such thirties English writers as W. H. Auden, C. Day Lewis and George Orwell. Ernest Mandel's *Delightful Murder* has recently continued the more card-carrying tradition.[2]

Numerous critics, from Dorothy L. Sayers to Geoffrey Hartman, have related the apparently fixed 'rules' of the detective form to those laid down by Aristotle. The structuralist Roman Jakobson's isolation of metonymy as a fictional method has made the form much easier to discuss, and Tsvetan Todorov's extension of Aristotle's story-plot distinction helps further to explain its split-level construction. The genre offers itself very effectively to attempts to deconstruct narrative more generally, Roland Barthes often turning to it for examples of the 'hermeneutic code', and Pierre Macherey using it to exemplify the self-abolishing tendency in all fiction.

Psychoanalytic approaches can be traced right back to Freud's description of the Oedipal 'family romance', to be shortly followed by Marie Bonaparte's analysis of Poe's Dupin stories. Geraldine Pederson-Krag, Charles Rycroft and Albert D. Hutter have related the form persuasively to the 'primal scene', while Jacques Lacan's 'Seminar on "The Purloined Letter"' and Jacques Derrida's riposte 'The Purveyor of the Truth' have turned Poe's story into a *locus classicus* of debates about the Freudian deconstruction of literature.

Typically, in these cases, the detective text is used as a clue, as readily grasped evidence of what is going on rather less clearly elsewhere. Paradoxically, this often makes for more precision about specific works than in the kind of study where the ground-rules are seen as given and the differences only as revealing local irregularities of terrain. A growing awareness of the benefits of such sidelong glances has recently been reflected in a number of full-length studies which set their parameters wider than received common sense about the genre's entertainment function might suggest.

Julian Symons's indispensable history, *Bloody Murder* (1972, revised 1985), also provides a useful introduction, at least up to a certain 'common sense' point, to the anglicised combination of social commentary, psychology and myth-criticism pioneered by his own thirties generation. John G. Cawelti's *Adventure, Mystery and Romance* (1976) situates the genre within a wider theory of popular formulae which permits scope for detailed analysis of specific texts from a range of thought-provoking angles. Dennis Porter's *The Pursuit of Crime* (1981) virtually exhausts the repertoire of recent literary theory, though this is then applied to a somewhat limited range of examples. Perhaps the best recent book, Stephen Knight's *Form and Ideology in Crime Fiction* (1980), sustains an enormously flexible political understanding of the form through a deceptively conventional-seeming series of close readings of specific authors. As well as such full-length studies there are now a number of critical anthologies, of which Glenn W. Most and William W. Stowe's *The Poetics of Murder* (1983) offers the most impressive array of current theoretical approaches.

While this book has some aims in common with all those just mentioned, it deals particularly with the relationship between detective fiction and established literature. At the outset, I should perhaps acknowledge that my main title embodies a deliberate confusion: in what sense and to what extent is detective fiction *not* literature? Since Raymond Williams pointed out that the notion of a 'literature' elevated above other kinds of imaginative and other writing was a construct born out of the Industrial Revolution alongside Romanticism (and, indeed, detective fiction), the word itself has become hard to use without visible or invisible inverted commas.[3] None the less, the normal assumption that detective fiction and literature *are* distinct is a revealing fact about our reading habits, and ultimately our society, which this book tries to explore by pushing to its limits. The much-enjoyed *différence* between the two literary realms is itself a structural fact of great importance to both: it is in repeatedly crossing this boundary while remaining aware of it that I hope this book achieves its chief 'sidelong' insights.

This is partly done through direct comparison of detective and literary texts, partly through a broader exploration of themes and contexts common to both, but perhaps chiefly through close discussion of detective works 'as if' they were literary ones. This last practice deliberately aims to bridge the gap between different established ways of talking about the two types of text: hence, for example, it routinely demotes the 'character' of the detective and his adherence to a prescribed procedure from their usual centre-stage position, and unapologetically gives away the endings of stories when this is necessary for an account of their overall construction. Equally routinely, it assumes that all texts *can* be discussed in equivalent detail, whatever assessment of ultimate quality may be being implied: this point seems well worth insisting on given a traditionally implicit critical rhetoric which equates discussability with 'literary' quality.

None of this is intended as a form of special pleading, or a way of continuously implying that *The Murder of Roger Ackroyd* is really 'as good as' *Oedipus the King*. Other books deal with that kind of thing, and for speed this one also sometimes voices its own brief assessments, but this isn't the point of the exercise. The argument is more simply that the various social and other issues dealt with by detective fiction are not wholly alien to those raised in other books, and that sometimes the 'formulae' by which detective fiction can so easily be defined have a wider relevance (as, of course, various 'literary' formulae have for detective fiction).

Though loosely chronological, this is not a comprehensive history: while linked, the chapters are best seen as separate essays, each coming at different material from a slightly different angle. The adoption of such a variety of angles seemed necessary in order to bring out something of the range of what detective fiction can tell us about the world we live in, about other fiction, and about ourselves. Hence the first two chapters aim to introduce some of the social, structural and psychological implications of the form, as a preliminary to the more chronological account which follows. Chapter 1 conducts a rapid survey of the genre's approach to crime as a source of scandal and shock, relating this to changing social conditions and to some other literature, while Chapter 2 looks closely at two texts widely separated in time – *Oedipus the King* and *The Moonstone* – to explore the structural and psychological issues mentioned earlier in this preface. The next two chapters deal with the seminal early detective writers Edgar Allan Poe and Emile Gaboriau, but pay particularly close attention to their respective uses of the short story and melodramatic novel forms. The next four chapters bunch round the years 1890–1914, the 'age of Holmes' but also of modernism. Chapter 5 explores the social content of the Sherlock Holmes stories and goes on to examine Arthur Conan Doyle's crucial creation of the 'series', while Chapter 6 considers the Holmes myth and then looks at the late novel *The Valley of Fear* as a significant link with subsequent English and American forms of detective writing. Chapter 7 argues that in the hands of four of Doyle's contemporaries detective fiction played a significant part in intellectual and social debate; while Chapter 8 shows how and perhaps why some important experiments of early modernism have a particularly significant relationship with the form. In a briefer treatment of the period after 1918, Chapter 9 deals with the English 'Golden Age' manner chiefly in the shapes of Agatha Christie and P. D. James, while Chapter 10 looks briefly at Raymond Chandler's handling of the American hardboiled form, before turning attention to some of the uses made of it in a range of recent British writing.

The book's subtitle, 'The Figure on the Carpet', is intended to apply to the content in several senses as a kind of mnemonic for the various ways in which detective fiction differs from respectable literature while also closely resembling it.

1

Detective Fiction and Scandal

The subtitle of this book has several purposes, but the first is to evoke a contrast between the world of high literature, as exemplified by Henry James's short story 'The Figure in the Carpet', and a genre bent on disfiguring the literary drawing-room with corpses. This first chapter, accordingly, will deal with detective fiction as a medium of scandal and shock, comparing its methods with the handling of bloody or shocking crime in other kinds of writing.

In aiming to cover such a large field comparatively rapidly, this chapter may not be the easiest introduction to the detective genre for readers completely unfamiliar with it. Detective texts that will be returned to more fully later on are discussed in the same breath as 'literary' texts which are dealt with equally quickly but once and for all, and such readers may prefer to come back to this chapter armed with the information more gradually provided in subsequent ones. My justification for introducing this material in this way this early is a sense of the need to situate the detective form as a whole within the kind of broad socio-literary context which can easily be overlooked once the attention has been diverted to the more formal and psychological issues the genre also raises, and which begin to be dealt with in the chapter after this. There is perhaps something of a chicken-and-egg syndrome in any such attempt to contextualise the facts before the facts themselves have been fully explored: my aim here is simply to introduce some of the large-scale implications of a form which in some sense claims to 'take on' the very large-scale issue of persistent criminality within a social formation which has been by and large concerned to think well of itself.

The element of scandal in detective fiction is not unique to it. On one hand, the form is only one branch of a much wider popular literature of sensation, and on the other the exposure of the running scores of the body politic has always been a major theme of 'serious' literature. The distinction between the two is worth stressing from the start: *initially*, at least, the two 'scandals' which the genre confronts seem to come from the bottom and from the top of society. First, there is the standing scandal of endemic crime among the lower classes, and the sense of a need to recruit literature in the battle against it; secondly, there is the more normal sense of 'scandal' concerning the illicit doings of the mighty.

Sensational descriptions of the activities of lower-class criminals are coterminous with popular literature itself. Cony-catching pamphlets, broadside ballads, gallows confessions and publications based on them such as *The Newgate Calendar* (1773 and after) establish a continuous line, with important changes in medium and emphasis, from the sixteenth century to contemporary news reportage. This early material has been well covered in many studies of detective writing (especially those by Stephen Knight, Dennis Porter and Ian Ousby), and at a deeper socio-historical level Michel Foucault's *Discipline and Punish* surveys the relations between crime as a mass-cultural phenomenon before and during the dawn of the 'detective' era.[1] To generalise, before the nineteenth century, the common criminal was him- or herself the 'hero' of such narratives, so that the radical innovation of detective fiction (in turn dependent on large changes in policing methods) was chiefly in shifting the focus further *away* from the direct contemplation of the commonest forms of crime:

> It was not only the broadsheets that disappeared with the birth of a literature of crime; the glory of the rustic malefactor and his sombre transformation into a hero went with them. The man of the people was now too simple to be the protagonist of subtle truths. In this genre, there were no more popular heroes or great executions; the criminal was wicked, of course, but he was also intelligent; and although he was punished, he did not have to suffer. The literature of crime transposes to another social class the spectacle that had surrounded the criminal. Meanwhile the newspapers took over the task of recounting the grey, unheroic details of everyday crime and punishment. The split was complete; the people was robbed of its old pride in its crimes; the great murders had become the quiet game of the well-behaved.   (Foucault, pp. 68–9)

Though I shall refer at times to these arguments, I make no claim in this chapter to cover the social background out of which detective writing emerged, or to develop any systematic history of its early stages: for this, readers should refer to the excellent accounts just mentioned. Instead, I shall start by looking briefly at a few moments where we can discern the seeds of the forthcoming genre in a shifting *rapprochement* between 'literature' and the 'popular culture' of crime, and then consider how the two elements coexist in some early examples of detective fiction itself. Though the embourgeoisement of crime stressed by Foucault will be taken up later, my initial emphasis will be on the literary treatment of the crimes of the common people. Three works often loosely recognised as having something to do with the genre's prehistory are by 'serious' writers but partake of some of the qualities of popular reportage. Defoe's *Moll Flanders* (1722), Fielding's *Jonathan Wild* (1743) and De Quincey's essay 'Murder Considered as One of the Fine Arts' (1827) all find interestingly different ways of presenting common crime to the reader, before the emergence of detective writing. I would suggest that in the way the narrative is conveyed all these works imply a growing demand for something like a detective function, in life but also in literature.

Moll Flanders's exploits as a thief and adventuress are described in the sustained pretence that she is the book's real author: Daniel Defoe has simply edited one more evangelical confession of a reformed sinner. While this factual, 'hands-off' approach produces one of the best accounts ever written of the *reasons* for criminality, it also raises problems which Defoe has to hedge over carefully in his introduction and which, arguably, the existence of the later detective mode would have prevented from arising in the first place. The non-judgemental description of Moll's criminal methods has to be justified in terms of social usefulness, and this is done by insisting that 'she' only describes them so we can be on our guard against them. In a simple and direct way, then, we are adjured as property-owning readers to become our own detectives in real life, but no convenient way has yet been found for us to test our mettle within the linear narrative of the book itself.

Henry Fielding's *Jonathan Wild*, by contrast, surrounds the exploits of a monstrous real-life criminal with an immensely deliberate satirical style whereby we *are* perpetually being put on our mettle, not against particular techniques, but against being taken in by a whole cultural tradition which blurs the distinction between criminals and heroes. If Fielding is concerned to turn his readers into *literary* detectives (and this includes their ability to 'detect' the figure of the corrupt Whig prime minister Walpole lurking within that of the gangster Wild), this can also be seen as part of a wider campaign on his part to rouse the London middle class against crime in all its branches: significantly, Fielding was instrumental with his brother John in setting up the Bow Street Runners, the ancestors of the modern Metropolitan Police. A very active concern with detection can then be seen as already presupposed in this particular use of the stylistic traps of the mock-heroic literary technique.[2]

Thomas De Quincey's 'Murder Considered as one of the Fine Arts' represents a further step in the involvement of 'literature' with the scandal of crime. The essay itself is a comical squib against the all-aestheticising tendencies of fellow Romantic writers such as Coleridge, prophetically showing how easy it would be to distance the horror of murder by judging it according to the laws of aesthetic taste. But just as interesting is the later and much more serious 'Postscript' (1854), where De Quincey attempts to 'take on' a new style of journalistic realism by pushing it to the limit in his own bloodcurdling history of Williams, the 'Ratcliffe Highway' mass-murderer. Abandoning the tongue-in-cheek tone of the essay proper, this account seems urgently to put onto us as readers the question of what we actually do, in our world of heightened sensibilities, with the horrified feelings aroused by such accounts. The drugged intensifications of Romanticism have constituted a kind of technological quantum leap in descriptive power, and De Quincey seems to watch himself putting it to use with a mounting Frankensteinian horror. To this extent he raises somewhat similar questions to Truman Capote's non-fiction novel *In Cold Blood*, where similar ambivalent feelings about 'new' literary-journalistic methods are tested against a family-slaying very like those commit-ted by Williams. Capote, however, makes far more use of reassuring detective-fictional techniques in presenting both the police hunt and his own amassing of evidence as a kind of buffer for his reader's feelings.[3]

None of these texts is a straightforward example of popular crime literature; but they do all show various ways of allowing that popular literature to impinge on 'high' literature (though the distinction is itself somewhat shaky in the case of Defoe). In all three cases there is a sense of scandal, not just over the endemic existence of crime but also over the techniques available for reporting it, to which the writers respond in different ways but with growing concern. The leap from such concern to the creation of detective fiction is still considerable but, if we now turn to the three 'Dupin' stories in which Edgar Allan Poe created the genre proper in the 1840s, we can see how some of the same sense of scandal, over the reportage as well as the crime, is confronted and summarily dealt with.

The actual 'Murders in the Rue Morgue' are easily forgotten in the excitement of Dupin's solution of them. They are, however, extremely grisly: Mlle L'Espanaye has been throttled and thrust up the chimney feet first, while her mother has been thrown out of the window with her head so nearly severed that it falls away when the body is lifted. The mangling of the corpses is made worse, if anything, by the threadbare banality of the petty-bourgeois setting. Though no one could claim the story was realistic, many techniques of realism are very rapidly deployed to make this setting as convincing as possible. But this is done by totally relegating the dreariness of the women's lives and the squalid horror of their deaths (both underlined by the name of the street) to the newspaper reports: despite much amusing picking-over of the corpses, neither the detective Dupin nor the narrator seriously registers the sense of outrage which has instead been conveyed to us through a convincing facsimile of popular reportage. The story seems to offer a way of bringing our responses under a new kind of automatic control, through a particularly well-planned alternation of narrative devices.

The less successful 'Mystery of Marie Rogêt' is interesting for pushing similar techniques to the furthest possible extreme, so that Dupin's inconclusive deductions constitute no more than an armchair gloss on a series of real newspaper reports about what appears to be an ugly sex-murder by a brutal gang. The story simply transposes the New York Mary Rogers case to Paris, but in so doing raises some interesting questions about the relations between popular reportage and the emergent detective genre. In discussing this story, Dennis Porter points out that the reportage of the Rogers case was instrumental in the establishment of New York's first 'Day and Night Police' in 1844, and that the press's new power in such matters was part of a recent decisive 'migration of tales of crime from ballad and broadsheet to newspaper *faits divers*' (Porter, p. 152). Seeing this migration as a 'phenomenon of the new industrial technology and the new wealth', Porter demonstrates a rising constellation of forces including systematic policing, a new awareness of New York as a great city on a par with London or Paris, and the press's assumption of a new responsibility to direct feelings of public outrage towards a careful sifting of evidence. Into this nexus 'Marie Rogêt' slots itself neatly in recognising the interchangeability of New York and the birthplace of detection, Paris; and, more significantly, in allowing Poe's new fictional form to respond directly to the new style of reportage in precisely the terms it expects: sifting every word and comma of it in the interests of public safety.[4]

Looking at these two stories in terms of Foucault's argument that the nascent detective genre marks the replacement of the spectacular punishment of the plebeian malefactor by the 'struggle between two pure minds', 'The Murders in the Rue Morgue' is especially instructive in that the ape/murderer combines the 'brutal' qualities we associate with the everyday crimes retailed in sensation reportage with the 'superhuman' qualities demanded of the criminal in order to match the brilliance of the detective. In a different way, 'Marie Rogêt' further postpones the entry of the master-criminal, largely through Poe's ignorance of the facts in the Rogers case; none the less, it is interesting to note that the redirected inquiry he calls for transfers attention from the plebeian 'gang' favoured by the press to one or other of Mary/Marie's more bourgeois admirers. (Ironically, the truth lay somewhere between, in a social reality overlooked by press and detective writer alike: a botched abortion.) In 'The Purloined Letter', where the hush-hush nature of the case precludes reportage of any kind, Foucault's 'pure mind' finally emerges at its most impeccable in the aristocratic genius, Minister D–.

In the two primary texts of the genre, then, popular crime reportage impinges on 'literature' in a new way. Allowed to take on itself the full burden of conveying the unpleasant details, it is sharply divorced from the 'literary' part of the text by a kind of collage technique which enables a fascination with 'real' crime to coexist with a fantasy of infallible detection which is clearly the reverse of realistic. While in some ways responding to the rising scandal registered by Defoe, Fielding and De Quincey, and bringing it under control, detective fiction also invites real, or realistically squalid, crime into the house of fiction in a schizophrenic formula which then comes to constitute a new kind of scandal within the walls of literature itself: the scandal of indifference.

As the form became familiarised, the jagged edges left by Poe were often smoothed off by moralising and sentiment, but a striking example of its innate schizophrenia can still be found in such stories as Conan Doyle's 'The Cardboard Box'. Here a particularly thoroughgoing display of Sherlock Holmes's wit and artistry (he reads Watson's mind *à la* Dupin, he is a spider responsive to every touch on his web) is juxtaposed with evidence of a particularly brutal double murder and mutilation: two severed but disparate ears, buried in salt, discovered in a cardboard box sent to the wrong address. The gap thus created is genuinely shocking, and it is significant that the original *Strand Magazine* story was, uniquely, excluded from the corresponding book-length collection *The Memoirs of Sherlock Holmes*, to have its bravura mind-reading episode lifted into a more innocuous context while the rest awaited more permissive times.[5]

It is also significant that the murderer Jim Browner, a jealous ship's steward who has caught his wife and her lover *in flagrante delicto*, is untypically followed almost to the foot of the gallows in a throwback to the much older tradition of the gallows confession. The return to this tradition, with its firm focus on the plebeian malefactor and 'his sombre transformation into a hero' testifies perhaps to an unease over the gap between Holmes's bravura ratiocinations and what is, not despite but because of its gory details, in many ways the most probable crime in the canon. The complexities of the case are not the result of Machiavellian brilliance but of a postal mistake, so that the normal conditions of the genre ('the criminal was wicked, of course, but he was also intelligent; and although he was punished, he did not have to suffer') are upset. Instead of Foucault's 'struggle between two pure minds', whereby the bourgeoisie sees its own face reflected in criminal and detective alike, we are left with a jagged mismatch between Holmes and the perpetrator of an everyday *crime passionel*. The sense of arbitrary severance between worlds is well caught up in the story's central imagery: the severed ears, disparate even from each other, crudely but flimsily boxed off from the world of the reader, but ever-open to surveillance once entered into such 'regular channels' as the postal system. That the story makes such a cheerful victory of its opening of this 'box' perhaps accounts for its unique position of disgrace within the larger 'canon'.

A further perspective on detective fiction's treatment of common kinds of crime can also be effectively illustrated from the Sherlock Holmes stories. First, it is worth briefly making the point that the rise of detective fiction coincided with that of 'Naturalism', the diffuse but important literary movement which aimed to look afresh, and 'scientifically', at certain common experiences, using the paired notions of 'heredity' and 'environment' as major guides. (With hindsight, the two axes can be seen as respectively Darwinian and Marxist.) Crime was often used as a quintessential example of the kind of experience requiring such analysis, as in the extraordinary case of Georg Büchner's *Woyzeck* (1837), written long before Naturalism christened itself as such in texts such as *Thérèse Raquin*, but only four years before Poe's 'Rue Morgue'. Though left in fragmentary form by the author's death (at twenty-three), the play examines a real-life *crime passionel* not unlike that of 'The Cardboard Box', but attempts to account imaginatively for the social and psychological pressures leading to a poor soldier's murder of his unfaithful common-law wife. While Woyzeck's detection and arrest are hinted at, in scenes describing bloodstains and so forth, the fragments remaining suggest that they are far less important than the revolutionary medical student Büchner's conviction that strong social, and equally evident mental, pressures powerfully explain a crime whose perpetrator should therefore not have been executed.[6]

There is a clear parallel between the 'medical' concerns of Büchner's kind of imaginatively fired Naturalism and those constantly represented by the Holmes canon. Both raise in different ways the issue of crime as an object of scientific inquiry, and can thus be seen as reflecting the shift emphasised by Foucault from spectacular but random punishment to an ideal of total and ever more intimate surveillance. Brilliantly, Büchner pounces on this whole theme by showing how precisely the type of surveillance which sees Woyzeck as a medical 'case' has turned him into one: the ghastly Doctor who feeds him exclusively on peas, and makes him wiggle his ears before a class of students, is largely responsible for his growing insanity.

Detective fiction's broad embrace of a similar ideal of quasi-medical surveillance is well exemplified in Sherlock Holmes, whose habit of reading off the intimate details of his clients' lives from signs only discernible to the specialist famously derives from the diagnostic methods of his Edinburgh medical professor, Joseph Bell. (The medical associations are carried through in Doyle's accounts of conceiving Holmes while waiting for patients, as well as in Holmes's claim to be the world's first 'consulting detective', and instinctive alliance with Dr Watson.) Bell's supra-medical methods emerge clearly in an anecdote concerning a human guinea-pig who vociferously denied Bell's diagnosis that he had once been a soldier. Dragged into an anteroom by powerful orderlies and stripped, he was discovered to carry the 'D' brand of an army deserter. Narrated to demonstrate Bell's infallibility, the story also neatly illustrates Foucault's identification of medical surveillance with political power, and chillingly recalls the Doctor's treatment of the poor soldier Woyzeck.[7]

A similar motif emerges very clearly from a particularly clearcut 'group' of Sherlock Holmes stories, of which the earliest is in many ways the most interesting and indicative. 'A Case of Identity' concerns a short-sighted young typist, Mary Sutherland, who has been wooed and then jilted by her disguised stepfather James Windibank, in order to keep her small inheritance in the family. Two other cases from the first twelve-story collection, *The Adventures of Sherlock Holmes*, concern very similar efforts by father-figures to secure their daughters' or stepdaughters' money: indeed, if we include two rather more loosely related stories, the theme occupies nearly half of the *Adventures*.[8] This suggests a very strong preoccupation on Doyle's part with the issue of father–daughter relations – gesturing in one direction at traditional 'paternalist' opposition to female independence, and in the other at possibilities of actual sexual abuse that may well have been as real in late nineteenth- as they are in late twentieth-century Britain.

'A Case of Identity' begins with Holmes expressing a wish to 'fly out of that window hand in hand, hover over this great city, gently remove the roofs, and peep in at the queer things which are going on, the strange coincidences, the plannings, the cross-purposes, the wonderful chains of events, working through generations, and leading to the most *outré* results' (Doyle, p. 191). On one hand, this introduction plainly indicates the origin of the word 'detection' itself ('remove the roofs'), but it also hints at a hush-hush approach in which sleeping dogs will be discovered but then let lie. This programme fits well with a story in which the central character is treated from first to last as a 'case': 'Oscillation upon the pavement always means an *affaire du coeur*' (p. 192). Having correctly deduced that his client has not only been virtually seduced by her stepfather but also betrayed to him by her own mother for money, Holmes lets Windibank off with only the symbolic threat of a horsewhipping, and resolves not to enlighten the victim herself, since there is danger 'for whoso snatches a delusion from a woman' (p. 201).

Drawing on one of the most powerful images in Foucault's *Discipline and Punish*, that of the concentric Panopticon prison in which the inmates are under surveillance at all times, Dennis Porter remarks that 'by the time of Doyle, the Great Detective of fiction had himself the essential qualities of the unseen seer, who stands at the center of the social Panopticon and employs his "science" to make all things visible on behalf of the forces of order' (Porter, pp. 124–5). This describes particularly aptly the hands-off approach of 'A Case of Identity', but can also be extended further to cover the wider 'father–daughter incest' group, where direct criminality is, of course, often punished, but where the subtext concerning the unlimited powers of the paterfamilias within his little kingdom is as normally just kept under observation as it is confronted head-on. Most of the other stories in the group are in fact much more derivative, either from Gothic ('The Speckled Band'; 'The Copper Beeches') or from Gaboriau ('The Beryl Coronet'), and hence simply demand a degree of stereotyped heroism on Holmes's part. 'A Case of Identity', with its firmly authenticated petty-bourgeois setting, is in many ways the most original, and hence calls forth the 'purest' response from whatever new forces Holmes is supposed to represent. And that response, made palatable by the class-inferiority of the 'villain' Windibank, is a perfectly managed blend of righteous civic concern with complete personal indifference.

After Doyle, the interwar 'Golden Age' of English detective fiction dispenses almost completely with the 'plebeian' malefactor: Foucault's 'struggle between two pure minds' now reigns supreme. While the Second World War and its aftermath may have thrown up the odd working-class villain (cf. the indicatively named Jack Havoc in Allingham's *The Tiger in the Smoke*), this fact is dealt with on principles going back through melodrama to Bill Sikes. Otherwise, especially in the interwar period itself, the plebeian malefactor only emerges as the ubiquitous but nonexistent 'wandering homicidal lunatic' whose entrance through the unguarded French window is a favourite postulate of the leading suspects.[9]

So far, the kind of 'scandal' chiefly discussed has related to the endemic existence of crime within the population at large. But obviously, a different set of problems arises when the criminality is perceived as occurring at the top levels of society.

We shall consider later some ways in which Sophocles's *Oedipus the King*, written in the fifth century BC, links tragedy and detection, but Elizabethan and Jacobean tragedy, which brings us nearer our end-point, also offers some suggestive parallels and distinctions. Not only shocking and gruesome crime but also a considerable degree of detection take place in many of these tragedies: Kyd's *Spanish Tragedy* and Shakespeare's *Titus Andronicus* and *Hamlet*, for instance, all offer us, in the revenger, a figure committed not only to punishing criminals but also to proving their guilt. Intercepted letters, messages deciphered from book references, entrapment through details known only to criminal and pursuer, the latter's disguise of imbecility: all these occur as prominently in these plays as in Doyle or Christie. In the anonymous *Arden of Feversham* an impromptu posse tracks down the murderers by following their footprints, and in Webster's *Duchess of Malfi* Bosola is a professional private eye, hired to report on the sex-life of his clients' sister.[10]

Of all the numerous differences from detective fiction which leap to mind, perhaps the three most prominent are that the crimes involved in such tragedies are usually also great matters of state, that the revengers are personally motivated, and that detection is only one element in a much larger sweep towards punishment and clarification. There are, in fact, exceptions to the first two of these differences: plays like *Arden* and the equally anonymous *A Warning for Fair Women* concern sexually-motivated real-life murders among the bourgeoisie and minor gentry, and their documentation of the inevitable road to the gallows puts them firmly in the broadside tradition.[11] As far as the revenger's personal motivation is concerned, Bosola is an interesting transitional figure in that he steps out of his designated role as the hireling of big political interests to become a free-standing agent, motivated (like the later agents of Hammett or Chandler) more by professional pride than by the mercenary commitment initially assumed in him. But despite such anticipatory exceptions the crimes of tragedy are primarily the affairs of the great, terrible precisely because their correction involves an unthinkable political rebellion which must then either itself be punished in the death of the revenger or vindicated in the establishment of a radically new order.

Writing emphatically from the Elizabethan left, Sir Philip Sidney stresses such points in his account of 'the high and excellent Tragedy, that openeth the greatest wounds, and sheweth forth the Ulcers that are covered with Tissue; that maketh Kinges feare to be Tyrants, and Tyrants manifest their tirannicall humors' (Draper, pp. 69–70). (This could also be seen as the programme of a slightly different branch of 'Naturalism' from that discussed earlier: Ibsen's *Ghosts*, which presents the misdeeds of a Victorian paterfamilias in terms of the environmental/hereditary riddle posed by congenital syphilis, harnesses the large emotions of tragedy to the procedures of medical detective work. In unconscious reminiscence of Sidney, reviewers termed the play 'a loathsome sore unbandaged'.[12]) A similar political motivation is clearly evident in one of 'high' literature's most important precursors of the detective genre, William Godwin's novel *Caleb Williams*. Written in 1794 as a radical exploration of current notions of political justice, the novel involves the servant Caleb's discovery that his aristocratic master, Falkland, is a murderer. His subsequent persecution at the hands of a social order which sides unquestioningly with the master takes up the body of the book, but the ending (over which Godwin remained deeply undecided) shows a broken Falkland confessing his guilt during a climactic courtroom scene in which Caleb's contrition is equally evident.

One of the book's great puzzles is its deep ambivalence about the initial act of detection: while on one hand Caleb's persecution is clearly unjust, on the other great stress is laid on Falkland's nobility and the guilty nature of Caleb's curiosity. The message is partly, then, that the extirpation of crime in high places will necessitate a change in the whole social order; but also that the older feeling of 'cursed spite / That ever I was born to set it right' remains valid for the individual whose knowledge pits him against that order. That the figure of the detective-hero is still decidedly unborn is indicated in the presentation of the bandit-turned-thieftaker Gines, whose Robin-Hood-like former colleagues are as noble as he is contemptible. The consistent reversal of normal notions of law and order is certainly part of the radical intention of the book, though its ambivalences also belong to a long broadside tradition. But in the presentation of Falkland as at once truly noble and as the representative of an unjust system, Godwin also seems to aim at a replacement of the whole notion of criminal justice by a full consideration of character and circumstance which, while dismantling the system Falkland heads, would also somehow still leave him heading it. The kind of analysis of class injustice towards which the book seems repeatedly to gesture never quite materialises, and certainly not in the narrating consciousness of Caleb, the would-be-loyal servant. Without this, we are thrown back on the dilemma of earlier tragedy: that the exposure of crime in high places must remain an act of rebellion which society cannot condone without fundamental disruption.[13]

It remains open to question how far Godwin, even in a revolutionary age, advocates such a disruption by presenting the problem as insoluble by other means; but in the post-revolutionary age of the mid-nineteenth century it can be argued that the creation of the detective hero offers a safe and acceptable way of confronting similar issues. By and large, this is done by releasing Caleb from his feudal obligations and assuring us that in so far as he is a murderer Falkland is also an abnormal monster who will collapse at the first touch of exposure. But in fact many early detective works retain traces of Caleb's difficulties when confronted with wrongdoing in high places. Poe's 'The Purloined Letter' successfully confronts such a criminal in one sense, but in another sense the blackmailing Minister D– is himself the detective of guilt at an even higher level, who must be punished while the knowledge he has gained is firmly suppressed. Furthermore, in his role as powerful criminal, he cannot be confronted openly for fear of scandal, so that Dupin resorts to the methods and, oddly, the motives of the classical revenger, as is suggested in his literary assumption of the role of Atreus to the Minister's Thyestes.[14]

The fact that such problems still affected not only detective fiction but also the newly created police forces whose activities it mirrors emerges in the police prefect's softly-softly approach, as well as in the fact that he is working for reward as, essentially, the Queen's private agent. A more extended reflection of police problems in this area is given in Emile Gaboriau's *Monsieur Lecoq*, where Falkland's threats to trample Caleb 'into atoms' (Godwin, p. 8) are echoed in the amateur Tabaret's warnings to the professional Lecoq about his quarry, the Duc de Sairmeuse: 'Free, this man is almost omnipotent, and you, an infinitesimal agent of the police, will be broken like glass' (Gaboriau, *Lecoq*, p. 365). It is significant that this part of Lecoq's quest ends with him turning, like Dupin, from a simple wish for a professional coup to a vow of 'revenge'. In this vow, Lecoq unknowingly aligns himself with the Jacobin Lacheneur family, so that beneath the reassuring *roman policier* carapace, his struggle with the Duc still carries some of the older implications of direct political rebellion.[15]

In England, too, early examples of the genre depict numerous confrontations between entrenched and police power. It is significant that in the laudatory *Household Words* articles which helped to

swing public opinion behind the new detective police, Charles
Dickens primarily praises their achievements in patrolling slums
and arresting professional crooks, whereas his main fictional
detective, Inspector Bucket in *Bleak House* (closely modelled on the
Inspector Field of the articles), is chiefly successful in uncovering
the secrets of the aristocracy.[16] While there may be some wishful
thinking in this, it is clearly important to Dickens that his revered
detective force should be shown to exercise a similar godlike
overview of society from top to bottom as he himself exercises in
his novels. Bucket becomes a metaphor for that ability to discern
connections across society's yawning gaps for which Dickens
repeatedly calls out, though with many indicative changes of
emphasis. Thus, comparing *Bleak House* to the earlier *Oliver Twist*,
we can see a sharp shift away from the *Newgate Calendar* tradition
in which a whole society, either as spontaneous mob or as more
deliberately 'mobilised' by the Mr Brownlows, comes to know itself
in the spectacular punishment of criminals like Sikes and Fagin.
Now, on the other hand, not just crime and punishment but
detection and a much subtler kind of guilt provide a new but yet
more effective imagery of social binding from top to bottom.

In his unintimidated bearing towards 'Sir Leicester Dedlock,
Baronet' and his exposure of his wife's secret, then, Bucket fulfills
an ideal function. None the less, he is privately hired and his duty
to his client pre-eminently involves the minimising of public
scandal. This ambivalent role of the policeman as employee rather
than truly godlike overseer emerges more clearly in Collins's *The
Moonstone*, where Sergeant Cuff is dismissed from the case when
he begins to suspect his client's daughter of the very minor offence
of stealing her own diamond. Collins's refusal to let 'the celebrated
Cuff' uncover the true solution of a case where he is so hampered,
despite his genuinely admiring portrayal, is perhaps a more accurate
reflection of the relations between policeman and wealthy client
than that portrayed in Dickens. The real-life Sergeant Whicher, on
whom Cuff is modelled, raised a social outcry leading to his forced
retirement when one such private inquiry led him to suspect,
rightly as it turned out, that his client's daughter, Constance Kent,
had murdered her stepbrother: as with Cuff, the disappearance of
a stained nightgown was the main evidence (see Ousby, p. 123).

The fantasy-figure of the amateur detective helps to do away
with such difficulties, if not completely. Building on Poe's Dupin
and Gaboriau's Tabaret, Doyle's Sherlock Holmes is the supreme

embodiment of this fantasy; but even here the social position is slightly ambiguous. Sufficiently independent to have his pick of cases, he is none the less for hire as the world's first 'consulting detective', a phrase whose medical tang seems partly designed to remove the sordid associations of real-life private detection, which was mainly involved with divorce cases. Accordingly we hear much more about *ennui* than about money, except when the client is sufficiently exalted. When this is so, however, the problems of the hireling start to kick in in the accustomed way so that, in such cases as 'A Scandal in Bohemia', 'The Priory School' and 'The Second Stain', Holmes's prime function is to suppress rather than to expose the materials of scandal. And here a trace-element looking back to Bosola and forward to Hammett's and Chandler's private eyes appears in Holmes's establishment of at least a vestigial 'revenge' on his noble clients, by way of chilly rebuffs or more explicit moral lectures.

The high-life scandals discussed above may all end in threats to the social order but, in their fictional forms at least, their origins are almost exclusively sexual. If we leave aside the sedate English 'Golden Age', with its general offer to induct us into the upper classes personally, then from the fatal passions of Falkland and Lady Dedlock to the many variants of the 'Purloined Letter' blackmail plot in Gaboriau, Doyle and the Chandleresque hard-boiled tradition, it is the existence of sexual feelings among the upper orders that ultimately lays them open to the public 'right to know' which detective fiction can still vestigially claim to represent. But since such slips are finally only those of individuals, and are then invariably covered up by other individuals – the detectives – it is far more as private 'I's than as the public 'eye' that we are then reverentially invited to inspect the 'Ulcers that are covered with Tissue'.

2

Oedipus and Aristotle; Freud and *The Moonstone*

OEDIPUS AND ARISTOTLE

Sophocles's *Oedipus the King* has acquired a special importance to our culture for two reasons only partly dependent on its merits as a play. The first is that it was the main model on which Aristotle based the generalisations of *The Poetics*, the founding work of Western literary theory. The second is that, as a text and not just as a story, it is the reference point for Freud's theory of the Oedipus complex, and hence a cornerstone of psychoanalysis. The fact that it also has a strong formal resemblance to a detective story makes it a natural focus of attention in a discussion of the relations between detective fiction and literature.

Sophocles's play was performed in Athens around 430 BC, and its outline is as follows. Fleeing his home after a prophecy that he will kill his father and marry his mother, Oedipus becomes king of Thebes and marries its queen, Jocasta, whose husband Laius has been killed on a journey shortly before. Many years later the city is smitten by plague, which the oracle says will only be lifted with the discovery and expulsion of Laius's murderer. Oedipus initiates an exhaustive inquiry, from which it begins to emerge that he himself unknowingly killed Laius on his travels. At this tense moment a messenger announces the death of Oedipus's 'father' in Corinth, but then reveals that Oedipus was actually a foundling: further interrogation of a terrified Theban shepherd confirms that he delivered to Corinth a royal baby he was supposed to put to death, following a prophecy that the child would one day kill its father and marry its mother. At these revelations, Jocasta commits suicide and Oedipus blinds himself before begging for banishment.

Aristotle's *Poetics*, written about 100 years later, is probably only part of a larger projected work setting out to describe the full range of imaginative literature. As we have it, however, the book moves rapidly through the other possibilities before settling on tragedy

16

as the best and highest of possible forms. Much of what Aristotle praises in tragedy is related specifically to its handling of plot.

The special importance of *Oedipus* to Aristotle's theory of tragedy is evident not just from the number of times he refers to it, but also from the fact that he refers to it at such crucial points in his argument. Thus he uses it to illustrate the combination of discovery with reversal (Dorsch, p. 46), the fall of the protagonist through error (p. 48), the arrangement of the plot to induce pity and fear (p. 49), the delayed realisation of the fearful act (p. 50), and the 'probable' emergence of the discovery from the incidents themselves (p. 54). Other references praise the play for sticking to the right sort of story (p. 48), for keeping Oedipus's improbable ignorance of previous events outside the action (pp. 52, 69), and for its compactness (p. 73). In some ways the first citation, to do with the combination of discovery with reversal, is the most important: though apparently just a technical point, it represents the apex of a card-house of 'bests' which puts plays like *Oedipus* at the pinnacle not only of tragedy but of all fictional narrative. On a general level, Aristotle permits us to apply his findings on tragedy downwards to other fiction, represented in his own day chiefly by the epic: 'Thus anyone who can discriminate between what is good and what is bad in tragedy can do the same with epic; for all the elements of epic are found in tragedy, though not everything that belongs to tragedy is to be found in epic' (p. 38). But more specifically, to combine discovery with reversal, as when 'the Messenger who came to cheer Oedipus . . . did the very opposite by revealing to him who he was', is to produce the best kind of complex plot, which is in turn the best kind of plot for tragedy, which is the best kind of serious narrative, which is the best kind of narrative full stop, since comedy is produced by 'more trivial' writers 'about the meaner sort of people' (pp. 35–6).

The technical point which wins *Oedipus* this prize status clearly arises from the element which most makes it resemble a detective story: its dependence on plot. Whether coincidentally or not, this particular plot derives its formal brilliance from a concealed secret, in fact the identity of a murderer, which is raised as the central problem at the beginning and solved at the end, with the interim being totally taken up by the inquiry. It is the way in which the Messenger's apparent interruption of the inquiry actually furthers it that provides the key instance of simultaneous discovery and reversal. Most of Aristotle's other references to *Oedipus* can also be linked to its 'detective' interest. The delay in understanding the nature of the deed of horror, the probable emergence of the discovery from the incidents themselves, the choice of the right sort of story, the removal from the depicted action of improbable elements necessary to the plot, and the general sense of compact causality could all be usefully prescribed for detective writing.[1]

The two remaining points, involving the protagonist's fall through error and the induction of pity and fear through the plot alone, can, however, only be made to fit the genre with some strain: the first if we see the protagonist as the criminal, and the second if we forget about pity but agree that the outline of a detective plot can produce in scaled-down form the same impact as a reading of the full text. Consideration of the protagonist and of the overall emotional effect provides a necessary reminder of the differences between tragedy and detective fiction. But *Oedipus* itself occupies a crucial position in bridging the gap: by an unrepeatable coup, the criminal is also the detective, as well as also being in many ways the victim, and hence combines in himself the three types of figure who could conceivably claim to be the protagonists of detective fiction. And it is arguably this tripling of functions ('where three roads meet') that produces the famous pity and fear: pity for someone caught in a trap, and fear that the claim to disinterested detachment, made by Oedipus as detective and ourselves as spectators, may at any moment prove unfounded.

Ordinarily, detective fiction demands a clear separation of the functions combined in Oedipus: it is the seventh commandment of Knox's 'Detective Story Decalogue' that 'the detective must not himself commit the crime' (Winks, p. 201), and when Agatha Christie made the criminal a figure as close to the detective as the narrator (in *The Murder of Roger Ackroyd*) she produced uproar in *aficionado* circles. This separation of functions ensures that, especially where a series is involved, no emotional problems attach to the figure of the detective, who is none the less clearly the protagonist. The two other figures who might concentrate feeling round themselves, the victim and the criminal, are drained of any such significance because we only become aware of them posthumously: the victim because he or she has died at the beginning of the book, and the criminal because his or her true character is only revealed at the end. Pity and fear are not only divided between these two figures, but also removed to the very fringes of the action: we are never, for instance, shown an execution. Thus it is arguable that detective fiction defines itself in large part by the programmatic separation of the functions and emotional challenges which Aristotle praises *Oedipus* for bringing together.

The actual history of detective fiction is not, however, quite as straightforward as such 'rules' might suggest. Numerous texts, especially from early and late in the history, either contravene this separation of functions or actively play with it. These texts include such acknowledged 'milestones' as Poe's 'The Purloined Letter', where resemblances between detective and criminal are constantly hinted at; Collins's *The Moonstone*, where Franklin Blake combines elements of all three functions; Doyle's 'The Final Problem', where Holmes becomes at once murderer and victim; Israel Zangwill's *The Big Bow Mystery*; Chesterton's 'The Secret Garden'; Gaston Leroux's *The Mystery of the Yellow Room*; and Christie's *Curtain* and *The Mousetrap*, in all of which the apparent detective (and in two cases the 'real' one) is the murderer; Hammett's *Red Harvest*, where a similar possibility is used to disturbing effect; most of Chandler, where the client often fills a detective–criminal role at one remove, and Marlowe adopts the stance of victim; and recent texts as diverse as Le Carré's *The Spy Who Came in from the Cold* and Stanley Ellin's *Mirror, Mirror on the Wall* where, as in numerous selconsciously 'postmodernist' works, further elisions of the three central roles produce effects of enhanced sophistication. Any list of the genre's 'classics' would include several of these texts which strain against the formula in the direction of a more *Oedipus*-like concentration of functions. While it would be hard to argue that they tend towards tragedy to the degree that they break the formula (though this may be Le Carré's aim), they are marked at least by a tendency to 'make you think', to raise the stakes of the game, which edges them towards a literature of challenge, and sometimes even of 'content'.

The importance of such works in the history of the genre demonstrates the limitations of *a priori* assumptions about the formula. None the less, a formula with limited prerogatives clearly does exist, and is worth considering further. Tsvetan Todorov has argued that the classical whodunnit 'contains not one but two stories: the story of the crime and the story of the investigation. . . . The first, that of the crime, is in fact the story of an absence: its most accurate characteristic is that it cannot be immediately present in the book. . . . [The second] is a story which has no importance in itself, which serves only as a mediator between the reader and the story of the crime' (Todorov, pp. 44, 46). In a brief allusion, Todorov relates this to the distinction between 'story' and 'plot', elaborated by the Russian Formalists, but also to be found in *The Poetics*.[2] Detective fiction works through an extreme extension of the 'hiding' of the story by the plot to be found in all fiction. Todorov draws attention to the second story's conscious awareness of itself, through the device of the 'Watson' or by other means, as a book: an awareness denied to the first story, which purports to be 'life'. It is in the rigour with which it maintains the division that the detective story is defined: existing at the level of the book, which is also that of the reader, the detective is inactive and invulnerable; the criminal is active but vulnerable because of his unconsciousness of the presence of the book. We could argue further that the rigorous exclusion of the first story by the second, at least until the end, involves above all a suppression of the 'action' which Aristotle saw as the philosophical essence of tragedy: 'the purpose of living is an end which is a kind of activity . . . it is by reason of their actions that [men] are happy or the reverse. . . . Tragedy is the representation of an action, and it is chiefly on account of the action that it is also the representation of persons' (Dorsch, p. 40). We might argue that detective fiction's 'representation of persons' by outward signs such as Holmes's pipe and Poirot's moustaches derives its empty and iconic nature from the fact that these things are substitutes for rather than expressions of a characterful 'action' which is really going on elsewhere.

In 'The Guilty Vicarage', which invokes Aristotle directly at several points, W. H. Auden describes the murderer in terms designed to recall the Greek tragic hero: 'Murder is a negative creation, and every murderer is therefore the rebel who claims the right to be omnipotent. His pathos is his refusal to suffer. The problem for the writer is to conceal his demonic pride from the other characters and from the reader, since, if a person has this pride, it tends to appear in everything he says and does' (Winks, pp. 19–20). This would be a fair description of Oedipus, whose characteristic pride 'in everything he says and does' and initial refusal to suffer are the only things that can be adduced against him, given the understandable conditions of the murder, through which, however, his royal status and what Aristotle would term his 'happiness' have been very directly 'created'. Auden's comment also pinpoints a key effect of the rigorous separation of action from narrative, or 'story' from 'plot', which Todorov identifies as the key to the detective genre: the direct emergence of 'representation of persons' from 'representation of action' is necessarily thwarted at the crucial point. (In some of the ironic texts listed above, however, most notably Zangwill's *Big Bow Mystery*, there is a satisfying elision of the conventionally unquestioned hubris of the detective with the 'demonic pride' which motivates his single crime.)

In both Aristotle and detective fiction there is a conservative appeal to stabilising laws and rules based on assumptions about the audience: a certainty as to the nature of audience reaction leads to a technical emphasis on a structure given in advance of the specific content but assumed to be well able to process it. The qualities of such an approach are perhaps best clarified by recalling moments of opposition, such as Coleridge's Romantic counterclaim in favour of an 'organic form' where content and form determine each other uniquely in each instance; or Brecht's call for a 'non-Aristotelian' theatre where the notion of a homogenous audience as the consumer of a prearranged, end-determined 'experience' is systematically attacked. Recent critical emphases on literature as 'process' rather than as 'product' have often used both Aristotle and detective fiction to represent the negative pole of the argument, and the recurrent postmodernist device of leaving an apparently detective-like quest deliberately unconcluded can be seen as part of a broader questioning of Aristotelian notions of unity and closure.[3] Even more apparently conservative fiction, such as the 'loose baggy monster' of the Victorian novel, can be seen to protest in its very prolixity against the moment when its various elements will be accorded their 'proper' places in accordance with Aristotelian notions of closure; and isolated earlier instances like Sterne's *Tristram Shandy* carry this protest to its limits.

An objection implicit in much of this work, but perhaps most sharply voiced by Brecht, is to the notion of literature as something to be consumed in line with an already known 'human nature'. The link between this foreknowledge of the audience and a conservative approach to content emerges clearly in Aristotle when he argues from the need to arouse pity and fear in the right proportions (by the fall of a hero who is 'the mean between' good and bad extremes) to the fact that 'at first the poets treated any stories that came to hand, but nowadays the best tragedies are written about a handful of families' (Dorsch, p. 48). This establishment of an increasingly conservative norm, after such primitive experiments as Aeschylus's 'factional' *Persians*, has its parallel in the restricted scope of the 'Golden Age' whodunnit, which replaced the far greater social range of such primitives as Poe, Doyle and Chesterton. In the course of this process a specific element, the plot, becomes evermore highly prized and carefully conserved. The shift from the prodigality of the earlier short stories to the heavily ritualised novels of the interwar period, with their lovingly hoarded and endlessly masticated scraps of evidence and their unique final twists, attests to this need to conserve that increasingly scarce resource, the 'good plot'. It is a persistent irony that the most memorable of such plots are those which threaten to undermine the conserving 'rules' by which the genre's continued existence is guaranteed. In Greek tragedy, of course, the plots are communal rather than private property; none the less, Aristotle does present them as properties of a sort, to be carefully worked and reworked in accord with an unchanging human nature.

Aristotle's central term for the way human nature consumes tragedy is catharsis, or purgation. Though the meaning of the term is much debated, most accounts agree that it refers in part to a psychological effect on the audience, whereby its emotions are raised to a high pitch and then released, in a way that can alternately be described as a 'tempering' (as for Milton) or a 'discharge' (in a more straightforward physiological metaphor). Some of the problems arise in describing exactly how this effect is created by, or mirrored in, the drama itself; a kind of problem which does not arise in describing the somewhat similar creation and release of tension in detective fiction. Here, clearly, anxiety is created by a system of supply and demand, where the need for a solution is urgently proposed but not satisfied until the end. The abrupt change in the direction of our feelings at this point can at least be compared to the exercising of the emotions which seems to be one point of catharsis: the emotions are not the same, but the abstract outline of their trajectory is. Furthermore, the achievement of this specific effect can be seen more clearly as the *aim* of these two forms than of any other (though a distinction should be made between tragedy as described by Aristotle and the often more complex effects of specific tragedies). In one attempt to relate catharsis to the content of Aristotelian tragedy, Augusto Boal has talked of Aristotle's 'coercive model', in which the audience is indoctrinated into right thinking through the cathartic alternation of emotional sticks and carrots, in parallel with the discovery and repudiation of the hero's error.[4] A somewhat comparable model for detective fiction is implied in Auden's emphasis on a 'dialectic of innocence and guilt', whereby the reader identifies with the suspects, all of whom 'must be guilty of something', to be finally repaid by the gratifying 'illusion of being dissociated from the murderer' (Winks, pp. 16–24). Auden's point that the classical whodunnit involves the restoration of an innocent society to a former state of grace through the casting out of a scapegoat, which also marks the restoration of the reader's peace of mind, suggests a comparably powerful 'coercive' machine to tragedy as perceived by Boal.

The gesture of casting out with which both forms end implies at least some parallel between the emotional purgation of the audience and the cleansing of a society. I shall conclude this part of the discussion by investigating the ways in which both tragic and detective 'models' of purgation seem to overlap in *Oedipus*. The plague with which the gods punish Thebes for Laius's uninvestigated killing can be seen as a powerful image for that pollution of a whole society which, in detective fiction, is represented by the mutual suspicion and disruption which falls on the microcosmic society of suspects. As in detective fiction, the authorities are called upon to lift the pollution, and society stands still while they do so. To this extent the chorus, frozen onstage for most of the play, their individual concerns forgotten in their flabbergasted concentration on the inquiry, can be compared to the suspended community of suspects, as well as to the audience, frozen in a similar semicircle, to whom they also act as a kind of mediating communal Watson. The accusation of two specific suspects early in the case, the powerful Creon and the revered Tiresias, confirms that no one is beyond suspicion or free to go about their affairs as usual. Oedipus, the authority in charge of the investigation, is, like the conventional detective, apparently an 'outsider' with no conceivable connection with the killing, though as king he can claim a kind of provisional insider status in so far as 'my spirit / grieves for the city, for myself and all of you' (Sophocles, p. 162, ll.75–6). He is called upon not only as embodying the state but also as a specialist, 'the best man alive at solving riddles' (p. 184, l.501), and hence combines the attributes of the police with those of the detective-as-genius. He proceeds to conduct a series of interrogations – of Tiresias, of Creon, of his wife Jocasta, of the Messenger and of the Shepherd –

which slowly reveal the identity of the murderer and the unsuspected factors of parricide and incest that made the crime particularly
heinous. These revelations are accompanied by further violence –
Jocasta's suicide and Oedipus's own self-blinding – which can be
compared to the second outbreak of violence by which detective
fiction often revives the tension near the end; and finally by the
solemn casting out of the criminal from the society which is starting
to reactivate itself at the end of the play. (The postponement of
Oedipus's physical exile at the last moment, for reasons relating
to the legend, does not really negate this movement but internalises
it at a deeper level in the 'untouchable' status to which Creon
relegates him by removing his children. The thwarting of Oedipus's
desire as king and detective to cast himself out as criminal is also
the most dramatic way of asserting that 'Here your power ends'
(p. 250, l.1676).)

The purging, then, is not only of our emotional suspense, but
also of the suspended society of which we have consented to
become a part. There is also, in Boal's reading at least, a moral
purging of hubris which, as we have seen, is particularly total in
Oedipus because we have been lured, as would-be problem solvers,
into a close identification with Oedipus's detective-like stance of
superior detachment. And these various purgings are all enmeshed
with the final repudiation and expulsion (albeit delayed) of the
scapegoat who is here not only the carrier of criminality but
also, appropriately, the king who began by claiming unique
responsibility for the plague-stricken city. It is because he is both
an interloping criminal, the archetypal outsider, and the king, the
uniquely representative insider, that Oedipus's expulsion satisfies
our contradictory needs to see society restored and turned inside
out. In most detective fiction the stakes are not nearly so high
since the criminal's outsider status is clear from the outset and his
final removal is purely restorative; in *Oedipus*, by contrast, every
movement has its opposite, so that the moment of Oedipus's
expulsion coincides with the intimation that, as legitimate heir, he
is the ultimate insider whose removal may be as catastrophic (in
ways explored in Sophocles's other two Theban plays) as it is
necessary. It is in this kind of doubling of each move by its opposite
that we find a specifically tragic meaning for Aristotle's discovery–
reversal combination going beyond the purely technical sense in
which we can apply it to detective fiction.

The other important body of theory linking *Oedipus* to detective fiction is the Freudian. For reasons which I hope will be clear, I intend to combine my discussion of this with a more prolonged examination of a second text where 'literature' and detection also overlap in many interesting ways: Wilkie Collins's *The Moonstone*.

FREUD AND *THE MOONSTONE*

Wilkie Collins's novel *The Moonstone* is another *locus classicus* in any discussion of the relations between detective fiction and 'literature'. While skilfully plotted on detective lines, it is also a substantial Victorian novel, with all the rich, rounded, social and psychological reverberations that implies. The questions raised by the coexistence of a relentlessly goal-directed detective structure and the 'loose baggy' discursiveness of the three-volume novel are clearly of interest: furthermore, the complexities of its content and structure are very interesting in themselves. These complexities have attracted the attention of both 'psychological' and 'social' critics, some of whose ideas can, with caution, be extended outwards to other detective works.

The Moonstone, an Indian diamond with a bloodstained history, is stolen from Rachel Verinder's room on the night of her eighteenth birthday. She refuses to discuss the incident, but has in fact seen it being taken by her cousin, Franklin Blake, with whom she is in love and who seems to be entirely unconscious of his own guilt. Her silence leads the able police detective, Sergeant Cuff, to suspect Rachel herself, but he also shrewdly draws attention to the importance of a smear on the newly-painted door, which must have stained the thief's garment, and to the probable involvement of Rosanna Spearman, a maidservant also in love with Franklin. In fact, it transpires, Rosanna had discovered Franklin's smeared nightgown and hidden it, before committing suicide because of his indifference to her. Cuff is dismissed from the case and Rachel banishes Franklin from her presence, becoming engaged to another cousin, the smarmy Godfrey Ablewhite. Through all this the oblivious Franklin remains the most tireless seeker of the missing diamond, until Rachel's direct accusation persuades him that he was himself the thief. With the help of Ezra Jennings, the assistant of the recently delirious Doctor Candy, he finally discovers that he was drugged by Candy on the fatal night (for tangential and innocent reasons) and took the diamond with the misguided aim of preserving it, only to be intercepted by Ablewhite, who relieved him of it in order to continue maintaining a mistress in the suburbs. Three Indian Brahmins, who have been pursuing the Moonstone throughout, kill Ablewhite to retrieve it, and the novel ends with the joyous marriage of Franklin and Rachel. The novel is constructed in the form of a series of narratives by central figures and more peripheral witnesses, commissioned and collated by Franklin himself.

The first approach I intend to consider is a psychological one, and it will be useful to introduce it by outlining some established psychoanalytic arguments about detective fiction which conveniently approach *The Moonstone* by way of *Oedipus*. Freud's description of the Oedipus complex in *The Interpretation of Dreams* addresses Sophocles's play specifically.[5] He sees Oedipus's curiosity and concern with riddles as reflecting the general human, or male, desire to uncover the tabooed and unconscious wish to kill the father and marry the mother. Specifically, Freud points to the moment in the play when Oedipus voices his fears of doing just this, and his mother–wife Jocasta replies 'Many a man before you,/in his dreams, has shared his mother's bed' (Sophocles, p. 215, ll.1074–5). This, for Freud, is an important clue to the story's universality: Oedipus enacts what others only dream of.

Freud's Oedipal theory has been applied to detective fiction by Geraldine Pederson-Krag, who argues in 'Detective Stories and the Primal Scene' that 'the unique feature of the detective story' is 'the curiosity it arouses'. Linking this curiosity to that of the child obsessed by the 'primal scene' of parental intercourse, she claims that the clues in detective fiction 'represent the child's growing awareness of details it had never understood, such as the family sleeping arrangements, nocturnal sounds, stains, incomprehensible adult jokes and remarks'. On this model 'the victim is the parent for whom the reader (the child) had negative oedipal feelings'; the criminal is 'the parent toward whom the child's positive oedipal feelings were directed, the one whom the child wished least of all to imagine participating in a secret crime'; and the detective, putting the clues together, the child him- or herself (Most and Stowe, pp. 15–16).

In 'The Analysis of a Detective Story', Charles Rycroft challenges Pederson-Krag's failure to draw the conclusion from her own argument that, if the victim represents the feared parent, 'then the criminal must be a personification of the reader's own unavowed hostility towards that parent. The reader is not only the detective; he is also the criminal.' Rycroft goes on to argue that detective fiction fails as art because 'this identification of the reader with the criminal remains denied': the reader is supplied instead with 'ready-made fantasies in which the compulsive question "whodunnit?" is always answered by a self-exonerating "not I"'. The ideal detective story, in which 'the detective or hero would discover that he himself is the criminal for whom he has been seeking' is *Oedipus*, whose cathartic effect 'depends on the fact that the guilt, which the typical detective story denies, is openly admitted' (Rycroft, pp. 114–15). The detective story is compulsively addictive rather than artistically therapeutic precisely because it fails to acknowledge consciously the truth at which it is always hinting. None the less, evidence of the true submerged content can be found in specific detective texts: a claim which introduces Rycroft's own analysis of *The Moonstone*.

For Rycroft, 'the theft of the Moonstone is a symbolic representation of the as yet prohibited intercourse between Franklin and Rachel and the loss of Rachel's virginity' (p. 119). Pointing to such details as the sexual symbolism of the diamond, 'with its central flaw and lunar changes in lustre', the tell-tale stain on Franklin's nightshirt, and Rachel's silence after the theft, Rycroft suggests that here, very nearly, is a story where, as in *Oedipus*, the hero discovers that he is pursuing the knowledge of his own sexual guilt. Although it is hard to see the sexual scene symbolised here as 'primal' in Pederson-Krag's rigidly Oedipal sense – something which Rycroft dismisses as unnecessary in any case – it is none the less surrounded by sufficiently heavy taboos to necessitate its translation into symbolic form and explain its appropriateness as the object of enough intense curiosity to fill a lengthy novel.

Rycroft goes on to argue that the novel evades the truth of the situation it evokes by providing each of the protagonists with a more darkly sexual 'double', on to whom a Victorian readership's feelings of moral disapproval about the central scene can be diverted. Thus Rachel's 'knowledge' of Franklin's deed is more actively asserted by Rosanna, who draws a sexual inference from Franklin's stained nightgown and whose self-abandoned passion for him leads to her symbolic death in a quicksand. Although Franklin has not consciously encouraged Rosanna, veiled references to a series of past liaisons indicate that he was capable of doing so, in line with the sexual double standard also represented in Rosanna's parentage: 'My mother went on the streets, because the gentleman who was my father deserted her' (Collins, p. 362). The double standard implicit in Franklin's behaviour is, however, more actively represented in the appropriately named Ablewhite, whose secret illicit liaison motivates his theft of the diamond. Any hostility we may feel towards the hypocrisy of Franklin's role as a 'hero' apparently oblivious to the nature and effect of his own actions (or perhaps even towards a book which so skilfully disguises its own sexual content) can be diverted on to Ablewhite, whose pretence of purity is so overdone as to constitute him a legitimate target for such hostility. We might further argue that in Rosanna and in Ablewhite, whose downfalls result from the use they make of having directly or indirectly *witnessed* the central event, we also have representatives of the tabooed witnessing of the primal scene on which Pederson-Krag lays such heavy insistence.

The more closely we consider the novel from this perspective, the more subtly we can see it as playing on the themes of frankness and self-delusion about sexual and other matters. I have already expanded his argument somewhat, but in starting to show how *The Moonstone* both exploits and circumvents the sexual hypocrisy of a specific, Victorian, culture, it seems to me that Rycroft comes close to undermining his own central contention that detective fiction fails as both therapy and art through its failure to be *Oedipus*. If the reason for praising Sophocles was that he brought the implications of a communal obsession further out into the open, it is hard not to see Collins, given the Victorian rules as to what was publishable, as doing the same. In indicating the novel's fairly complicated relationship to a specific culture, Rycroft raises important issues which demand to be pursued beyond the disapproving argument they are meant to demonstrate.

In a more recent article, Albert D. Hutter argues that such critics as Rycroft and Pederson-Krag are confined to an outmoded 'wish fulfilment' model of literary psychoanalysis, which he proposes to replace by 'a model of conflict resolution'. Agreeing that many incidents in *The Moonstone* have 'primal' or at least sexual overtones, he is more interested in the ways these are mediated to us by conflicting, uncomprehending or falsifying witnesses. As well as Rachel's blocked response to the initial 'theft', Hutter discusses Rosanna's more outspoken conclusions about the same event, and the lubriciously prudish account given by the confessed 'suppressed hysteric' Miss Clack of the moment when Rachel submits to Ablewhite's embraces. For Hutter 'the specific early psychological configuration called "primal scene" does *contribute* here to the novel's dominant concerns with looking and with the problem of knowledge; but it does not *determine* those concerns'. Thus, while the content of Miss Clack's thought may be sexual, it is more important that her 'obsession with seeing and not seeing, hearing and not hearing, reproduces that "detective fever" which has gripped us from Collins's time to our own' (Most and Stowe, p. 249).

In connecting this reading with the novel's multiple-narrative technique, Hutter certainly gives a fuller account of the importance of structure than those proposed by his predecessors. Instead of seeing simple wish-fulfilment or self-exonerating fantasy as the main organising principle, Hutter argues that *The Moonstone* embodies in its series of overlapping unreliable narratives the same kind of 'process' that Freud found in *Oedipus*: a 'process of revealing, with cunning delays and ever-mounting excitement – a process that can be likened to the work of psychoanalysis' (Most and Stowe, p. 249, quoting Freud's *Interpretation of Dreams*). Pointing specifically to Ezra Jennings's reconstruction of an ordered narrative from Dr Candy's fragmented ravings, Hutter argues that Jennings 'has hit upon the quintessential method of the modern detective and also on something which sounds remarkably like psychoanalytic free association . . . the reconstructive core of detective fiction' (p. 241). Jennings's 'reconstructive' function is also apparent in the climactic re-enactment of the novel's primary, if not primal, scene, where Rachel and others witness, this time without trauma, the original circumstances under which Franklin removed the diamond. In taking the reader through an analogous process of constant questioning and reinterpretation of conflicting, partial and self-deluding accounts, Collins instils a necessary technique of continually resolving (or re-solving) early conflicts at a higher level.

Though Hutter's emphasis on 'process' has an overall tendency to marginalise the novel's content, he also argues briefly that it reflects 'the nineteenth-century Englishman's fundamentally new perspective of himself, both politically and psychologically'. Thus the story concerning the Moonstone's eventual destiny reflects doubts about colonial exploitation which are also apparent in a frequent reversal of prejudices about racial characteristics, especially dark skin; and on both political and psychological levels, though the novel does end with a solution, 'the reader's experience of *The Moonstone* is weighted the other way: it encourages us to distrust closure' (pp. 237–88). The points about Empire briefly indicated by Hutter have been more forcibly made by John R. Reed, who points out that the central 'theft' only re-enacts the greater crime whereby the novel's secure and wealthy English milieu rests on systematic imperial plundering.[6] The obsession with the nominal crime, the mystery surrounding it, the spreading of the suspicion over as many people as possible, including those we identify with most closely, all point to an uneasy awareness of what really underpins the apparent idyll of the Verinder household. The sense of fatality hanging over the diamond, the bloody circumstances of whose acquisition decree its eventual return, perhaps covers a half-conscious demand for the return of India itself, the 'jewel in the crown' first of Mogul and then of English conquerors, to its original owners. The imperial theme is subtly underpinned by the main narrator Betteredge's comic dependence on *Robinson Crusoe*, a novel which postulates a hero of colonial enterprise as a mythic Everyman. The opening quotation from *Crusoe* about 'the Folly of beginning a Work before we count the cost' (Collins, p. 39), comically applied by Betteredge to the writing of his own narrative, is also dramatically juxtaposed to the Prologue's account of the bloody cost of Empire.

To this allegorical background we can add the emphasis on dark-complexioned outcasts Hutter mentions: not only the three Indian Brahmins but also the half-caste Ezra Jennings, the victim of unnamed accusations which perhaps refer to the tabooed interracial reality he represents. Another wrongly accused and physically stigmatised outcast, Rosanna Spearman, the offspring of an illicit relationship between classes rather than races, connects the imperial theme to that of class exploitation, and the 'Shivering Sand' with which she is particularly associated becomes, as seen through her eyes, a potent symbol for the mass of humanity excluded by the privileged world at the centre of the novel: 'It looks as though it had hundreds of suffocating people under it – all struggling to get to the surface, and all sinking lower and lower in the dreadful deeps!' (p. 58). The Sand, which, as Hutter points out, can also be seen to symbolise Rosanna's suppressed sexual longings, functions throughout the novel as a complex image of the deceptive surface which masks oppression and turmoil on both the social and the psychological levels. By allowing the Sand such prominence in the geography of the Verinder estate, as well as through his repeated reversal of our prejudices concerning such outcasts as the Brahmins, Jennings and Rosanna, Collins ensures that the enjoyable detective surface of his novel never quite obscures the dreadful deeps.

It seems to me that the kinds of Freudian approach discussed up to now are very useful tools for understanding detective fiction well beyond the confines of *The Moonstone* itself, and I shall continue to refer back to them throughout this study. But I propose now to abandon the specifically psychoanalytic line in order to examine further some of the questions of 'content' to which it has already started to lead.

It is arguable that the ideal detective story has no metaphors, no reference beyond itself, and therefore no concealed content: that the story of the crime – Todorov's 'first story' – occupies and should occupy exactly the space which in another work would claim to be occupied by its 'meaning'. In postmodernist hands this emptiness of content, or at least the implied possibility of such emptiness, constitutes a kind of negative glory, and it is arguable that the same possibility of 'unalloyed' reading contributes to the more general addictive lure of the form. How does this admittedly ideal template fit the apparently content-laden *Moonstone*?

We can make the initial point that, in the image of the Shivering Sand and elsewhere, Collins himself deliberately plays on the incompatability of detective and other interests. The Sand's alternately smooth and 'dimpled' surface can be seen as reflecting the blank detective dimension we are invited to share with Franklin and, to some extent, with the ever-loyal Betteredge. The complicity of these two leading narrators in the suppression of the 'dreadful deeps' is excellently conveyed when Franklin commissions Betteredge to skim through the suicidal Rosanna's last letter to him for evidence bearing on the 'truth' of the case, in order to spare himself knowledge of the truth of her feelings. Thanks to Betteredge's censorship of much of the letter, Franklin is able to include it in his final narrative without needing to encounter it directly, other than in the brief editorial remark that 'I can leave the miserable story of Rosanna Spearman . . . to suggest for itself all that is here purposely left unsaid' (p. 380). For the reader interested in the detective mystery there is, as Betteredge tells Franklin, 'nothing' in the letter; at the same time, in describing other instances of precisely this indifference on Franklin's part,

Rosanna's ghettoised narrative can be seen to 'suggest for itself' a commentary on the official narrative that carries his seal of approval.

The continued presence of such a dimension of 'suggestion' can clearly be linked to the possibility of meaning and metaphorical depth we have been discussing. This in turn can be related to the multiple-narrative construction which differentiates *The Moonstone* from many later detective works. As already argued, Franklin's persistent self-blindness is evident throughout the novel; at the same time, it is only through his work as commissioner and editor of all the disparate narratives that we attain the total picture. As with the Moonstone itself, numerous facets are organised round a centre which is elusive and possibly flawed. In this decentring of the controlling consciousness the novel differs sharply from most detective stories, where a stable distance between the detective's central consciousness and the consciousness which narrates is normally seen as essential. The crucial difference is perhaps the simple and obvious one that no single 'great detective' dominates *The Moonstone*: instead the detective function devolves on virtually the whole society of the novel, even including the deluded perceptions of Miss Clack.

Despite some partial exceptions (Bentley's *Trent's Last Case*; perhaps some of Christie's Miss Marple novels), one might argue that the detective story 'proper' evolved negatively, out of the jettisoning of the old sense of communal responsibility for crime with which Collins is still in touch, as much as through the positive creation of brilliant individual detectives such as Sherlock Holmes. Sergeant Cuff, usually cited as 'the' detective of the novel, anticipates Holmes quite precisely in several ways (not least in Betteredge's Watson-like narration of him), but his uneasy hireling role in the Verinder household is accurately reflected in his dismissal at an early stage for daring to tamper too intimately with its social balance. The forlorn drug addict Jennings, who suggests several aspects of Holmes's Bohemian 'other half', also fades from the picture after performing the key act of detection, ensuring that the space later to be filled by the great detective remains empty. Into this space, we might provisionally argue, the emotional and symbolic meanings of a particular social vision are still allowed to pour.

The alternative claimant to the 'central' role in most detective fiction is the criminal who has created the basic *mise-en-scène* in which the narrative takes place. Godfrey Ablewhite's failure to fit this organising and shaping role can partly be explained by the comparatively trivial nature of the crime itself: unlike the murder which becomes increasingly statutory in later works, his semi-accidental acquisition of the diamond is not what stops the society of the novel in its tracks. What does so is the breakdown of confidence when the diamond disappears: the burden of mutual distrust is far greater and more destructive than the burden of loss, or even of fear (which is neatly diverted towards the Indians). It is in the quest to expel this circling distrust in an acceptable way that the society of the novel pulls together: the unacceptability of Cuff's solution (with its echoes of the real-life Sergeant Whicher's scandalous accusation of Constance Kent in the notorious 'Road Murder' case) is what ensures his dismissal as a cure worse than the disease. The determination *not* to accuse Franklin entirely dictates the movements of Rachel and Rosanna, and the spirit of this determination is not abandoned until a harmless first cause of the mystery is discovered in Candy's amnesia. Ablewhite's place in the chain of cause and effect is comparatively secondary, and in structural as well as psychological terms there is little reason to dismiss Rycroft's account of him as a somewhat nominal scapegoat.

In the absence of the central balance of forces between detective and criminal, *The Moonstone*'s 'centre' becomes that of the society it depicts. As in a long comic-novelistic tradition this is supplied by the continuity of the Verinder estate as it it revitalised by the wedding of Franklin and Rachel and the expected birth of their first child. Around this centre are arranged the other figures whose efforts have been as much to bring about this event as to recover the diamond (Jennings, in particular, combines his detective role with that of Hymen). Seen from this schematic distance, the novel is simply one more of those celebrations of an organic landed society which dominate the English literary tradition, with Betteredge ushering us into and out of the premises like the butler of a house party: 'I am the person (as you remember no doubt) who led the way into these pages, and opened the story. I am also the person who is left behind, as it were, to close the story up' (p. 518). What has also been demonstrated, however, is the dependence of this settled order on the lonely and rootless figures whose non-integrated and often (again, Jennings and Rosanna are the clearest instances) desperate perspectives have contributed so essentially to the outcome. It is also significant how few of the peripheral figures survive to partake in that outcome: to the deaths of Rosanna,

Jennings, Ablewhite and both of the happy couple's surviving parents can be added the impairment of Candy's faculties and of Cuff's career, the banishment of Miss Clack, the alienation of Limping Lucy (another of the book's emblematic cripples), and the continued wanderings of Murthwaite. The tenuous 'society' of the beginning of the book, which leaves its ghostly traces in the documents of which it is composed, has all but vanished by the end: just as the Brahmins are scattered in permanent exile on achieving their goal of restoring the Moonstone to its rightful place, so the collective authors of *The Moonstone* are expelled from the restored world they have laboured to bring about.

The detective investigation, in which numerous witnesses contribute their evidence and depart, is a useful way of maintaining the dual focus which is one of the great achievements of the Victorian novel: on the need for integration and on the facts of disintegration, on 'community' and on individual alienation from that community as it is actually constructed. Dickens, who uses a wider range of methods to achieve a similar dual focus, came through Collins's influence to rely increasingly, as T. S. Eliot suggested, on the detective plot as at least one of those methods from *Bleak House* onwards.[7] By finding ways to give weight and density to the perspectives of its various 'witnesses', then, the three-volume Victorian detective novel valuably clogs the pure 'reading for the plot' of the subsequent genre. None the less, in *The Moonstone*, reading for the plot demands certain rituals of catharsis and expulsion: not, as in *Oedipus* and the pure whodunnit, of a single tainted individual, but of a too complex, difficult, and tenuous society.

In following up some lines of inquiry, it is inevitable that one will displace others which may be logically just as important. Here, in pursuit of some vital links between *Oedipus* and *The Moonstone*, I have overshot some of the chronological evidence for my generalisations about the 'pure' detective form. In returning now to the two writers who influenced Collins most deeply in this field, Poe and Gaboriau, I shall draw unapologetically and copiously on some of the positions just established. The Oedipus complex will continue to raise its ugly head, but just as persistent will be the more diffuse question of metaphor as a vehicle of social meaning: does detective fiction dispense entirely with the notion that literature needs to have a wider 'meaning' and, if so, how far does it succeed? No completely cut-and-dried answer can be given to this question, but

I shall argue that Poe, the most metaphorical of writers, makes a determined effort to destroy all such meanings, whereas Gaboriau, a much more original writer than is usually recognised, successfully fits the very 'abstractness' of detection into a wider perspective, in which a dense social symbolism remains alive and well and living, usually, in Paris.

3

Poe

Edgar Allan Poe invented the detective story. He also virtually invented the English short story itself, as well as propounding an anti-didactic, anti-mimetic theory of 'the poem for the poem's sake' which looked forward to the aesthetic concentrations and distillations of early modernism. The connections between these facts will be a continuing concern of this book, and accordingly I propose to approach Poe's detective fiction first by way of his literary theory and then by way of his more general practice as a writer of short stories.

In 'The Philosophy of Composition' (1846), Poe makes a famous attempt to explicate his poem 'The Raven' in terms of the fact that William Godwin's ur-detective novel *Caleb Williams* was written, roughly speaking, backwards. The 'indispensible air of consequence, of causation' Godwin gained by keeping 'the *dénouement* constantly in view' can and should be extended to all literary forms by replacing *dénouement* with 'the consideration of an *effect*' and the concomitant search for 'such combinations of event, or tone, as shall best aid me in the construction of the effect' (Poe, p. 978). The subsequent relentlessly intentionalist account of the genesis of 'The Raven', which itself reads like a detective story, stresses the primacy of effect over meaning or didactic purpose.

While a didactic concern with truth is 'heresy' in poetry, 'Truth is often, and in a very great degree, the aim of the tale. Some of the finest tales are tales of ratiocination'. ('Tales of ratiocination' was Poe's name for his own detective stories, which he had begun writing the previous year.) The superiority of the tale in general over the novel is established in terms of the latter's sacrifice of 'the immense force derivable from *totality*'; like the defunct epic, because 'it cannot be read at one sitting' the novel is 'the offspring of an imperfect sense of art' (review of Hawthorne's *Twice-Told Tales*, Poe, pp. 949–50).

Tales of ratiocination, then, are fully artistic in happening to aim for the specific effect of Truth, whereas poetry aims for Beauty and other tales may aim for 'terror, or passion, or horror, or a multitude of other such points' (p. 950). Thus presented, 'Truth' emerges as a highly specialised and relative object, one among the many sensations and flavours to be procured separately in the cafeteria of literature. Though in some ways restating Romantic precepts, Poe makes a decisive break with his predecessors in rejecting any overall demand on literature to be a mixture of Truth, Beauty and 'The Moral Sense' (p. 1026). Instead we have a world of intense specialisation which, we might argue, ties in logically with the marketplace in which Poe worked: an increasingly voracious magazine readership demanding an increasingly differentiated and clearly packaged product.

This is perhaps only another way of describing what is often called 'sensationalism', a word which Poe ironically associates with the demands of magazine readership in 'How to Write a Blackwood's Article': 'Should you ever be drowned or hung, be sure and make a note of your sensations – they will be worth to you ten guineas a sheet. If you wish to write forcibly, Miss Zenobia, pay minute attention to the sensations' (p. 236). In this usage, 'sensation' encompasses at once the public's demand for excitement and the concentrated sensibility of the aesthete. In the ensuing article, 'A Predicament', where Miss Zenobia describes having her head cut off in minute detail, Poe mocks the attempt to combine two aims which should be kept separate: powerful sensation and the effect of truth.

Specialisation of effect is at the root of Poe's general project, then, and out of that specialisation the detective story, among other things, is born. It will be one of the main concerns of this chapter to explore the kinds of unity of effect Poe's detective fiction offers. Before doing so, however, it will be useful to see how the search for concentrated and specialised effect works out in the kind of tale for which Poe is most famous: the Gothic horror story.

Perhaps the most famous of these, 'The Fall of the House of Usher', concerns an unnamed narrator's visit to the mansion of the reclusive Roderick Usher, the evocation of whose gloomy surroundings and nebulous fears takes up much of the tale. The fears seem eventually to concentrate around the dimly glimpsed figure of Usher's twin sister Madeline, a sufferer from catalepsy who in the course of the narrator's visit apparently dies and is entombed in the vault beneath the house. At the climax, while the narrator reads a Gothic tale to calm his host, Madeline breaks from her coffin, ascends the stairs and falls dead into the arms of her brother, who in turn dies of shock. As the horrified narrator leaves, the house splits along an ancient fissure and collapses into the pool at its feet.

The story's apparent absurdity when reduced to this bald outline indicates how little it depends on its 'plot'. Instead, it derives its dynamic from the gradual coming together of the nebulous terrors suggested at the beginning, in the climax and subsequent collapse described at the end. This is done through a comprehensive cross-referencing of one thing with another, so that, for instance, the early bewilderment of the narration is echoed in Usher's moods of 'tremulous indecision', as well as in his apparent invention of atonal music and abstract painting: he improvises on his guitar 'a singular perversion of the last waltz of Von Weber' and paints 'pure abstractions' full of 'vaguenesses at which I shuddered the more thrillingly, because I shuddered not knowing why' (Poe, p. 268). A similar cross-referencing accompanies the approach of the climax: as the suspense of 'Mad Trist', the tale the narrator is reading, mounts, so do the storm outside and Usher's terrified 'reading off' of the sounds announcing that his sister is mounting the stairs for a different kind of tryst. Finally, as the last two members of the Usher family fall to the floor in a single death, the 'House of Usher' and the tale itself collapse in their wake.

An important unifying factor is that the protagonist's own personality is split along the same emotional lines as the tale itself: the 'tremulous indecision' of the beginning and the 'collectedness and concentration' (p. 269) of the end are also the twin aspects of Roderick, particularly as shown in his rapidly 'varying' voice. We might suggest that these two traits also describe the two tasks confronting Poe as author: first creating a vague sense of fear with which to beckon and confuse the reader, but then needing to produce a resolving embodiment of the fear so that the tale can end effectively. It is relevant that these two functions are explicitly combined in a single figure, in a way that stops them from pulling apart, and also that that figure is an artist who, rather like Poe himself, pushes the specific emotions he works with to the verge of abstraction. We shall see later how a similar split in Poe's detective, Dupin, is equally closely related to the twin poles round which the ratiocinative tales are constructed.

This brief account has omitted much discussion of the two other chief characters: the narrator and Madeline. If we ignore the argument that the whole story is a self-projection on his part[1] it is easy to see the narrator, whose flabbergasted responses place him halfway between Usher and the reader, as a parallel figure to the ur-Watson who narrates the Dupin stories. As for Madeline, the causes of her sickness, like her feelings on awakening in the coffin, can only be guessed at – although clearly in some ways the creative core of the story. Surmises may well arise that she represents the lost possibility of regenerating the 'house' through incest, or that she is a projection of Usher's or the narrator's suppressed anima, but they are nowhere alluded to in the text. One of the results of Poe's concentration on singleness of effect, then, is the exclusion of other and different kinds of experience; and it is very relevant that this deliberately excised experience is that of a woman.

Another story, 'The Black Cat', also enacts such an exclusion in the name of a concentrated obsession, but at the same time seems implicitly to comment on the fact that it does so. Briefly, the story concerns the crazed narrator's love–hate relationship with a cat, which he maims in the eye and then hangs. After a strange incident in which the house burns down and the figure of a cat somehow appears in the plaster above the bed, he adopts another cat, clearly a reincarnation of the first, with which he goes through a similar cycle. When his wife tries to stop him from killing it, he murders her instead and bricks her body up in the cellar. In the presence of a search-party he confidently raps on the cellar wall with a stick, to be greeted by an inhuman shriek which leads to the wall being removed and the corpse revealed, with the shrieking cat perched on its head.

It is not hard to surmise a sexual displacement in the central object of the narrator's obsession: the cat, a present from his wife in the early days of marriage, changes slowly from an object of love to one of hatred, which he finally kills '*because* I knew that it had loved me, and *because* I felt it had given me no reason of offence' (Poe, p. 478). The cat's subsequent reappearance in the plaster above the marriage-bed, and the final perch of its reincarnation on the head of the dead wife, enforce an identification of wife and cat which is underscored by the wife's own reference to black cats as 'witches in disguise'. The cat's 'red extended mouth' (p. 483) and black fur in which, in its devilish reincarnation, a hangman's noose can be glimpsed with growing clarity, clearly expresses a vaginal phobia common in Poe's tales. Given this subtext, the complete textual blankness about the wife herself, innocent, loving and barely glimpsed, is as striking as the passions aroused by the cat over whom the narrator expresses such agonies of remorse.

But in fact the narrator issues a direct challenge to the reader to become the kind of detective of psychological projections and motivations he himself is incapable of being:

> Hereafter, perhaps, some intellect may be found which will reduce my phantasm to the commonplace – some intellect more calm, more logical, and far less excitable than my own, which will perceive, in the circumstances I detail with awe, nothing more than an ordinary succession of very natural causes and effects.   (pp. 476–7)

As Marie Bonaparte remarks in her classic Freudian study of Poe, this reads like a prophecy of 'the remote advent of psychoanalysis', given that the 'natural causes and effects' mentioned could only conceivably concern mental projections (Bonaparte, p. 459). Any other kind of explanation of the tale's events seems comically beside the point, as when the narrator attempts to 'expound' the cat-like shape which appears above his bed after the fire. A neighbour, clearly, had tried to rouse him by throwing the hanged cat through the window, and a gravely described confluence of lime, heat and ammonia must have done the rest. 'Although I thus readily accounted to my reason', the narrator continues, the incident still made 'a deep impression on my fancy' (Poe, p. 479). In this context, the fancy is clearly the right horse to back: the attempt at scientific detection can only be a joke in this shadow-world of psychic retribution.

The concentrated and specialised effects of 'The Fall of the House of Usher' and 'The Black Cat' arise from more or less analysable obsessions on the part of their protagonists. The earlier tale 'Berenice' (1835) is interesting for the narrator's firm declaration that his condition bids 'defiance to anything like analysis or explanation' (p. 147). Very briefly, the Berenice of the title is the first of Poe's cataleptic, prematurely interred heroines, in this case the beautiful cousin and fiancée of the narrator, Egaeus, who is so obsessed with her teeth that he raids her tomb in order to extract them. Though reluctantly acknowledging that his momomania is a 'disease', Egaeus initially presents it to us in terms of a heightened perceptual capacity and philosophical curiosity which in some ways resemble the special interests of the detective: 'This momomania, if I must so term it, consisted in a morbid irritability of those properties of the mind in metaphysical science termed the *attentive*.' In a style riddled with the circumlocutions of special expertise, he goes on to expound the '*intensity of interest* with which, in my case, the powers of meditation (not to speak technically) busied and buried themselves, in the contemplation of even the most ordinary objects of the universe' (p. 147).

Egaeus inhabits a world of paradox ('*certum est quia impossibile est*', p. 148) and insists that his mania does not fix itself on anything whose significance can be explained or understood. It is distinguished from the speculations of the mere daydreamer in that the objects on which he concentrates are 'invariably frivolous' in themselves; indeed, that their lack of relation to normal canons of moral and emotional significance is a prerequisite of his interest. It is not hard, in fact, to suggest an unconscious significance for the teeth he extracts from the mouth of his unfortunate fiancée shortly before the intended wedding: fear and envy of the *vagina dentata* presumably play their part here too, as Bonaparte inevitably suggests (Bonaparte, p. 218). None the less, it is as insignificant objects, objects metaphorically as well as physically 'cut off' from Berenice herself, that the teeth come to obsess Egaeus to the point where '*tous ses dents étaient des idées*' (Poe, p. 150).

Another story which recounts the abstraction of a single fragment from a reassuring context of significance is the story Poe wrote immediately prior to the first Dupin story. 'The Man of the Crowd' (1840) describes the narrator's pursuit through the London crowd of a man who 'does not permit [him] self to be read' (Poe, p. 308). Everyone else carries such clear professional stigmata as the clerks who 'all had slightly bald heads, from which the right ears, long used to pen-holding, had an odd habit of standing off on end' (p. 309). The existence of one man who defies such 'reading' impels the narrator to follow him and discover, with growing horror, that despite an 'absolute idiosyncrasy of expression' (p. 311) he seems to have no identity or wish other than to remain part of the crowd. As such he comes to represent the ultimate threat of the city, 'the type and genius of deep crime' (p. 314).

I have described these four stories selectively, in a way designed to bring out certain parallels with, but also some differences from, Poe's three detective stories featuring C. Auguste Dupin. Thus the use in 'Usher' of an admiring narrator and a noble recluse enamoured of darkness and inhabiting a house 'tottering to its fall' is closely duplicated in the relationship between the narrator and the decayed aristocrat Dupin. Perhaps even more relevant is the split personality expressed in the voices of both protagonists: the mixture of elements we have discussed in connection with Usher's personality and voice is also strongly evident in Dupin, whose vocal variations from 'rich tenor' to 'petulant' treble suggest 'the fancy of a double Dupin – the creative and the resolvent'. As with Usher, these two aspects of personality seem to correspond very clearly to the two functions of the type of story being told. In the short story, designed to be read 'at a sitting', the crossover from creation to resolution is particularly tangible, but perhaps most of all in the detective story, where the difference between 'creative' mystery (the realm of the criminal) and 'resolvent' final solution (the realm of the detective) is, if anything, even more clearcut. Poe's attempt to hold the two functions together in the figure of Dupin is, as we shall see, both crucial and problematic.

The obliteration of female experience which programmatically accompanies the focus on 'unity of effect' in so many Gothic tales is also evident in all three Dupin stories. In all of these the sufferings of women are fundamental, but somehow never brought centre-stage: only reaching us through dispassionate third-party accounts. In the Gothic tales the all-too conscious sidestepping of female experience is expressed in the repeated image of premature interment or bricking-up, and it is arguable that in the detective stories the firm structural wall dividing crime (that is, violence against women) from detection serves a similar function. 'The Black Cat' narrator's yearning for a scientific theory of causes and effects which would account for his own inexplicable violence also seems relevant here: it's arguable that this is exactly what detective fiction provides.

The two other stories considered contain some rather more elusive points, which are perhaps best taken together. Both 'Berenice' and 'The Man of the Crowd' seem to raise quite specifically the idea of fragments, and their relation to the whole. Both narrators possibly resemble the reader in their claim to be detached observers, attentively perusing the world at large. But while disavowing any specific personal interest, each becomes caught up with a single part of the whole, whose challenge seems to consist precisely in its 'unreadability' in any other context than its own. Such *disjecta membra* arguably resemble the short story form itself, cut off from the organicist claims for a general literary usefulness which Poe the theorist so firmly rejects. If so, the dread of not being able to 'read' such fragments is allayed in detective fiction, where the clues carry a similar meaning of meaninglessness until finally fitted into place by the detective. Their 'specialness', in which they resemble the odd challenges of the short-story form itself, is subdued to a wider specialism, in which they 'permit themselves to be read' in a totally new kind of literary context.

In concluding this brief general discussion of Poe's insistence on specialisation of effect, it is worth asking whether the detective story is *specially* specialised in any way, in terms of content as well as form. On several simple counts it is fairly clear that it is. Poe's detective, Dupin, is pre-eminently a specialist, with one faculty, the faculty of analysis, developed to a high degree. Like many other Poe heroes, Dupin emphasises his specialism by excluding extraneous elements from his physical environment, such as company and daylight. The nature of the stories, too, is relentlessly concentrative: our search for the solution involves, by definition, a progressive exclusion of the contingent and the inessential, focusing our interest ever more tightly on a single issue. None the less, as I hope the following more detailed discussion will show, Poe's invention of the form also in some ways constitutes a determined *attack* on the monomaniac preoccupations of the Gothic tales.

The first Dupin story, 'The Murders in the Rue Morgue' (1841), opens with a long disquisition on the superiority of 'analysis' to 'ingenuity' and then introduces C. Auguste Dupin, a scholarly recluse with whom the narrator once shared an apartment in Paris. An example of Dupin's analytic powers is given in an episode where he reads his friend's thoughts, and then we are introduced to the main story. Two women have been horribly murdered in an upper apartment, and witnesses heard two voices, one gruff and one shrill, before breaking down the door. Since the apartment was firmly locked and no one was discovered except the corpses, the police and press are baffled. Dupin visits the scene briefly, places an advertisement in a newspaper, then calmly proves to his astonished colleague that the killer escaped through a window everyone thought locked, and must have been an orang-utan. At this point a sailor enters, lured by Dupin's advertisement claiming that the ape has been found, and confirms the story at pistol point: the ape, which was his, escaped one night with a razor and climbed up a lightning-rod to the Rue Morgue apartment. Climbing after it in pursuit, the gruff-voiced sailor expostulated from the window but then fled as the shrill-voiced ape killed the women. It then escaped in its turn, kicking shut the window which fortuitously locked itself thanks to a concealed spring. The sailor is exonerated, an innocent suspect released, and the ape captured and put in the zoo.

Rather than exploring the specifically 'detective' aspects of this story (which has often enough been done),[2] I should like first to stress its continuity with the Gothic tales by drawing attention to what several critics have noted as a kind of concealed motif: a *doppelgänger*-like connection between Dupin and the ape whose guilt he uncovers. Looking at the tale in terms of Poe's own biography, Marie Bonaparte presents the horrific murder as an equivalent of the 'primal scene' of parental intercourse, interpreted as violent by the child who inadvertently witnesses it and who is represented in the story both by the sailor at the window and by the 'resolvent' Dupin. In 'envying' the sailor his possession of the ape, Dupin is really recalling the happy time 'when the small onlooker might still identify with that savagely potent "father"!' (Bonaparte, p. 456). More recently, Richard Wilbur has pointed to the similarity between the two voices of the 'double Dupin' and those heard at the scene of the murder, and concluded that Dupin 'uses his genius to detect and restrain the brute in himself, thus exorcising the fiend' (Wilbur, *Responses*, p. 137). Wilbur adduces such textual details as the similarity between the tale's three two-member households, all living *au troisième* and all carefully secluded (pp. 136–7), and points out elsewhere that the narrator's phrase about handling Dupin's whims – '*Je les ménageais*' – further underlines the resemblance with the sailor's animal *ménagerie* (Carlson, pp. 168–9). Looking forward more generally to the detective genre's 'double current, irrational and rational', Stefano Tani has yet more recently interpreted the riddling phrase about 'a double Dupin – the creative and the resolvent' as meaning that the 'creative' side constitutes a Gothic residue secretly in sympathy with the ape, which the 'resolvent' side struggles hard to keep in check (Tani, p. 4).

Further secret links between detective and ape are perhaps hinted at in the story's strange epigraph from Sir Thomas Browne:

'What song the Syrens sang, or what name Achilles assumed when he hid himself among women, although puzzling questions, are not beyond *all* conjecture.' The ape who has concealed his identity, if not himself, among the corpses of women, also resembles Achilles in being an incarnation of physical strength. And immediately after this epigraph, we are told how the Dupinesque analyst glories 'as the strong man exults in his physical ability, delighting in such exercises as call his muscles into action' (Poe, p. 315). The murders are mysterious because of just such motiveless 'exulting' on the ape's part; and whereas the epigraph hints at a puzzle in the hero's name, 'Dupin' connotes both criminal 'duper'[3] and apelike 'pinetree-dweller'. And, pursuing the mythopoeic line one last step further, the ape's 'wound in the foot' (p. 338) perhaps recalls not only Achilles' heel but also the wound from which the ur-detective Oedipus derived *his* mysterious name.

But all such arguments, however interesting, tend to return the story to Poe's dominant Gothic mode. The metaphorical identity between detective and ape, once spotted, can then be seen to have a similar concentrative effect to the self-obsessions of Poe's Gothic protagonists. This impression is strengthened by the narrator's suggestion that Dupin's strange behaviour is 'the result of an excited, or perhaps of a diseased, intelligence' and that to an outside observer 'we should have been regarded as madmen – although, perhaps, as madmen of a harmless nature' (p. 318). Their seclusion, love of darkness, and 'time-eaten mansion . . . tottering to its fall' can all be seen to confirm this effect. Yet the story contains a pronounced counter-movement to such images of distillation, perhaps observable in the fact that the love of darkness is a 'whim', to be broken or (as in 'The Purloined Letter') exploited at will, and that the apparently doomed Gothic house, 'long deserted through superstitions into which we did not inquire', remains upright at least long enough to house a three-story series.

The brief page or so listing these apparently Gothic elements ends with the denial 'that I am detailing any mystery, or penning any romance' (p. 318). We can begin to trace the ways in which the tale is not a romance by returning to the question of Dupin's doubleness. Here is the relevant passage in full:

He boasted to me, with a low chuckling laugh, that most men, in respect to himself, wore windows in their bosoms, and was wont to follow up such assertions by direct and very startling

proofs of his intimate knowledge of my own. His manner at
these moments was frigid and abstract; his eyes were vacant in
expression; while his voice, usually a rich tenor, rose into a treble
which would have sounded petulantly but for the deliberateness
and entire distinctness of the enunciation. Observing him in
these moods, I often dwelt meditatively upon the old philosophy
of the Bi-Part Soul, and amused myself with the fancy of a
double Dupin – the creative and the resolvent.   (p. 318)

Though Dupin is clearly 'possessed', it is less clear which of his
two aspects is actually the demonic one (Bonaparte and Wilbur
simply attribute both to Poe). While Tani is sure that the 'frigid
and abstract' side is also the creative one, the actual sequence of
ideas in this and other passages[4] suggests that it belongs instead
to his resolvent aspect, leaving the 'creative' as the normal, given
personality expressed in his usual 'rich tenor'. This is consistent
with a systematic downgrading of what may well seem creative in
other tales, in favour of the resolvent faculty of 'analysis'.

The superiority of 'resolution' to creativity as normally conceived
is at any rate the gist of the long, quasi-scientific preamble, which
begins with the assertion that 'The mental features discoursed of
as the analytical, are, in themselves, but little susceptible of
analysis' (p. 315). The second paragraph identifies this faculty with
that of 're-solution', and the passage as a whole contrasts it forcibly
with a lower faculty described as 'ingenuity', which is further
associated with 'the constructive or combining power . . . frequently seen in those whose intellect bordered otherwise upon
idiocy'. That both these faculties are in a sense 'creative' can be
seen in an invocation of Coleridge's famous contrast between
Fancy and Imagination: 'the ingenious are always fanciful, and the
truly imaginative never otherwise than analytic' (p. 317).[5] The
distinction is revealing in that the 'constructive or combining
power' of fanciful ingenuity is specifically associated with the
intense 'concentration' and 'attentiveness' elsewhere attributed to
Poe's Gothic heroes. Thus whereas Usher at his most uncannily
perceptive manifests 'an intense . . . concentration', and Egaeus
an exceptionally *'attentive . . . intensity of interest'*, here the merely
ingenious chess-player is marked by his 'attention' and ability to be
'concentrative rather than . . . acute' (p. 315). And in a later passage
Dupin himself disparages his real-life precursor Vidocq[6] who, he
says, 'erred continually by the very intensity of his investigations'

and in being 'too profound' (p. 326).

In many ways these pronouncements are the reverse of what we might expect in the founding work of the detective genre. Concentration, attention, profound intensity of investigation and above all perhaps 'the constructive or combining power' would all seem to be prerequisites, yet it is these which Poe inaugurates the form by systematically downgrading. Qualities which constituted the demonic glory of his Gothic heroes are here the province of the Paris police. While it is important to notice that the analyst 'comprehends' these qualities and is, in passing, 'necessarily ingenious' (p. 317), the import of the whole passage is to relegate them to an uninteresting subordinate level.

To understand this relegation it is necessary to look more closely at the advantages of re-solution or analysis. Roughly the distinction appears to be between being in the grip of the tendency to let one idea lead to another (seen by Locke, for example, as the motivating force of literary creation)[7] and having enough grasp of other contexts to direct that tendency at will. This seems to be the point of the approving references to the games of draughts and whist where, because of their very simplicity, 'it is in matters beyond the limits of mere rule that the skill of the analyst is evinced. . . . Our player confines himself not at all' (p. 316). The merely ingenious chess-player, by contrast, is confined by rules variously characterised as 'elaborate', 'bizarre', 'complex', 'manifold' and 'involute', which limit him obsessively to the terms of his starting-point. If the terms applied to the confining rules of chess evoke the inwardly turning complexity of Gothic, the analyst 'glories' in his freedom from such rules, a freedom which comes suggestively close to cheating in its attention to a 'casual or inadvertent word; the accidental dropping or turning of a card' (p. 316).

I would like now to suggest that not only does the resolvent Dupin evade the rules of 'fancy', but that his endless powers of recontextualisation are inimical to them at a deeper structural level. We can perhaps recall here how the 'vaguenesses' of 'Usher' and the misdirected emphases of 'The Black Cat' seem to cry out for explication by 'some intellect more calm'. And though Egaeus claims that his monomania bids 'defiance to anything like analysis or explanation' and the Man of the Crowd does not permit himself to be read, their strange quests to possess or to become meaningless fragments cry out all the more to be expounded as 'essences' of mania and crime. The Dupin whose powers are so 'little susceptible of analysis' can of course be unravelled in the same way if we choose, but it is instructive to consider the ways in which the tale at least tries to constitute him as an unreadable reader or unanalysable analyst, through a rigorous rejection of metaphor.

The Prague Structuralist critic Roman Jakobson famously drew attention to the difference between 'metaphor' and 'metonymy' as narrative procedures.[8] In metaphor, one thing stands for another by sharing with it some essential quality. The Gothic tales, with their numerous cross-references between cat and wife, or house and owner, can be seen as intensely metaphorical, unifying all the tale's elements in line with Poe's aim of singleness of effect. In metonymy, by contrast, one thing stands next to another in a temporal sequence, and this in turn involves a use of synecdoche whereby an aspect or fragment of a whole 'stands in' for it as an exemplary instance: realistic narratives expect us to relate these fragmentary instances back to the known wholes from which they come. This can be seen as one of the key procedures of the detective story, where our ability to deduce the whole ape or sailor from a scrap of fur or greasy ribbon is constantly put to the test. We move not so much from similarity to similarity as from difference to difference, in a world where everything is defined by its distinguishing, or 'tell-tale', features.

The two dimensions, metaphoric and metonymic, doubtless coexist in all texts to some extent, but it is arguable that the dominance of metonymy in detective fiction makes the genre fundamentally hostile to metaphor. As a narrative procedure, the analytic or 'resolvent' approach to the 'tale of ratiocination' radically *denies* the need for any symbolic explanation of its action and any further 'resolution' of its images than that offered us by Dupin. The metaphoric dimension of the Gothic tales, in which a single image or situation is dwelt on with growing intensity up to a climactic manifestation, is replaced by a metonymic dimension in which everything depends for its significance on its position in a temporal sequence of cause and effect.

The clearest example of this replacement of metaphor by metonymy is perhaps the mind-reading episode in which we are first introduced to Dupin's analytic powers. On a stroll through Paris, Dupin astounds the narrator by chiming in with his thoughts about a would-be tragic actor named Chantilly, who has not previously been mentioned. He then traces the narrator's complete train of thought back to a collision with a fruitseller fifteen minutes before. 'The larger links of the chain run thus — Chantilly, Orion, Dr Nichols, Epicurus, Stereotomy, the street stones, the fruiterer' (Poe, p. 319). Dupin's subsequent explanation of all this invokes a series of scientific, literary and contemporary Parisian contexts with which even the most erudite reader is unlikely to be familiar. Bonaparte gives a bravura Freudian reading, centring round the inadequate Chantilly's resemblance to Poe's actor-father, but it seems clear that one deliberate point of the passage is to put us completely under Dupin's thumb as far as the power to explain the workings of the human mind is concerned.

The glittering array of specialised knowledge from which we are excluded partly demonstrates the ground-level of creative speculation the two friends share, but also emphasises the many different contexts of which Dupin's 'larger links of the chain' are metonymic fragments. They are, however, only important as they contribute to the chain: the main point of the passage is to sweep us from earth to heaven and from the mundane present to the fabulous past by way of a series of metaphorical connections whose enticements towards fuller explication we are precisely being taught *not* to explore. To do so is to fall prey to the 'constructive or combining power', bordering on idiocy, in whose grip the narrator is arrested red-handed by Dupin. Though Dupin's analysis comprehends this power, it is also what has made the narrator transparent, laying his mind open to analysis as if he 'wore a window in his bosom': the rich simultaneity of metaphorical association is overcome by being reduced to the successive moments of a metonymic sequence of differences.

Interestingly, the 'Stereotomy' which forms one of the links is a system of tidily juxtaposing paving-stones to avoid falling, as the narrator has just done, into the 'holes and ruts' created by the old cobblestone system. And the prohibition of *depth*, or profundity, is the main point of Dupin's strictures on Vidocq: 'Truth is not always in a well. . . . she is invariably superficial'; 'By undue profundity we perplex and enfeeble thought; and it is possible to make even Venus herself vanish from the firmament by a scrutiny too sustained' (p. 326). Leaving aside the swipe that the reference to Venus seems to take at Poe's future Freudian analysts, we can say that in such passages we are being taught to feel for a different order of meaning, where 'direct' access to metaphorical depth is replaced by our willing acceptance of the horizontal metonymic *surface* of the narrative.

I would suggest, then, that the demonic aspect of Dupin, which makes him so different from the rest of us, is not his reassuringly 'creative' but his almost inhumanly 'resolvent' side: indeed, it is perhaps this inhumanity that links him most clearly to the ape. Both, in this story, enact that overlooking of the L'Espanaye's sufferings which seems one of the points of the story, the ape by treating them as rag dolls and Dupin by calmly picking over the bodies for clues, leaving the signifying exclamations of horror – 'sacré', 'diable', 'mon Dieu' – to their keepers and the sensational press.

Dupin's assertion that truth is 'invariably superficial' can be reasonably related to the programmatic superficiality its critics object to in the detective genre as a whole. It resembles the semi-cheating whereby the adept at whist places the events of the game in more contexts than the rules seem to indicate. By his constant invoking of such contexts, beyond those apparently given, Dupin also in a sense cheats us in our expectation that the specific short story will exhibit some overall unity of meaning. It is by *not* concentrating on what seems to be before him, by suddenly invoking zoological treatises and Maltese hairstyles, that he asserts his dominance over our more narrowly focused vision. As with most later detective stories, this element of cheating is accompanied by a sense of formal disappointment or even outrage on our part. Though later writers usually undertake not to conceal the main clue until seconds before the main revelation (as Dupin does with the scrap of fur), few avoid a feeling of let-down when we discover that the criminal is 'only' Mr X or Miss Y, rather than some distillation of all the tantaslisingly displayed possibilities. Poe's ape is thus a fitting precursor of all later culprits in being, after all the kerfuffle, 'only' an ape.

We can summarise the above arguments by saying that 'The Murders in the Rue Morgue' operates on two levels. On the first, there are numerous parallels between detective and criminal which, when followed up, tend to 'concentrate' the story into a richly metaphorical psychodrama not very different from those of the Gothic tales. On the second level, however, this form of Gothic concentration is prohibited: instead, we pursue the solution by reference to numerous disparate fragments broken off, as it were, from a number of different contexts but all lying on, rather than under, the surface of the tale. The new genre, then, radically replaces one kind of formal unity with another. The synchronic uncovering of a unified meaning operating throughout the text becomes a diachronic juxtaposition of fragments whose originating contexts have no satisfying or 'deep' meaning in themselves, but only as they provide stepping stones to the next fragment and context. Poe's annexing of the grand name of Coleridgean 'Imagination' to this faculty is startling, but seems to indicate his pride in finding a new source of formal unity which can claim to be comprehensive rather than confiningly intensive, in which the proposed special effect of 'Truth' can be attained without the tautologies of Gothic, whose elements are only significant in so far as they all connote each other.

The much briefer discussion of the two other Dupin stories that follows will only be in expansion of some of the points already made. The second story, 'The Mystery of Marie Rogêt', was avowedly written as an attempt to solve the case of Mary Rogers, a New York shop assistant whose apparently assaulted body was found in the Hudson River after an elaborately prepared solo outing. Stressing the 'scarcely intelligible coincidences' between this and his lightly fictionalised Parisian version, Poe in the guise of Dupin directs suspicion on to an ex-lover of Marie/Mary in preference to the thuggish 'gang of miscreants' espoused by the press (Poe, pp. 397, 406). John Walsh has demonstrated fairly conclusively that the truth lay between the two theories, but not in a way either anticipated: the elaborate arrangements were to conceal an attempted abortion at a New Jersey inn, whose drastic failure led to the rapid disposal of Mary Rogers's body by the innkeeper and her sons, who then crudely faked the evidence of a gang-murder in some nearby woods.[9] While Poe drew important attention to the improbabilities of this evidence, his main conclusions were disproved by the dying confession of the innkeeper herself, which led him to a confusing last-ditch attempt to overlay his original deductions with hints at what really happened in the second, most widely-published version of the story. Because of its documentary content, and perhaps because the final additions induce almost total narrative incoherence, this story is much less discussed than the other two.

The 'factional' issues raised by the story are fascinating, particularly in the contrast they highlight between the press obsession with lower-class gangs and the nascent detective genre's counter-balancing obsession with the deep-laid plots of the Foucauldian mastermind: the margin with which both theories miss the every-day reality of abortion confronting working women, and its attendant enormous dangers, is almost exactly equal. None the less, I propose for the rest of this brief discussion to treat the story 'as if' it were a work of fiction, for reasons which I hope are obvious, given its important position in the context of the development of detective fiction as a whole. Seen in this way, the story becomes strikingly postmodernist in its acceptance of a kind of intertextual relativity at the centre of its narrative method, in which Dupin's 'strong exertions of intellect' are scarcely more than footnotes to a series of contradictory newspaper reports. So strong is the emphasis on method rather than results that the actual detection of the criminal is 'omitted' from the text to be replaced by a so-called editor's note justifying the omission on the fictionally ludicrous grounds of its irrelevance to the factual Rogers case, where the culprit had not yet been caught.

The story's peculiarity, when read as fiction, can be interestingly related to the overlapping of metonymic fragments from disparate contexts observed in 'Rue Morgue'. Appropriately enough, the main clues are fragments of Marie's clothing, on the probable methods of whose tearing Dupin expounds at length. This dwelling on the traces rather than the experience or significance of what seems to be a brutal sex-murder (though the fact is very euphemisti-cally handled) is typical of Poe; and here the inability to move on from these traces, owing to the lack of a clear solution, gives rise to a sense of fetishistic obsession not wholly under the story's control. But Dupin's main philosophical contribution, which can be related to the 'cheating at whist' theme already discussed, confirms the importance of transgressing the limits of the given context by adducing others:

> a vast, perhaps the larger, proportion of truth arises from the seemingly irrelevant. It is through the spirit of this principle, if not precisely through its letter, that modern science has resolved to *calculate upon the unforeseen*. . . . It is no longer philosophical to base upon what has been a vision of what is to be. *Accident* is admitted as a portion of the substructure.   (pp. 417–8; italics as in the original)

Dupin's main action, accordingly, is to incorporate accident into the substructure by adding further, apparently irrelevant reports which throw the given narrative into greater disarray. The 'openness' of the resultant text, decreed by the factual uncertainties of the Mary Rogers case, strikingly resembles some of the postmodernist deconstructions of detective certainties described by critics such as Michael Holquist and Stefano Tani.[10]

The last Dupin story, 'The Purloined Letter', concerns a compromising letter stolen from the French Queen (though her rank is not spelled out) for purposes of political blackmail. The police acting privately for the Queen ransack the thief's apartment in vain, whereupon Dupin undertakes to find it for a share of the reward. Visiting the thief, the high-ranking Minister D– with whom he is acquainted already, Dupin instantly notices the letter in a place so obvious the police overlooked it, and on a second visit replaces it with a similar letter bearing a vengeful message to the Minister, whose political downfall is now assured. Returning the original to the police chief, Dupin pockets the reward.

This tightly structured story has attracted much critical attention in the wake of Jacques Lacan's famous 'Seminar' on it. Without wading deeply into the complex issues raised by Lacan, Derrida and others,[11] I intend to look chiefly at the way the story extends some of the themes of 'Rue Morgue'. The contrast established there between a mere 'ingenuity' of depth and a superior 'analysis' of surface here clearly constitutes the major programme. In expanding this contrast, Dupin uses a series of explanatory analogies: the game of 'even and odd', in which a clever player is always one step ahead of his opponent's bluff or counterbluff; the fact that mathematics works by 'truths within the limits of *relation*' rather than '*finite* truths' (Poe, p. 603); the fact that small street-advertisements and names on maps are easier to read than large ones. In all these instances the analytical adept does not ransack the logical hiding-places of truth, but scans the 'surface' of the problem in the knowledge that concealment and obviousness are constantly interchanging poles within a single binary system.

The story is marked by a comparable firming-up of Dupin as a 'character', bringing the Gothic and analytical traits of 'Rue Morgue' into a more carefully constructed harmony. Thus his addiction to darkness, a Gothic trait mentioned but not much exploited there, here becomes an active aid to perception, allowing him to see without being seen. When the Prefect G. first announces the problem, Dupin observes 'we shall examine it to better purpose in the dark', and proceeds to wrap his ironies at the prefect's expense in 'a perfect whirlwind' of tobacco smoke (p. 596). The same idea crops up in the 'green spectacles' from behind which he cases D–'s apartment while complaining of weak eyes. His decayed fortunes are now also made good use of, both in his eagerness for reward and his apparent social parity with his exalted antagonist.

This parity, which further extends from their shared initial to their shared abilities in poetry and mathematics (p. 602), consolidates the much more covert linking of detective and criminal in 'Rue Morgue'. The thoroughgoing binarism of this story, in which every parallel is also an opposition, admits the hidden links to the surface where, like the letter, they are perhaps most effectively concealed. Thus Dupin's account of the game of 'even and odd' emphasises the importance to victory of the 'identification of the reasoner's intellect with that of his opponent' (p. 601). Many further parallels between Dupin and D– are persuasively demonstrated in Lacan's seminar, which particularly stresses the way in which Dupin's substitution of one letter by another mirrors the original theft. This is part of a broader argument in which Lacan presents the letter itself as a 'pure signifier' whose only meaning derives from its intersubjective context as it moves from hand to hand, rather than from its unread erotic content (Most and Stowe, p. 29). As in 'Rue Morgue', the various clues acquire their meanings through being recontextualised rather than through what Dupin here calls their 'finite truths'.

The final aspect of the Dupin series I would like to look at is the fact that it *is* a series. The influence of Dupin on later literary detectives, and pre-eminently on Sherlock Holmes, is generally acknowledged, as is the way the stories 'struck out at a blow' most of the genre's basic plot formulae, as Dorothy L. Sayers put it (Winks, p. 57). It is especially significant, however, that Poe did this through writing three short stories with the same hero. I shall argue later that Doyle's extension of this practice was fundamental in establishing the dominance of the genre. But Poe's creation of the first single-hero series (excluding legendary romances and such spin-offs from chronicles as *The Merry Wives of Windsor*) can be seen as the first example of that endless re-enactment of the same situation by the same central cast that has become through Doyle and then through television the staple narrative form of the twentieth century.

But the way Poe ends the series is also perhaps significant.

Dupin's final message to D–, inscribed in the substitute letter which is to lead to his downfall, casts himself in the role of the classical revenger Atreus and D– in that of his brother Thyestes, whose punishment at Atreus's hands was notoriously worse than his crime.[12] The encodement in an unexplicated scrap of French verse of this ancient revenge plot, where hero and villain cannot be disentangled, returns us suddenly to the demonic Dupin and perhaps reminds us that both his and D–'s actions are equally treasonable. Perhaps it is no accident that this sudden deconstruction of Dupin back into an amoral, personally involved revenger not too far from the demonic heroes of Gothic, puts an end to the series in which he has so briefly starred. The quasi-mythic struggle silently enacted in his final ciphered message can be compared to a later struggle between *doppelgängers* which was also at least intended to silence the hero for good: Sherlock Holmes's final battle with Moriarty at the Reichenbach Falls.

4

Gaboriau

The other 'founding father' of detective fiction was the French novelist Emile Gaboriau (1833–73), who can be credited with creating the detective novel in the wake of Poe's invention of the detective short story. In introducing Gaboriau, a certain amount of old-fashioned partisan literary-critical grumbling would seem to be in order. His novels are now very difficult to come by in English, and critics who discuss him in passing tend to move rapidly from acknowledging his invention of the detective novel to strictures on his failure to confine it tightly enough within some of its later limits. We shall see in the next chapter how this cardinal sin made Sherlock Holmes 'positively ill', in the first of the novels for whose broken-backed construction Gaboriau's influence is, ironically, routinely blamed. The common charge is that he mixes tightly plotted 'pure' detection à la Poe with other kinds of novelistic interest, and in particular with lengthy background narratives which virtually constitute novels within novels. That many of these complaints depend on received wisdom rather than first-hand knowledge is apparent in frequent confusions between his various books and between his two leading detectives, Tabaret and Lecoq.[1]

I hope that what follows will start to show how Gaboriau anticipated much of what is interesting in later crime writing: in Collins, whose multi-faceted mixture of narrative approaches owes a great deal to him; in hardboiled writing, whose self-doubting confrontations with money and power often throw detection itself into question; in numerous post-Freudian texts (like those of Ross Macdonald) whose *familial* Oedipal themes he anticipates a good deal more directly than either Poe or Collins; and in the modern 'police procedural', where the duel to extract a confession is as important as determining guilt at an abstract level, and casts as many reflections on the apparatus of control as it does on the criminality of crime.

I propose to discuss Gaboriau not just as a 'bungling' precursor of Conan Doyle but as a novelist who uses the sometimes awkward clash between single-viewpoint detection and omniscient historical

or psychological narration for serious novelistic purposes. Though
this clash occurs at its most extreme and challenging in his last
major detective novel, *Monsieur Lecoq* (1869), I shall begin with the
first, *L'Affaire Lerouge* (1865),[2] where the two narrative levels are
less obtrusively separated, but where the reasons behind the
mixture are already clear and interesting. Before doing so, I should
perhaps point out that I shall not systematically follow up the
arguments about metaphor and metonymy raised in the preceding
discussion of Poe (see pp. 48–9). The detailed procedures of detection
are, indeed, primarily metonymic; but with a figure so much 'on
the carpet' as Gaboriau, it seems more useful to stress the elements
of connection and interrelation which demonstrate that, at least at
novel length, detective writing is capable of handling 'themes',
'topics' and 'issues' in a way for which it doesn't always get credit,
and particuarly not from those enthusiasts who deplore all such
complexities as impurities.

The powerful Count de Commarin has a wife and a mistress,
each of whom bears him a son. Preferring the mistress, Mme
Gerdy, he arranges to have the babies secretly swapped so that
hers can inherit his fortune. The novel begins many years later
with the murder of the nurse, Claudine Lerouge, who performed
the exchange. In a display of brilliance on which some of Sherlock
Holmes's performances are very clearly modelled, the amateur
detective Tabaret concludes that the killer was a gentleman, anxious
to destroy some of her papers. By an apparent coincidence,
Tabaret's lodger Noel Gerdy claims a strong interest in the case:
he has recently discovered that he is the Count's legitimate son;
the acknowledged heir, Albert, must have murdered the nurse to
conceal the fact of the swap. As the reluctant Count installs Noel
at the château, Albert is arrested and interrogated by a magistrate,
Daburon, who happens also to be his rival in love and once came
close to murdering him. Finally, Albert's fiancée Claire gives him
the alibi he was too honourable to request; and Tabaret realises
that the apparently upright Noel, desperate for money because of
his mistress's extravagances, murdered the nurse because her
evidence was the opposite of what he had claimed. Though
intending to exchange the babies, she was prevented by her
husband, who now returns from sea to tell his story and clinch
the case against Noel. Fleeing for his life, Noel is tracked down by
Tabaret to his mistress Juliette's apartment, where he shoots
himself.

Apart from its detective interest, the novel is clearly dominated by the two closely intertwined themes of the thwarting parent and the unhappy love-affair, particularly as these are highlighted in a society obsessed by status and by money. The main thwarting parent, the repulsive Count, blames his own unhappy but prestigious marriage on 'the barbarity of our parents', while his discarded son Noel unjustly but obsessively blames his mother for the poverty which has prevented his 'marriage with a young girl I love' (Gaboriau, *Lerouge*, pp. 61, 58). The extravagance which drives Noel to crime only expresses his mistress Juliette's frustration with their clandestine relationship; her childhood in turn was 'a long alternation of beatings and caresses, equally furious' (p. 96). The semi-secrecy of Albert's engagement to Claire, which deprives him of an alibi, is imposed by the patrician arrogance of his father and the pride of her noble but poor grandmother, the Marquise d'Arlanges. Even the nurse's absconding husband, Lerouge, 'almost wanted to kill' his father for trying to prevent his marriage to Claudine (p. 378), which none the less turned out badly and culminated in his preventing her from switching babies, thereby becoming in a sense yet another of Noel's thwarting parents.

Similar pressures are just as clearly evident in the lives of the two leading figures on the detective side of the fence. Old, ugly and apparently halfwitted, 'Père' Tabaret is a prototype of such 'unimpressive' detective heroes as Father Brown and Hercule Poirot. Where he differs from them is in a still active desire for marriage and children, cruelly frustrated in his youth by a miserly father whose pretence of poverty prevented him from marrying. On his father's death he became a detective out of a 'mania' for crime literature quite consciously adopted 'to replace the interest in life I despaired of gaining' through sexual fulfilment (p. 38). Indeed, Noel's savage outburst against his mother for condemning him to 'waste his affection' in undeserved poverty, comes hot on the heels of Tabaret's equally shocking outburst against the father who 'ruined my youth, wasted my manhood' for the same reason: crime and detection (and perhaps also the 'mania' for reading about them) would seem, then, to spring from very similar sources (pp. 35, 57). Daburon, the examining magistrate with whom Tabaret works in close conjunction, owes his legal eminence to a comparable combination of parental inadequacy and sexual disappointment: it is his father's perverse failure to acquire a noble title that has hindered him from declaring his love for Claire d'Arlanges until too late, and driven him to seek fulfilment in his work.

The sexual frustrations of the two detective figures make them thoroughly fallible. Tabaret's failure to suspect Noel is the result of a stifled passion for his mother, which he expresses by treating Noel as his own son and heir: ironically, given the prevailing level of father–son relations, perhaps his most paternal act is to drive him to his death. Meanwhile, Daburon's interrogation of Albert is so confused by the fact that he once nearly killed him out of jealousy, that he mentally reverses their roles, obsessively muttering to himself that 'I am going to appear before the Viscount de Commarin' (p. 147). Both detectives, then, are blinded by their emotional involvement in the case, and though they eventually see justice done it is in traumatic opposition to their personal desires. They both retire from the law: Daburon in search of forgetfulness and to his friends' hopes of 'some time inducing him to marry', and Tabaret into a kind of terminal eccentricity in which he 'doubted the very existence of crime, and believed that the evidence of one's senses proved nothing' (p. 436).

In striking contrast to the 'pure' whodunnit, then, the detectives share a common plight and an overlapping history with the protagonists of the murder intrigue. Such identifications across the legal and narrative divide can to some extent be subsumed under the heading of 'there but for the grace of God go I', or 'Poor humanity!', as Tabaret's favourite saying has it (pp. 47, 48, etc.). But they also drive towards a deeper questioning of the presumed divisions between innocence and guilt, man-hunting and fortune-hunting, parental love and patriarchal tyranny. The most insistent questioning centres on the novel's supreme father-figure, the Count de Commarin, whom Noel finally denounces in a climactic rechannelling of his earlier unjust attacks on his mother: 'Adieu! my father: you are the true criminal, but you will escape punishment. Ah, heaven is not just! I curse you' (p. 420). The appalling Count, at this point simultaneously offering his son five thousand francs for his silence and a pistol to kill himself with, becomes a self-parodying emblem of the two alternatives of paternal (and aristocratic) power: to make or, most usually, to break.

I have tried to show that, however melodramatically or schematically, *L'Affaire Lerouge* has a thematic content which goes beyond the simple detective interest of the case. It is perhaps this as much as anything which has caused confusion to *aficionados*: arguably the purest detective fiction replaces 'content' entirely by a process whereby a single tightly focused consciousness reduces all meaning into a single causal pattern. If *L'Affaire Lerouge* refuses this model at the level of content, it does so just as dramatically at the level of narrative technique. It begins, certainly, according to a formula which it helps to establish: our viewpoint moves rapidly up a chain of command from the victim's neighbours to the braggadocio police chief (Gevrol) and only then to the star amateur detective, Tabaret. From here we stay with Tabaret for the first four chapters, seeing not only the case but also the important new characters, Noel and Mme Gerdy, through his eyes. From the fifth chapter on, however, the novel becomes a free-for-all in which the careful feeding out of evidence alternates with omnisciently narrated scenes, often flashbacks, which privilege us over the detectives and enable us to sympathise with all the characters equally, whether detectives, criminals, or people only tangentially related to the case, like the impressively analysed Juliette or the comic but thematically significant Marquise d'Arlanges.

This dual focus in the narration permits a restless, questioning movement in which one perspective criticises the other. The detective quest which reveals the hidden connections between a low-life village murder and the upper reaches of the aristocracy is not in itself enough unless we also register the conflicts of desire and frustration in the 'respectable' middle ground which motivate criminal and detective alike. We are prepared for this mutually critical technique by a neat piece of symbolism: Noel leaves Tabaret's house, in which he is such a respectable tenant, by a secret exit of which the great detective remains himself unaware throughout the book. Breaking away from the detective-centred narrative by this act, Noel leads us to the very different world of the dream-palace-cum-torture-chamber he has created to satisfy the longings of his mistress, but which also expresses a great deal of himself. As the pointed and sympathetic analysis of Juliette's motives makes clear, she demands money as a substitute for social recognition, which is also Noel's own position *vis-à-vis* the parents who conceived him in a similar love-nest (and indeed, further down the line as it were, also the position of his victim, the blackmailing Claudine Lerouge).

The lingering description of Juliette's apartment, with its Louis Quatorze *salon doré* and its oriental smoking-room, can be interestingly related to Walter Benjamin's attribution of the detective genre to the new importance of interior décor in the nineteenth century, and pre-eminently in Paris: 'For the private citizen the space in which he lives enters for the first time into contrast with the one of daily work . . . the traces of the inhabitant impress themselves upon the *intérieur* and from them is born the detective story, which goes after these traces.'[3] The love-nest, Juliette included, constitutes Noel's chief escape from the cramped home which he uses as an office, and his reason for never inviting company to it is its absolute incompatability with his career as a lawyer: 'What client would confide his interests to an imbecile who permitted himself to be ruined by the woman whose toilettes are the talk of Paris?' (p. 103). It is, appropriately, in this apartment, which his years of experience as a pawnbroker's clerk enable him to price in a series of 'significant glances', that Tabaret finally becomes aware of Noel's guilt: an awareness only underlined by Juliette's complaint that 'he hides me like a secret crime' (p. 411).

We might even argue that the apartment is an emblem of the suppressed state of mind of a whole society as embodied in the good bourgeois lawyer Noel. The luxury of the rooms stands for a general fantasy of social aggrandisement which the pseudo-Bonapartism of Second-Empire society encourages but can never permit to be realised. The fact that this hidden life in someone assumed to be 'one of us' goes unrecognised by the detective constitutes a crucial failure of perception on his part. It is significant that Tabaret's bravura uncovering of the criminal links leading from low to high society is succeeded by a long period of blindness to the destructive forces operating at the supposed point of balance represented in his own 'frugal' residence. It is arguable that the trail of murder and destruction that Noel creates is only one way to bridge social divisions which Tabaret, and the detective genre he presides over, are trying, with equally limited success, to bridge in another.

Before turning to *Monsieur Lecoq*, it will be useful to consider very briefly the way Gaboriau's chief detective novels fit together as a rough series: another area in which he expanded greatly on Poe, though a more immediate model may have been the *Comédie Humaine* of Balzac. The next two novels, *Le Crime d'Orcival* (1866–7) and *Le Dossier no. 113* (1867), star the famous and well-established Monsieur Lecoq of the detective police. Though a Lecoq also appears briefly in *L'Affaire Lerouge* as 'an old offender, reconciled to the law' (p. 10), he is a peripheral figure with a different history to that of this later Lecoq, who has no criminal record and whose professional ambition is fuelled chiefly by a desire to regain a lost social status. In *Le Crime d'Orcival*, which conforms most fully to the later conventions of the 'pure' detective novel, Lecoq is at his closest to such disinterested sleuths as Dupin and Holmes, while in *Le Dossier no. 113* he rather resembles Tabaret in his paternal attitude towards the chief suspect, Prosper, as well as in a passion for Prosper's mistress which makes him conduct the case in such heavy disguise that his true identity is not revealed even to the reader until the end.

The theme of the struggle between generations, and particularly fathers and sons, is explored at its fullest in *Monsieur Lecoq*, both at a literal and at a more symbolic level. This long novel is divided into two parts, *'L'Enquête'* and *'L'Honneur du nom'*, which are normally published separately in English as *Monsieur Lecoq* and *The Honour of the Name*: a confusing separation since the end of the second part is the dénouement of the first.[4] The novel takes us back to the beginning of Lecoq's career, over which the retired Tabaret now presides as a kind of guru, and ends with assurances of his future glory; the fact that this is thus at once the beginning and the end of the series (apart from some later 'social' novels where some of the same characters reappear) lends an added dimension of cyclical myth to the numerous encounters between youth and age which form a thematic link throughout.

A police patrol investigating a triple killing in a drinking-den arrests an apparent ruffian, May, who pleads self-defence but is reticent about other details. The young policeman Lecoq, who disarmed and captured him, feels there is more to the case and brilliantly demonstrates that a lady and others have left the scene. Despite opposition from his chief, Gevrol, and the magistrate d'Escorval, who mysteriously drops the case on seeing the prisoner, Lecoq persists in trying to prove that 'May' is of high rank. When all these efforts fail, the prisoner is deliberately allowed to escape so that Lecoq can follow him. He runs him to ground in the town-house of the powerful Duc de Sairmeuse but his search, graciously permitted by the duke, who is glimpsed shaving, reveals nothing. In despair he consults the oracular Tabaret, now retired, who confirms his growing suspicion that 'May' is Martial, Duc de Sairmeuse, himself. Lecoq prepares to gather more information on the duke's rural estate, before returning for his 'revenge'. In the second part, to be discussed in more detail later, it emerges that Martial and d'Escorval were once rivals for a woman who was later murdered by Martial's wife Blanche. The tavern brawl was a trap set by the murdered woman's brother, and Martial clung to his disguise to save his wife's name.

As Ernest Mandel points out, 'social and political problems are far more prominent in [Gaboriau's] novels than in the stories of Poe or Conan Doyle, in particular the conflict between monarchist conservative landowners and the liberal bourgeoisie' (Mandel, p. 19). It is in its challenging juxtaposition of such problems to the comparatively smooth detective narrative that the second part becomes indispensable to the effect of the book as a whole. Before approaching these issues directly, however, I shall spend some time exploring what seems to me a deliberately implanted mythical dimension in the first part of the book, which emphasises in its own way the conflict between the old and the new. This conflict is accompanied by a pronounced use of seasonal imagery, as well as a carefully established context of church festivals which serves to reinforce numerous parallels with the passion of Christ.

The killing in the drinking-den takes place around midnight on Shrove Sunday, after a heavy fall of snow which is just beginning to thaw. (The murder in *Lerouge* takes place around the same date, on Shrove Tuesday, though the orgy-before-penance overtones of the date are not so fully developed.) Despite the bluster of the ageing Gevrol, it is the young Lecoq who captures the murderer and goes on to uncover vital clues which undermine his chief's face-value acceptance of the case. Eyes sparkling like those of 'a conqueror taking possession of an empire' (Gaboriau, *Lecoq*, p. 22), he rapidly acquires an ascendancy over his elderly sidekick 'Father Absinthe' by reading the marked snow round the hovel like 'a white page upon which the people we are in search of have written, not only their movements . . . but their secret thoughts' (p. 38). At first incredulous, Absinthe compares himself to St Thomas – 'I have touched it with my fingers, and now I am content to follow you' – and Gevrol to a mere 'John the Baptist' in comparison to Lecoq (pp. 41, 44).

Lecoq's early triumphs over age, winter and darkness are followed by a protracted struggle to establish the prisoner's identity, which lasts throughout Lent. Like Christ in Gethsemane, Lecoq

has a dark night of the soul 'about mignight' on Shrove Tuesday,
when he stumbles alone through the streets, believing that 'There
only remains now for me to withdraw, with the least possible
damage and ridicule, from the false position I have assumed'
(p. 201). For several days in Easter week, he lies stretched out in a
loft to spy on May, to whom, however, he is betrayed, Judas-like,
by a Gevrol 'not worthy to unloose the latchets of [his] shoes'
(p. 348). May's escape takes place on a 'balmy' April morning close
to Easter, and although his final disappearance in the ducal hotel
is Lecoq's darkest hour, it also leads to the breaking of the case
when he turns in 'rage and despair' to Tabaret, otherwise known
as Père Tirauclair, or Father Bring-to-light (pp. 295, 332). Excited
by Lecoq's gloomy description of the prisoner – 'if I were super-
stitious, I should say he was the very devil himself' – Tabaret
assures him that he has 'conducted this affair like an angel' and,
in an echo of the quest for an heir which characterised him in
Lerouge, declares that now 'I shall have a successor' (pp. 345–8).
With the help of his omniscient knowledge of history, which he
adjures his successor to acquire if he is not to remain 'a common
detective', Tabaret confirms the identification of May which Lecoq
hardly dared to contemplate but which now determines him to
'remain in shadow until the day when I can remove the veil from
this mystery; then I will appear in my true character' (p. 366).

The omsicient narrative of the second part emerges at precisely
the point where Lecoq decides to seek fuller knowledge. It is
'exactly one month to a day' after this that he returns, rips off the
last of many disguises, and wrests a confession from the duke.
The conclusion of the case, which vindicates both antagonists
simultaneously, takes place a week later, that is, within a few days
of Ascension Day. Lecoq's final coming into his kingdom is
underscored by his adoption, on the day of his elevation to
inspector, of 'a seal, upon which was engraved the exultant rooster'
(Gaboriau, *Honor*, pp. 583–5).

Similar though more ambiguous links with the life of Christ and
seasonal resurrection myths can also be found in 'May', whose
assumed name connotes the month of high spring just as Lecoq's
name connotes the bird of morning. His role as prisoner, technically
innocent of crime but repeatedly interrogated about a claim to high
birth which he denies, recalls the inquisitions of Christ concerning
his claim to be the son of God. His 'last supper' before being
imprisoned is bread and wine, and there may even be a sly point

in the fact that he communicates with his followers outside the prison through messages contained in pieces of bread (Gaboriau, *Lecoq*, pp. 149, 264). The magistrate d'Escorval's abrupt abandonment of the case recalls the hand-washing Pilate, and his replacement, Segmuller, fleetingly resembles Herod in wishing for the torture implements of the Inquisition (p. 253). As we have seen, May's 'escape' takes place around Easter, whereupon he resumes his true rank and position. This victory is, however, accompanied by the death of his wife, over whom he prays 'may God forgive you as I forgive you – you whose crime has been so fearfully expiated here below!' (Gaboriau, *Honor*, p. 576). Lastly, the narrative as a whole finally works to vindicate him as well as Lecoq, and it is notable that the Ascension period at which this vindication takes place is in mid-May.

The duke's role is ambivalent, however, owing to the mystery and deceit with which he surrounds himself. Thus the significance of his name could be that he is the *false* May, an idea borne out by what seems like an unconscious slip in Gaboriau's chronology. Though his initial appearance as a 'young man' is never questioned despite Lecoq's tireless surveillance, and though he is fully capable of leaping a wall and killing a young attacker with his bare hands, his birth in 1791 puts him in his seventies if we accept a contemporary 1868 setting, and even if we don't, other internal evidence puts him at least in his mid-forties. His aura of supernatural deceitfulness is reinforced by an ability to adopt roles, histories and languages at will, from polylingual circus-barker to hardened convict, familiar with prison layouts and using a criminal *argot* 'which it is impossible to render, so changeable and so diverse is the signification of its words' (Gaboriau, *Lecoq*, p. 320). This versatility is matched by the extraordinary changeability of what seem, and in fact are, his real emotions, whereby he attempts suicide at one moment and appears perfectly relaxed and cheerful the next.

In his shape-shifting powers the ageing duke resembles Proteus, the old man of the sea from whom Hercules has to wrestle the secret of his own future, and it is appropriate that we are ushered into his presence by the *masked* Shrove Sunday revellers who set the scene for his arrest. In the somewhat *Golden Bough*-ish perspective adopted so far, he effectively fits the role of old-year-masquerading-as-new, the priest-king whom the young hero defeats but also replaces after learning his methods: it is as a similar adept at disguise that Lecoq finally triumphs, affirming his newly 'exultant' identity by renaming 'May' in a way which relegates him to a discredited past.

As a young hero triumphing over the deceits or inadequacies of age, Lecoq can also fruitfully be compared to Oedipus, the mythic ancestor of all detectives. This Oedipal parallel is evident not only in Lecoq's riddle-solving abilities, but also in the particular psychological intensity of his struggles with a series of father-figures. Born of well-to-do parents who died when his father became bankrupt, the young Lecoq became secretary to a brilliant astronomer, Baron Moser, an ambivalent Laius who expelled him from his house on discovering his potential genius for crime. It is to reverse these two traumatic falls from grace that Lecoq has channelled his ambition into police work, and their combination perhaps underlies his obsessive conviction that the 'mystery' of the prisoner's identity lies in the high social circles to which both Moser and his own father belonged. May's mysterious growth from young hooligan to ageing duke can thus perhaps be related at a fantasy level to Lecoq's growing awareness that it is the father, with his twin attributes of age and power, who is the antagonist he really seeks in the guise of the ruffians it is his usual business to pursue.

The sequence by which he becomes aware of the duke's real identity is suggestive. Pursuing 'May' through the duke's bedroom he has 'the honour of seeing M. le Duc de Sairmeuse through the half-open door of a small, white, marble bath-room' (p. 331). Unrecognisable after shaving, the duke ironically asks 'is the fugitive still invisible?', to which Lecoq mumbles a respectful yes. The intimate setting combined with the tangible presence of power, the riddling irony of speech, perhaps even the act of shaving, all evoke the child in the presence of the father. Lecoq's subsequent suspicion is surrounded by a strong sense of taboo: the duke's guilt is 'a strange, absolutely inadmissible thought' (p. 338). And it is then very much in the tones of a psychoanalyst trying to break through a strong mental defence that the suggestively named 'Father Bring-to-light' exclaims: 'You know as well as I do, that May resides on the Rue de Grenelle-Saint-Germain, and that he is known as Monsieur le Duc de Sairmeuse' (p. 359).

As the most powerful father-figure in the book, who is also the murderous foe to be tormented and interrogated, the duke constitutes, perhaps, the centre of Lecoq's Oedipal quest on a symbolic level. But another quasi-psychoanalytic probe of Tabaret's – 'What connection do you see between the fall of the judge and the prisoner's attempt at suicide?' – further reminds us of the duke's initially mysterious links with his rival d'Escorval, with whom he shares so many experiences and secrets (p. 352). It is, in fact, d'Escorval who seems to arouse some of Lecoq's most identifiably Oedipal emotions. He is the first high-ranking legal official to recognise Lecoq's brilliance, but at the same time he 'overawed and froze him to such a degree that his mind seemed absolutely paralysed in his presence' (p. 89). At their second meeting d'Escorval delivers a rebuff which leads Lecoq to some very Oedipal suspicions: '"Can it be," he murmured, "that he holds the key to the mystery? Does he not desire to get rid of me?"' (p. 105). The 'mystery' seems here to ramify outwards from the particular case to a whole hidden world of power and knowledge from which Lecoq remains excluded. (D'Escorval's method of getting rid of this over-inquisitive junior, however, is not to shatter his feet like Laius but to give it out that his own leg is broken.)

In the general welter of father-figures, Lecoq's treacherous superior Gevrol, firmly subordinated sidekick Absinthe and true spiritual father Tabaret all have their clear but different places. Before moving on from the Oedipal theme, it is perhaps relevant to insert that the ultimate French whodunnit, Gaston Leroux's *Mystère de la chambre jaune*, essentially describes a very young detective's discovery that the victim and perpetrator of a series of vicious quasi-sexual assaults are his parents, and that for good measure his criminal father is also his chief rival as a detective. Though the appearance of such a rampantly Oedipal text forty years after *Lecoq* may prove little in itself, it perhaps indicates that certain Anglo-Saxon taboos were never quite so necessary in a French literature where the link between power, sex and the search for identity is fairly standard.

Before turning to the very different world of the second part of the novel, the world which Lecoq seeks to penetrate, it is important to insist on its distinctness from the 'world' of detection of which he is the hero. With its endlessly repeated quests, its series organisation and – here at any rate – its theme of youthful regeneration, detective fiction resembles the timeless mode of heroic or chivalric romance. The world of the second part, by contrast, is far more timebound, both in the way in which its 'dates' are those of an irreversible history rather than the cyclical calendar, and in its much greater resemblance to a very different tradition of romance. Its apparently melodramatic plot conforms closely to the 'prose' romance tradition from which, for example, Shakespeare's Last Plays derive: what, if Freud had not taken over the term for slightly different purposes, we might call 'family romance'.[5] With their once-for-all quests to reunite shattered families and inheritances, such stories are bound up with time and history in a way in which the endlessly repeated exploits of heroic romances are not. They are also very clearly bound up with an aristocratic world order in which the family bodies forth the state. While this involves a definite limitation of subject-matter, I would none the less argue that '*L'Honneur du nom*' makes very effective use of prose romance conventions to explore the traumatic aftermath of the French Revolution, an aftermath systematically marked by divisions between classes on one hand, and between generations on the other.

In the following outline and hereafter, I shall follow Gaboriau in giving the Duc de Sairmeuse, otherwise 'May', his real Christian name, Martial: as we shall see, his plethora of names is one of the points of the book. The story concerns a family feud sparked off during the Bourbon Restoration by the ingratitude of Martial's father, the old duke, towards a faithful steward, Lacheneur, who has preserved the Sairmeuse estate for him throughout the revolutionary period. Mortally embittered, Lacheneur foments an abortive rebellion in which he is killed, but his son Jean and daughter Marie-Anne survive, the latter secretly marrying the liberal aristocrat d'Escorval and giving birth to a son. Suspecting her Byronically uncommunicative husband of being the child's father, Martial's wife Blanche murders Marie-Anne; a crime for which, many years later, when Martial is one of the most powerful men in the country, she is still being blackmailed by the family of the poacher-turned-spy Chupin. Tracing her to Paris through this family, the hate-crazed Jean Lacheneur arranges to have both her and Martial ambushed in a drinking-den, and it is here that the disguised Martial is arrested by Lecoq after killing his attackers and giving Blanche time to escape. Despite having loved Marie-Anne, Martial stays silent in prison to protect his wife's honour, though she kills herself in remorse on his escape. Marie-Anne's long-lost son, who disappeared at her death, is now reunited with his father d'Escorval, who withdrew from the 'May' case out of scruples at having his former rival in his power. Finally trapping Martial into confessing that he was May, Lecoq exonerates him, while still acquiring enough kudos to embark on a triumphant police career.

To deal with the political dimension first, it is possible to read the above story as an allegory of the hopes and fears of the liberal-bourgeois audience Gaboriau is primarily addressing. Like the idealised figure of Marie-Anne,[6] their France is the daughter of a Revolution which has finally paid back its debts to the old nobility. In its reactionary revanchist form (the old duke), however, this nobility has ignored the Revolution's achievements (Lacheneur's improvements to the estate) and thereby provoked renewed outbreaks (Lacheneur's revolt, anticipating those of 1830 and 1848), with which young people of all classes have sympathised in varying degrees (Marie-Anne's three suitors: the noble Martial, the liberal d'Escorval and the radical peasant Chanlouineau). Though these further outbreaks have revealed the decrepitude of the old order (the old duke's increasing subservience to Martial and the actual imbecility of Blanche's even more reactionary father), they were doomed to failure. France's future depends on a liberal ruling class in touch with the people (d'Escorval's marriage to Marie-Anne, which her embittered father tried to prevent), though it will accept the chaste devotion of peasant (Chanlouineau, who bequeaths her his house) and monarchist nobleman (Martial, who repeatedly protects her). But that ideal balance is being destroyed by a renewed vendetta between ultra-rightist aristocrats (Blanche) and embittered revolutionaries (Jean Lacheneur), a destruction aided by an opportunistic lower class ready to betray anyone for a price (the blackmailing Chupin family).

Just as insistent as the class allegory is the repeated stress on the embittered relations between fathers and children. (It is significant that apart from the liberal d'Escorval none of the younger generation protagonists have mothers.) Though at first morally swayed by his daughter, old Lacheneur (in a plot perhaps taken from *The Jew of Malta*, with which there are several other parallels[7]) more or less prostitutes her for the sake of revenge, while cruelly snubbing his fanatically devoted son Jean. In a contrary movement the dominance of father over child is virtually reversed in the aristocratic families, where Martial and Blanche reduce their once-domineering fathers to various kinds of mental collapse, a situation echoed in the case of the spy Chupin, who is regularly beaten by his sons. A different kind of unsatisfactory father is represented, perhaps less intentionally, in d'Escorval, whose pusillanimous flight from the endangered Marie-Anne results in her murder and the disappearance of their son, whose whereabouts he makes only the feeblest efforts to discover.

The prose romance traditionally centres on the disruption of families through the sins or mistakes of parents which are then healed by their children. In this case the partial redemption of one generation is attained through the emblematic figure of Marie-Anne, but her murder leads us to seek a more final redemption in her missing son, who should by rights be at the centre of the ending of the story as a whole. His parentage by Marie-Anne and d'Escorval, along with what we may call his shadow-parentage by Martial, Chanlouineau, and even the penitent Blanche (who has spent years looking for him) allegorically constitutes him as the new future of France herself. And we discover at the end that to this parentage must be added his devoted fostering by his vengeful uncle Jean Lacheneur, the chief surviving emblem of the Revolution at its most unalloyed. It is, then, perhaps (in a novel written three years before France's last Revolutionary attempt for a century, the Commune)[8] a young Jacobin whom the noble magistrate d'Escorval finally embraces as his son.

This significant reunion, however, is never personally witnessed either by us or by Lecoq, who tactfully withdraws from a scene of emotion from which he is separated 'only by a velvet *portière*' (Gaboriau, *Honor*, p. 582). This brief moment of overlap between the two levels of detective/'heroic' and historical/'prose' romance suggests an oblique connection between them which deserves to be pursued further. Lecoq's embarrassed indecision 'whether to remain or retire' reinforces, I think, our feeling that the real long-lost son is, or ought to be, Lecoq himself, the 'exultant rooster' who also symbolises France resurgent. On the other hand, remembering d'Escorval's earlier attempts to 'get rid of' him, we might suggest that the Family Romance in which d'Escorval is so central is itself a kind of literary Laius, struggling to the last to curtain itself off from this threatening parvenu which is detective fiction.

Finally, Lecoq cannot be a long-lost son because he is a policeman, a professional lacking even a Christian name who represents an opposite (serial, continuous) social model to that proposed in the reintegrated noble families of domestic romance. It is significant that on discovering that the real son bears his father's first as well as his second name, and is furnished with 'all the proofs necessary to establish his identity', Lecoq also appropriates d'Escorval's identity by forging his seal and handwriting in the trick which forces Martial to identify *him*self (p. 582). And Lecoq's apparent failure to find a new name for himself in the aristocratic romance plot is followed almost immediately by the blazoning of the rooster-emblem which flings the one name he has defiantly in the world's teeth.

It is worth taking this question of Lecoq's 'name' a little further. Initially simply 'the youngest' member of Gevrol's patrol, he is not named at all until he has captured 'May' and begun to challenge his chief's deductions. His lack of Christian name even then confirms him as 'a policeman' first and foremost, but as the novel progresses the professionalism marked by this lack of the full name becomes more and more a positive rather than a negative aspect of his identity. The next turning-point comes when his disciple Absinthe projects him into history by unthinkingly adding the 'Monsieur': 'Although unintentionally, the good man had certainly become the young policeman's godfather. From that day forward, to his enemies as well as to his friends, he was, and he remained, Monsieur Lecoq' (Gaboriau, *Lecoq*, p. 68). This title, significantly, angers the similarly unforenamed Gevrol, whose own soubriquet, 'General', highlights his position within the force but also confirms his lack of status outside it. Lecoq's 'Monsieur', by contrast, establishes his identity within the world at large and thereby regains for him the status a cut above the police lost by his improvident parents. 'Monsieur' in its origins, of course, indicates actual aristocracy: prefixed to 'Lecoq' it becomes a legendary instance of the policeman's right to respectful recognition within a society still unprepared to grant him a fully individual status. The rooster-seal is the final stage in the honouring of Lecoq's name: the still unforenamed professional identity which through its triumphant history constitutes an entitlement in itself.

If a vital *process* of self-identification underlies Lecoq's development, it runs parallel to the protracted but single *act* of identifying the prisoner 'May' as the elaborately entitled Anne-Marie-Martial de Tingry, former Marquis and present Duc de Sairmeuse. On the virtual completion of this act, the novel to do with establishing a new name, *Monsieur Lecoq*, is interrupted by the volume about defending the honour of an old one. Despite the importance of the much-insulted honour of the Lacheneurs, 'The Honour of the Name' primarily denotes the name of Sairmeuse, a name which, particularly as borne by Martial's father and wife, the narrative contrives to dishonour at every step. It is only after Martial has expiated this dishonour by taking it on himself, by enacting the circus-barkers and hardened crooks those other bearers of the name have already become, that he redeems it.

But the clear point which does emerge from the novel's repeated stress on identification is the power of a noble name in a class society. As Tabaret exclaims, 'do you think of going to arrest the Duc de Sairmeuse? Poor Lecoq! Free, this man is almost omnipotent, and you, an infinitesimal agent of police, will be broken like glass' (p. 365). This complete reversal of the roles assumed earlier by Lecoq and 'May' demonstrates the limits of police power, 'that mysterious power whose hand was everywhere' (p. 19), as the young Lecoq once believed. The novel's apparently triumphant conclusion can hence be seen as something of a stand-off between the two incompatible forms of power represented by the two types of name, professional and hereditary. And the same feeling of an unresolved stand-off also applies to the two versions of romance: as long as he never does penetrate this other world of aristocratic power, Lecoq is condemned to the endless repetition of triumphs in other people's stories which will constitute his glory as a professional detective hero. And as long as it conceals itself behind *portières*, aliases and tales of broken legs, the world of 'family romance' is condemned to becoming the repository of decadence and scandal, a world of which detective and reader alike can still exclaim that it 'will be in my power again on the day I learn its secret' (p. 365).

In summary, we might argue that the split narrative of *Monsieur Lecoq* establishes an equality, but at the same time a difference, between two principles, two types of identity, two social forces. Lecoq's youthful winning of spurs occupies, as it were, the horizontal dimension of the novel, a dimension which finally subsumes everything else; whereas *L'Honneur du nom*'s vertical plunge back into identity as history involves, if only allegorically, an awareness of sources of power which the triumphant horizontal present tense ignores at its peril. The final social 'message' is, perhaps, simply one of a tempered meritocracy: let 'the forward youth who would appear' adopt the French rooster as his emblem, in the confidence that it also symbolises individual self-advancement within an egalitarian profession. But let him also learn, like that unseen child of the family romance which he at once is and is not, 'the assistance history gives' (p. 363).

5

Sherlock Holmes – The Series

Sir Arthur Conan Doyle's Sherlock Holmes is the supreme 'character' of nineteenth-century detective fiction. As such he has inspired two very different critical traditions: the biographical and the archetypal. The first consists of the lugubriously tongue-in-cheek following-up of minor inconsistencies about dates and names which accounts for the bulk of 'Holmesian' literature. The second, more critically respectable, avoids getting sucked into the labyrinth of particular cases by concentrating on the archetypal Holmes formula – drawing attention either to the famous 'methods' or to the romantic–scientific blend which accounts for Holmes's overall appeal as a 'personality'.[1]

In the face of these two powerful traditions, I hope I am not simply being perverse in attempting first of all to introduce the 'canon' (a phrase I gratefully borrow from the Holmesians) without an initial close-up on the figure of the great detective himself. I shall eventually get round to him, but it seems to me that such a discussion will be more meaningful after some attempt to establish the social concerns and tendencies of the full range of stories he appears in. This synoptic approach has at least the benefit of nodding both to the minutiae of the Holmes industry and to the abstracting tendencies of archetypal criticism – but here it seems important to establish early that there are about ten basic formulae at work, and not just one. Some of these are best explored by looking closely at particular cases, but some emerge most clearly in the lump. Indeed, if we substitute 'story' for 'man', Holmes's own pronouncement in *The Sign of Four* provides what could almost be the motto for this approach:

> While the individual man is an insoluble puzzle, in the aggregate he becomes a mathematical certainty. You can, for example, never foretell what any one man will do, but you can say with precision what an average number will be up to. Individuals vary, but percentages remain constant. So says the statistician. (Doyle, *Complete Adventures*, p. 137)

The Contents and Outcomes of Holmes's Cases

A = Arrest (18)
P = Providential punishment (11)
E = Escape (7)
L = Let off by Holmes (9)

1. *Secret Societies* (11)
(a) American: *A Study in Scarlet* (P), 'The Five Orange Pips' (E), 'The Dancing Men' (A), *The Valley of Fear* (E), 'Wisteria Lodge' (E), 'The Red Circle' (L).
(b) European: 'The Six Napoleons' (A), 'The Golden Pince-Nez' (P), 'His Last Bow' (A).
(c) British (Moriarty): 'The Final Problem' (P), 'The Empty House' (A).

2. *Colonial or Seafaring Conspiracies* (5)
The Sign of Four (A), 'The Boscombe Valley Mystery' (L), 'The *Gloria Scott*' (E), 'Black Peter' (A), 'The Solitary Cyclist' (A).

3. *Gangs* (9)
(a) Conspiratorial: 'The Engineer's Thumb' (E), 'The Greek Interpreter' (E), 'The Resident Patient' (E)
(b) Fool's errand: 'The Red-Headed League' (A), 'The Stockbroker's Clerk' (A), 'The Three Garridebs' (A)
(c) Other: 'Lady Frances Carfax' (A), 'The Mazarin Stone' (A), 'The Three Gables' (L).

4. *Inside Jobs* (5)
(a) Espionage: 'The Naval Treaty' (L), 'The Second Stain' (L), 'The Bruce-Partington Plans' (A).
(b) Other: 'The Beryl Coronet' (L), 'The Priory School' (L).

5. *Solo villains* (15)
(a) Savage squires: 'The Speckled Band' (P), 'The Copper Beeches' (P), 'The Reigate Squires' (A), *The Hound of the Baskervilles* (P), 'The Dying Detective' (A), 'The Devil's Foot' (P).
(b) Sexual jealousy: 'The Cardboard Box' (A), 'The Norwood Builder' (A), 'The Veiled Lodger' (L), 'The Retired Colourman' (A).
(c) Thieving servants: 'The Blue Carbuncle' (L), 'Silver Blaze' (P), 'The Musgrave Ritual' (P).
(d) Sexual predators: 'Charles Augustus Milverton' (P), 'The Illustrious Client' (P).

6. *Non-criminal cases* (15)
(a) Returned lover: 'The Noble Bachelor', 'The Yellow Face', 'The Crooked Man', 'The Abbey Grange'.
(b) Cover-up: 'A Scandal in Bohemia', 'A Case of Identity', 'The Man with the Twisted Lip', 'The Three Students', 'The Missing Three-Quarter', 'The Blanched Soldier', 'The Sussex Vampire', 'The Creeping Man', 'Shoscombe Old Place'.
(c) Other: 'The Problem of Thor Bridge', 'The Lion's Mane'.

What follows only makes full sense in conjunction with the list on p. 75. To include specific titles would have been cumbersome, but my general categorisation aims finally to illuminate every single story by indicating underlying themes which might otherwise be overlooked. While some cases inevitably straddle categories or fail to match up in every detail I have tried to cut as few corners as possible in the name of symmetry or neatness. As a final explanatory point: I have put 'weak' and/or late works on a par with more obviously important ones because, though some stories read like simple copies of others, the repetition of a formula still indicates its comparative importance for author and readers alike.

There are sixty Holmes stories in all, including the four novels. Of these the clearest-cut sub-category is the 'secret society' story concerning a full-blooded secret organisation with countless members, an initiatory code, and the will and power to destroy its enemies. There are eleven such stories, in nine of which the main secret society featured is foreign. In six, which include the two novels *A Study in Scarlet* and *The Valley of Fear*, the secret society is American, and in three, European (though some of the American groups have European origins). The American stories run quite rigidly to type: a fugitive from the society either kills or (more usually) is killed by its agents. Despite Holmes's best efforts, the society usually evades him. The European groups – Russian anarchists, the Italian Mafia, a German spy network – are less predictable in their behaviour and final treatment. The British group which is central to only two stories (though it also crops up in *The Valley of Fear*), the Moriarty organisation, forms an apparently unique bridge between the American-style secret society and the more miscellaneous indigenous crimes described in other tales.

A related group of stories concerns a conspiracy of silence between those in the know about a crime committed in the colonies or at sea, which leads to the blackmail or revenge-killing of some apparently respectable resident of the Home Counties. There are five stories (including the novel *The Sign of Four*) which conform to this pattern. In these stories the idea of a silent bond, whose actual or threatened betrayal is the subject of the story, constitutes a significant link with the 'secret society' stories. In both types the notion of foreign evil coming to roost on British soil is crucial. Lumping the two types together, this broad theme of 'conspiracy' is the subject of sixteen of the sixty stories. Furthermore, it is the subject of three of the four novels, and helps to account for their greater length, so that in raw bulk it occupies a good third of the total Holmes canon.

The next large group of stories to be considered involves professional criminal gangs. There are nine of these. In two, which partly overlap with the foreign conspiracy group, a young man is secretly hired to do a job for a ruthless gang of mixed nationality, who violently threaten his life before fleeing abroad. In another story a British gang takes a 'conspiracy'-style revenge on a former member. Apart from these cases, British gangs are not homicidal, or only incidentally so, but are far more likely to be caught. In three closely related stories, a team of two (or in one case the survivor of a duo) removes an innocent party from the scene of a proposed robbery by sending him on a skilfully fabricated fool's errand. Though appealingly clever, these duos contain firmly delineated 'outsider' elements: an effeminate aristocrat, two Jewish brothers, an ex-Chicago gangster. Other professional gangs are more miscellaneous, but all partly foreign: an Australian husband-and-wife team, an incompetent duo headed by an Italian count, a largish gang of thugs denoted mainly by its one black member. Except for this last one, professional gangs operating on British soil are small: two or three as against the massed hordes of the foreign-led secret societies.

A further clear-cut group of five stories about criminal associations, if not about gangs, is the 'inside job' group. In three very similar cases a man in a position of trust has a vital government document stolen by a member of his family for foreign spies. In two other stories the missing object is not a document but has similar overtones of grave national importance. In all five cases Holmes recovers the object of trust and, in all but one, hushes up the family scandal, though foreign spies and lower-class confederates may be arrested and hanged.

Criminal groups, including conspiracies and inside jobs, then, account for thirty of the sixty Holmes stories: exactly half. There are fifteen stories dealing with individual criminals. Five, including *The Hound of the Baskervilles*, deal with an apparently prosperous gentleman, often of the squirearchy and/or a good colonial position, who murders, or in one case imprisons, a relative for money. This group is characterised by an innate savagery expressed in a reliance on vicious animals and/or tropical drugs, and accounts for most of the occasions in the canon when Holmes is threatened personally. (A single story, 'The Reigate Squires', resembles these in atmosphere but has equally strong links with the 'conspiracy' group.)

Four stories deal with actual or attempted murder from motives of sexual passion or jealousy: these are confined to the lower middle class, and always involve some striking physical disfigurement as a symbol of the ugliness within. Three stories deal with a thieving servant, also something of a Don Juan, who loses his booty and sometimes his life, even before Holmes enters the scene. Two deal centrally with a man who preys professionally on women, either as blackmailer or seducer, and is destroyed by a past victim whom Holmes allows to go free.

This leaves no less than fifteen cases where no technical crime has been committed, at least by the living. The most clear-cut group consists of four 'returned lover' stories. An apparently happily married woman is confronted by an earlier lover, husband or, in one case, child. While her present husband's response ranges from the understanding to the homicidal, the wife's loyalty to her past commitment is applauded, and in two cases where the husband dies as a result of his own violence, it is only on Holmes's discretion that the lovers are ruled innocent. This category has some interesting resemblances to the 'conspiracy' category, in that the old affair which now comes home to roost took place in the 'freer' world of the colonies or America.

Though otherwise diverse, most of the other non-criminal cases involve a cover-up of some kind. A king tries to hide his past from his fiancée; a man woos his own stepdaughter in disguise; a beggar hides the source of his income from his wife; a servant protects a cheating student; a sportsman hides his marriage from his uncle; a leper is concealed by his family; a woman covers up for her twisted stepson; a professor conducts a secret rejuvenation experiment; a squire conceals his sister's natural death from his creditors. Once unravelled, Holmes almost always perpetuates the cover-up on being assured that the peccadilloes involved will cease. Eluding all my categories so far are a well-plotted whodunnit where the only technical crime is suicide, and a story about a giant sea-anemone.

In summary, then, the Holmes canon divides into four almost equal groups: sixteen conspiracies, fourteen gangs, fifteen solo villains and fifteen non-criminal cases. Of the forty-five punishable cases, only eighteen actually end in the arrest and legal punishment of the main offender (that is, ignoring henchmen). Of the remaining twenty-seven, eleven end in the culprit's 'onstage' death or maiming, which is generally seen as providential. In seven further cases the culprits escape, only to be providentially struck down later. Finally, there are no less than eleven cases where Holmes deliberately lets the criminal go (admittedly this includes two technically 'non-criminal' cases where, however, the technical judgement has been made by Holmes himself).

Reviewing the canon for the class attitudes it reveals, we can briefly generalise that the working class, barely visible in most stories, proves strikingly incompetent when it does step out of line; the lower middle class suffers from dangerous tensions, but chiefly in the sexual domain; the professional class, when it is what it seems and not providing a mask for tainted gentry like Professor Moriarty and Dr Roylott, tends to align itself with the detectives; the aristocracy, British and foreign, supplies a number of black-sheep cads and seducers who are rarely brought to book unless by their victims, just as the real magnates can depend on Holmes to conceal their peccadilloes although they may have to endure a tongue-lashing or, worse, his silent contempt. By far the most dangerous class is the one to which both the savage squires and the ex-conspirators belong: the rural gentry. Fortunately, in obedience to the Gothic traditions at work in these particular stories, they tend to be graphically and horribly hoist by their own petards.

For future reference, it will be worth looking a little more closely at the two largest categories: the 'secret society' and the related but distinct 'colonial conspiracy'. In the secret society stories three distinctive elements emerge. First, the society is almost supernaturally powerful; secondly, its agents (and/or sometimes its enemies) manifest their presence by a use of codes and secret signs which Holmes occupies the foreground of the story in deciphering; and, thirdly, Holmes's efforts are largely ineffectual, since the threatened deaths usually take place and the killers usually escape, their final punishment belonging either to God or to a revenge-cycle outside Holmes's control. In so far as there is one, the message seems to be that these alien activities are no concern of British justice, though they are of God: hence the blustery weather conditions frequent in these stories. Britain's task, as embodied by Holmes, is to *monitor* rather than antagonise these powerful forces: hence Holmes's bravura displays of decipherment, which can be read as surrogates for the protection he never in fact extends to the threatened victims. We shall see later how the Moriarty stories ring certain changes within these basic conventions.

In the 'conspiracy' category, the past crime also sometimes involves a special code, but here Holmes's decipherment is effective at least in procuring rough justice. The ex-criminals run very much to type: rugged and battered, with names like Black Jack of Ballarat or Black Peter Cary. Such a figure has made an illicit pile thanks to the rough-and-ready conditions obtaining in the colonies or at sea, and is either being pursued by an equally rugged ex-partner or blackmailed by an oily witness of his crime. (It is an interesting testimony to the strength of these formulae that in an apparently very different case, the *crime-passionel* story 'The Cardboard Box' discussed in an earlier chapter, the almost arbitrary combination of a rugged sailor and a sinister witness – here 'Jim' Browner and his Iagoesque sister-in-law – brings in its wake the severed ears which constitute a particularly gruesome version of the conspiratorial 'secret code'.) The Home-Counties setting of many of these stories, plus the common presence of an innocent daughter, suggests an imagery of the crimes of Empire coming home to roost in the respectable heartland, which can be compared to that of *The Moonstone*. The crime itself is often ambivalently portrayed, however: as an Indian co-conspirator remarks in *The Sign of Four*, 'We only ask you to do that which your countrymen come to this land for. We ask you to be rich' (Doyle, *Complete Adventures*, p. 147). The fortunes seized by the freebooters seem to be held out to them as the inevitable reward of their enterprising spirit (an implication further confirmed if we include the 'returned lover' category as a subgroup of this one). Accordingly, though the crime eventually claims the lives of its perpetrators, a frank confession can be enough to seal Holmes's lips, while the booty stays in the mother-country, in the redeeming hands of a new generation. A striking case of such collusion is 'The Boscombe Valley Mystery', where Holmes allows an innocent man to remain under suspicion of parricide so that he and his rich bride may remain 'in ignorance of the black cloud' of *her* father's record of banditry and murder (p. 217).

It would be possible to carry on, delineating in ever more precise detail the family traits of each subcategory. Of course there are detailed exceptions, but there is also very little doubt that the Holmes 'world' breaks apart into a strictly finite range of possibilities. I would suggest further than this finally leads to a view of the world as thoroughly 'knowable': whatever our surprise at this or that detail, it is more important that, over the whole range, certain expectations are confirmed. Keeping this general background in mind, I propose now to discuss in closer textual detail the 'methods' through which this very specific world is created.

'Now, in my opinion, Dupin was a very inferior fellow. That trick of his of breaking in on his friends' thoughts with an apropos remark after a quarter of an hour's silence is really very showy and superficial. He had some analytical genius, no doubt; but he was by no means such a phenomenon as Poe appeared to imagine.'

'Have you read Gaboriau's works?' I asked. 'Does Lecoq come up to your idea of a detective?'

Sherlock Holmes sniffed sardonically. 'Lecoq was a miserable bungler,' he said, in an angry voice; 'he had only one thing to recommend him, and that was his energy. That book made me positively ill. The question was how to identify an unknown prisoner. I could have done it in twenty-four hours. Lecoq took six months or so. It might be made a text-book for detectives to teach them what to avoid . . . There are no crimes and criminals in these days.'(Doyle, *Complete Adventures*, pp. 24–5)

Whether deliberately or not, this passage from the first Holmes novel, *A Study in Scarlet*, pays strong indirect homage to both the predecessors it claims to dismiss. The attack on Dupin directly echoes Dupin's own attack on his own precursor Vidocq, for not being superficial *enough*. And the grumble that 'there are no crimes and criminals in these days', which follows the attack on Lecoq, is a verbatim translation from Lecoq's own mentor, Tabaret.[2] While Doyle's many debts to Poe and Gaboriau are not his main claim to interest, a brief examination of them provides a convenient introduction to his technique within individual stories: partly because they also help to pinpoint some significant differences.

It is often pointed out how closely Holmes's character, circumstances and relations with the narrator and the police, are modelled on those of Dupin.[3] But the same can also be said of such celebrated early *cases* as the second novel, *The Sign of Four*, and the first short story, 'A Scandal in Bohemia'.

The murder of Bartholomew Sholto in *The Sign of Four* clearly echoes the double killing in 'The Murders in the Rue Morgue'. Each takes place in a locked upper room inaccessible to anyone of normal physique; each turns out to have been committed by a superhumanly agile but subhumanly savage being, whose keeper, a rough seafarer, has climbed to the window after him but been powerless to prevent the murder. In each case the detective finds evidence on the body of the killer's primitive nature, and further evidence contradicting the police theory that the window was not used. And in each there is a moment of special horror when the narrator almost, but not quite, identifies the perpetrator: 'I felt a creeping of the flesh. . . . "A madman," I said, "has done this deed"' (Poe, p. 334); '"Holmes," I said, in a whisper, "a child has done this horrid thing"' (Doyle, *Complete Adventures*, p. 112).

In general, however, Doyle tones his model down and blurs its outlines. Where part of the horror of Poe's murder is its total arbitrariness, as shown in the heaps of money left untouched near the bodies, Doyle's is just the unplanned offshoot of a robbery; where Poe's baffling locked window is caused by an unprecedented combination of the ape's non-human behaviour and blind chance, Doyle's pigmy Tonga is subhuman enough to instill a general sense of fear but human enough to tidy up after himself, pulling up ropes and shutting windows like any other cat-burglar; where Poe's ape and sailor leave a genuinely sealed-looking room, Doyle's pair leave an open skylight and a superabundance of clues, from coils of rope to wooden-leg-prints, with which to solve the minimal problems as to their means of access.

'A Scandal in Bohemia', concerning a foreign king's attempt to recover a compromising photograph from his ex-mistress, closely reproduces the basic situation of 'The Purloined Letter'. Though the sexes of royal personage and potential blackmailer are reversed, many other details, down to the bungled initial searches and the rigged disturbance in the street, remain the same. But the philosophical underpinning of Poe's story, the interchangeability of concealment and exposure, disappears completely, to be replaced only by some rather rickety assumptions about female psychology.

Though the two cases mentioned are by no means Doyle's best bits of plotting, the contrast with Poe perhaps brings out how much less interested Doyle is in philosophical puzzles. Action comes before elegance, and Poe's probings into the nature of reality are replaced by the 'certainties' that all women reveal where they hide their treasures in a crisis, and that all savages are savage. In these two cases there seems to be a direct link, whether or not intentional, between the specific changes Doyle has made to Poe, and some particularly blatant kinds of social prejudice. The substitution of the defenceless Irene Adler for the powerful Minister D– aligns Holmes with the king's sexist bullying for most of the tale (despite some belated signs of compunction); and the substitution of the pigmy Tonga for Poe's ape provides a kind of 'I told you so' support for *The Sign of Four*'s generally gloomy view of such benighted human groups as Indians ('black devils') and dockworkers ('dirty-looking rascals') (pp. 145, 137).

As far as Doyle's borrowings from Gaboriau are concerned, there are numerous passages where Holmes imitates the behaviour of Tabaret or Lecoq very closely: one such is in 'The Boscombe Valley Mystery', where his almost physical transformation into 'a dog who is picking up a scent' (p. 211) follows a similar description of Lecoq almost point by point (Gaboriau, *Lecoq*, p. 37); another is in *A Study in Scarlet*, where his 'little cries suggestive of encouragement and of hope' (Doyle, *Complete Adventures*, p. 31), are identical to Tabaret's 'little cries of triumph or self-encouragement', as he makes virtually the same deductions about the criminal's height from the spacing of his footprints (Gaboriau, *Lerouge*, p. 26). The other unacknowledged debt of the novel which dismisses Gaboriau with such contempt is its use of the 'split-narrative' novel form: I shall return to this later in the context of *The Valley of Fear*, where Doyle at last manages to exploit it effectively. But even when spending 'twenty-four hours', rather than 'six months', in the short stories in which Holmes really came into his own, Doyle continued to borrow plot-ideas freely from Gaboriau's novels.

One case in which he does this very well is 'The Beryl Coronet', an economical and thought-provoking reworking of the Lecoq novel, *Le Dossier no. 113*. The banker Holder, Holmes's client, accuses his own son of stealing part of a coronet entrusted to him as security for a loan by a royal personage. Holder's beloved niece, who lives with him and his son, tries to throw blame on her maid's lover, but finally turns out to be the real thief together with her own lover, the dissolute Sir George Burnwell. The son had just wrested most of the coronet from Burnwell when 'caught' by his father, but kept silent to shield his cousin. Holmes recovers the rest of the coronet, though to avoid a national scandal the villain goes unpunished.

In Gaboriau's *Le Dossier no. 113*, on which this story is clearly based, an aristocratic villain deposits money in a bank and then arranges to have it stolen by the banker's wife, so that he can put pressure on the banker to give him his daughter's hand. The wife has been persuaded by the villain's accomplice masquerading as her long-lost illegitimate son. Until the end, the chief suspect of the theft is a bank clerk called Prosper, which also happens to be the unusual name of the suspected lover of the maid in Doyle's story. The noble rank and gambling habits of Gaboriau's villain and the 'angelic' appearance of his sidekick are clearly combined by Doyle in the single figure of Burnwell, while the desired daughter and guilty wife merge into the desired and guilty niece.

In both stories the choice of a banker's household is particularly appropriate because it is precisely his position of public trust that blinds him to the realities of his family's private feelings, and the presence of the all-important safe or bureau in the very home which epitomises his 'security' permits the robbery to strike at the heart of the bourgeois power he represents. But in both stories also, the threat from within is activated by a very specific kind of threat from without: the unregenerate aristocrat postulated by a long melodramatic tradition as the chief enemy of bourgeois order.

Doyle's concentration of cast whereby the banker's mother and daughter are merged in the more ambivalently placed figure of his niece, adds a source of pressure absent in Gaboriau. In Gaboriau we are placed first in the emotional positions of the young lovers (the daughter and Prosper) and then in that of the banker's wife; in Doyle our point of view is confined more straightforwardly to that of the banker himself. But Holmes's inquiries soon clearly establish that the doting Holder keeps his niece a virtual prisoner, while apparently unconscious of the sexual feelings clearly involved on his part: when Holmes points out that her apparent readiness to stay at home is 'unusual in a young girl', Holder is unaware of the irony of his insistence that 'she is not so very young. She is four and twenty' (Doyle, *Complete Adventures*, p. 307). As long as she calls him 'dad' and passes 'her hand over his head with a sweet womanly caress', he is sure she will willingly marry his son and perform all the other female roles he expects of her, from doting daughter to motherly angel. The reasons for her final elopement with the deplorable Burnwell are very clearly established in terms of the quasi-incestuous pressures to which, like other young women in the early Holmes stories, she has been subjected.

Though Doyle forfeits the brilliant irony whereby Gaboriau's noble bank-client pulverises bourgeois notions of security by stealing his own money, he creates a slyer circularity of his own which obliquely queries the acquiescence of late-Victorian society in the escapades of its future monarch. The august customer who has started to pawn the crown jewels to pay his gambling debts recalls the future Edward VII, 'Bertie', as clearly as does the shamefacedly-masked 'Bohemian' monarch of the first short story (especially as illustrated by Sidney Paget). It is also relevant that the banker's name is Holder, since his main task is to 'uphold' the good name of a disreputable upper class at whatever cost to his own family and feelings, by 'holding' its property in pawn. Holder's enthusiastic readiness to sacrifice his own son on the alter of the prince's extravagances exactly echoes the blindness which has already 'sacrificed' his beloved niece to another noble gambler, Burnwell. If 'Holder' denotes the obsequious wait-and-see conservatism of the middle classes in the last years of Victoria, the reworking of Gaboriau's depositer-thief into a mixture of 'Bertie' and the most memorable robber of bourgeois tragedy is even cheekier. 'Sir George Burnwell' transcribes into suitably hellfire terms the fate of Lillo's anti-hero George Barnwell, hanged for robbing (like the niece in this story) a notably thrifty uncle:[4] the knighthood and the final lack of punishment perhaps just indicate how dangerously respectable this kind of figure has become.

Tracing the ways in which Doyle varies source material in individual instances only takes us a short way in determining what, if anything, is new about his handling of the detective genre. I would argue that his real distinctiveness lies in his development of the 'series' mode which is only rudimentary in his predecessors. Poe's three Dupin stories certainly suggest the possibility of an infinite series of further cases, but he takes it no further, and Gaboriau's five loosely linked novels featuring Tabaret and Lecoq do not induce the same sense of insistent formulaic repetition as the extended short story series which was really Doyle's invention.[5]

With other fictional developments, such as the rise of the novel, early manifestations of a new form often betray a self-consciousness tending at times to self-destruction (or indeed 'self-deconstruction'). In two very different contexts, *Don Quixote* and *Tristram Shandy* dramatically exemplify this as far as the novel is concerned. It is arguable that with the ending of 'The Purloined Letter' Poe threatens to kill off the infant detective-series genre by converting it back into something more Gothic and personal in the duel between doubles, and that Gaboriau works (especially at the beginning and end of the Tabaret–Lecoq cycle, in *Lerouge* and *Lecoq*) to make us 'doubt the very existence of crime', at least as something that can be adequately solved by detectives.

Coming along at a later stage, Doyle evinces a more workaday faith in his form, although arguably (as I shall describe later) the second Holmes novel virtually contradicts the first and, once established, the series makes the largest such attempt before *Dallas* to kill itself off. But despite such hiccups, Doyle's importance as the creator, not of a single hero but of the epic single-hero short-story *series*, cannot be overemphasised.

The series is by definition indeterminate along the axis which links the separate stories together. But there is also the axis in which each story taken as a unit is necessarily highly determinate and finite: any flow onwards from one unit to another would threaten to undermine the required equivalence of each unit by subordinating some to others. I would like to argue that this structure of the series as a whole, whereby an indeterminate axis repeatedly crosses a single or unitary one, is also a vital element in the structure, and even the subject matter, of each story taken individually. At times other related words perhaps better describe this 'indeterminacy': depending on the context these can include anonymity, generality and reproducibility. And whereas the opposing axis on the broad structural level is the particular case or the single story, at the level of subject matter it can be variously represented by the precise clue, the exact name, the 'singular' detail. I would argue that some of the most memorable and characteristic stories are memorable precisely because of the persistence with which they juggle these two axes together.

'The Red-Headed League', the original 'fool's errand' story, concerns a red-headed pawnbroker, Jabez Wilson, who is lured into working for the eponymous league while his innocent-seeming assistant Spaulding and new red-headed 'employer' dig a tunnel from his shop to the bank next door. Guessing the truth from the street layout and the mud on the assistant's trousers, Holmes lays an ambush in the bank, where Spaulding is revealed to be the brilliant mastermind John Clay.

What might be called the 'indefinite' axis of this story is, as often, imaginatively coterminous with London itself, the sprawling anonymous city perceived as virtually unknowable. The opposite axis, of 'singularity', is provided on one level by Holmes's correct identification of the criminals and their intentions, but on another level by the comic specificity of the story's opening imagery to do with the bizarre 'red-headed league' which the crooks have invented to decoy Jabez Wilson from his shop. Wilson's experience of the league juxtaposes the countless or anonymous with the singular or specific in a number of ways. Indeed its very name, and hence that of the story, suggestively confuses the two ideas by attaching a grammatically 'singular' adjective to a collective noun: there is a paradoxical suggestion, which turns out in one sense to be justified, of an innumerable body with a single head. The point of intersection whereby the strikingly peculiar invades Wilson's hitherto conventional life is the newspaper advertisements column which, like London itself, houses the ultimate in singularity within the ultimate in infinitely reproducible anonymity. The singular item brought to his attention by these means is one which professes all the weight and authority of a general advertisement to the public at large, but has in fact been devised to single him out from the mass by way of his one individual trait, his red hair.

In the comic scenes which follow it turns out that within the vast mass of London even this attempt to bestow the required uniqueness on the otherwise undistinguished Wilson is only the first stage in his blatantly rigged selection from a quasi-apocalyptic horde of other red-headed men 'from north, south, east and west. . . . I should not have thought there were so many in the whole country as were brought together by that single advertisement . . . – straw, lemon, orange, brick, Irish-setter, liver, clay' (p. 180). Wilson's reward for his 'uniqueness' is to be set to work copying out the *Encyclopaedia Britannica* verbatim in an empty room. This task too combines the notion of an endlessly reproducible series (not only Wilson's act of copying but also the Encyclopaedia's status as mass-object) with that of the odd and the singular. The jostling juxtaposition of 'Abbots, and Archery, and Armour, and Architecture, and Attica' comments equally on the old-world individuality of Wilson's scholastic task and on its mass-produced modern arbitrariness. In a further surreal touch, the contrast between imagined organic whole and actual mechanical part is reinforced in Wilson's eventual discovery that the 'league is dissolved', and that an elaborately laid trail of false names and addresses leads only to a 'manufactory of artificial knee-caps'

(Doyle, *Complete Adventures*, p. 182).

Holmes's intervention begins to resolve the cacophony of the reproducible and the unique, but initially does so by simply extending the methods of the crooks. Thus he individuates Wilson from the start on five counts which distinguish him even more precisely than the obvious red hair which gave the gang their handle: 'Beyond the obvious facts that he has at some time done manual labour, and he takes snuff, that he is a Freemason, that he has been in China, and that he has done a considerable amount of writing lately, I can deduce nothing else' (p. 177). By singling Wilson out on these very specific counts, Holmes asserts the same kind of power over him as the crooks have done, and the final 'nothing else' expresses the same simultaneous dismissal of him as otherwise utterly undistinguished. This fundamental dismissal of Wilson, returning him to the faceless ranks from which he has been plucked, is expressed by the 'league' in the brusque announcement of its dissolution which effectually, since Wilson is its only real member, 'dissolves' him. Holmes too (or rather the story itself, if they are distinguishable) abandons Wilson as of no further interest once his most striking claim to singularity, namely the story he has to tell, has been drained from him.

The dénouement revolves round Holmes's awareness that what really makes Wilson singular is the fact that his pawnbroker's shop backs on to a bank. Again this is a knowledge, or a type of knowledge, which Holmes shares only with the gang. It is a knowledge of relationships rather than entities; an ability to discern the hidden connections between Wilson's 'faded and stagnant square' and 'the line of fine shops and stately business premises' which 'presents as great a contrast to it as the front of a picture does to the back' (pp. 184–5). Such a knowledge of connections, commonly expressed by Holmes's A-to-Z familiarity with London streets and districts, is the magic solution of the impasse between the ungraspably amorphous and the irreducibly singular from which the problem seems so dramatically to arise. His realisation that the source of Wilson's singularity is not him but his shop, and then only in its relation to the bank, implies a means by which the whole cacophony of London might eventually be comprehended: the apparently singular ceases to be so when juxtaposed correctly to something else (and therefore moved on from, with the hint of callousness by which Holmes moves from client to solution, and then from case to case), and the amorphous ceases to be amorphous when grasped as the sum total of all such juxtapositions.

As we have seen, Holmes shares this knowledge with the crooks, and it is their concealment of the hidden connections underlying the amorphous/singular dichotomy that creates the mystery. One of the most entertaining aspects of the 'league' is the solemn mimicry of a large and impersonal organisation by what turns out to be a gang of two; of which, moreover, one member is so clearly the boss that his colleague virtually fades out at the end. The finale's somewhat surprising focus on John Clay as a superstar criminal, a 'personality' with some of the makings of a Moriarty, provides the necessary opposite pole to the impersonality so successfully mimicked by the league as well as to the role of harmless underpaid assistant Clay himself has adopted in previous appearances. (Glancing for a moment at that role, the trait which most distinguishes 'Spaulding' is the passion for photography which drives him repeatedly into the cellar. He is of course really digging a tunnel, but it is typical that he should mask this *connecting* activity behind a harmless 'singularity' involving a mass-reproduction technique.)

The unmasked Clay is shot through with the contradictions he has so ably exploited. Despite his virtual invisibility to his employer he is characterised by effeminate, possibly homosexual traits – a smooth face, pierced ears, a 'white, almost womanly hand', and a defiant solicitude for a partner 'lithe and small like himself' – which, especially in the 1890s context, could be taken to imply a particularly flamboyant individualism. His noble rank and place 'at the head of his profession' imply further claims to distinction, reflected in the idiosyncratic demand that even the arresting police call him 'sir'. But such marks of singularity are also linked with counteracting elements of chameleonlike variety implying a deeper de-individuation or undistinction: mixed sexual identity; the class mixture expressed in his thieves' slang; even a lack of fixed criminal abode whereby 'he'll crack a crib in Scotland one week, and be raising money to build an orphanage in Cornwall the next' (pp. 186–9). His very name, John Clay, in contrast to the far more distinctive names of 'ordinary' characters like Jabez Wilson or even his own *alter ego* Vincent Spaulding, implies the common clay of average undistinguishable man (as hinted when 'clay' closes the list of decreasingly red hair-pigments), and perhaps even the distinction-in-indistinction of Adam himself.

But the simultaneity of the singular with the amorphous can

also be read as mastery of the connections between worlds normally conceived of as distinct: seen thus, 'Clay' also implies the connecting element on which the walls creating the network of distinctions which is the city are superimposed. Such an undermining of the notion of the city, by burrowing beneath the dividing walls but through the connecting clay, is perhaps the real 'essence' of what the Poe of 'The Man of the Crowd' calls 'deep crime'. But as we have seen, Sherlock Holmes is also a master of such connections, as witnessed by his initially exclusive interest in the earth on Clay's trousers, and his reading of the ground under the pavement by rapping it with his stick. Holmes also possesses much of his antagonist's chameleonlike versatility-within-singularity: it is in this story that we learn that (in close echo of Dupin) 'In his singular character the dual nature alternately asserted itself, and his extreme exactness and astuteness represented, as I have often thought, the reaction against the poetic and contemplative mood which occasionally predominated in him' (p. 185). Holmes's fluctuations from langorous musicianship to bloodhound-like energy, which constitute a major part of his pattern, imply a protean ability to hold disparate aspects of experience in easy connection with each other: to that extent it is like the power of disguise which he exploits in other stories. And again, as with his antagonists here and elsewhere, it is precisely this *doubleness* which constitutes 'his singular character'.

The structure of the ending, in which the two 'singular characters' of the criminal and detective confront each other, represents a struggle for the ultimate singularity to be bestowed by the final spotlight. With his arrest and relegation to the class of prisoners the criminal loses the uniqueness which has briefly challenged that of the detective. But to put it another way, the detective has for the first time forced uniqueness in the form of identification on to the criminal who has hitherto sheltered behind anonymity. The criminal then leaves a trace of his singularity in the sense of providing Holmes with a 'singular case' ('one of the most singular which I have listened to for some time', as he calls this one) which affords him a respite from the *ennui* and 'conventions and humdrum routine of daily life'.

But Holmes's disgust with routine, as well as containing a continuing claim to match the 'aesthetic' interest of the criminal, perhaps also expresses a self-reflexive awareness on Doyle's part that within the series structure of which he is the first embodiment,

Holmes *is* routine incarnate. It is a paradox of these stories that the great and unique Sherlock Holmes, penetrator of all that anonymous London fog, master of the singular detail and the specific identification, represents in his infinite reproducibility (in stories which resemble each other as closely as the houses of a London terrace) the very spirit of endless sameness against which he seems eternally to battle.

As well as clarifying the underlying structure of the series formula, the notions of reproducibility and singularity can also be helpful in understanding Holmes's famous deductive 'methods'. Poe's 'The Man of the Crowd', written just before 'Rue Morgue', already laid down the basic logical lines whereby a generally known fact (such as that all clerks' right ears are bent) is used to spotlight the 'unreadable' exception. But where Poe uses this basic dichotomy to highlight the terrifying mystery of urban man, Doyle generally uses it as a reassuring and clarifying mechanism.

A classic instance occurs near the beginning of 'The Blue Carbuncle', where Holmes draws an amazing string of deductions from a hat picked up in the street. In its status as an arbitrarily detached fragment from the attire of a man who is himself only an arbitrarily detached fragment of a similarly clad mass, the hat would seem to represent the ultimate in anonymity. But, singled out by Holmes's magical scrutiny and emblematically hung on a chair in the middle of the room, it becomes instead the trumpet of its owner's unique life-history.

The most striking fact, that the owner's wife has ceased to love him, is proved by collating the hat's singularly unbrushed state with collateral general evidence of marriage. In this instance, clearly, the 'proof' of singularity assumes a very high degree of its opposite in society in general: hat-brushing only inevitably equals marital affection in the world of ideal conformity which, perhaps, it is one of the subliminal aims of detective fiction to create. A truly singular household in which a wife loved her husband while not caring about his hat would be a monstrosity as 'unreadable' as Poe's Man of the Crowd. This household, on the other hand, offers just enough singularity to be identifiable, but cannot even be imagined to break the more fundamental principle which equates wifely love with hat-brushing.

We can express all this more philosophically by remembering that all deduction depends on the syllogism. In this case the syllogism is: the unbrushed hat's owner has a wife; all loving wives brush their husband's hats; therefore this wife is not loving. A similar middle term or 'known rule' is present in all of Holmes's deductions, properly so called, and hence I would argue that wherever these deductions touch on matters of social relationship there are always some very large-scale assumptions about unbreakable social rules implicit in them.[6] Though a lot more could be said, this is perhaps enough to demonstrate the generally conservative swing of the 'purely' deductive mode which Doyle bequeathed to most of his English successors.

6

Sherlock Holmes – The Valleys of Fear

Endless repetition is, of course, the soul of the series as a form. The sometimes unnoticed effect this has on other aspects of narration can be highlighted if we contrast it with the somewhat haphazard beginning of the Holmes series and the 'death' with which it was intended to end. The first two Holmes novels contradict each other at almost every point as if blithely unaware that between them they are founding a series. Indeed, *The Sign of Four*'s conversion of a briskly philistine ignoramus into a fountain of pessimistic literary-philosophical quotation, and its near-annihilation of Watson as a Poesque narrator by marrying him off, can be seen as part of a more deliberate attempt to strangle the series–impulse at birth. But then, interestingly, the full-blown series–structure virtually founds itself on the need to enshrine these seminal incoherences within a stable continuum. Thus Holmes's 'dual nature', while borrowed from Dupin, can also be read as a permanent and ongoing attempt to reconcile the opposite qualities of thinking-machine and aesthete displayed in the first two novels. Even more strikingly, the inconvenience of Watson's marriage leads to the early assertion of a freedom to shuffle chronology from story to story, which then becomes a vital device for maintaining the *indeterminacy* by which the series fights free of the possibility of temporal closure, or unidirectional movement towards an ending, which would threaten to turn it into a seri*al* or extended novel.

Within the series structure any elements making for organic completion need to be either jettisoned completely or at least frozen in a permanent adolescence of non-development: as with the retardation of Watson's learning faculties whereby, though eternally lectured to by Holmes, he never advances that step in applying his methods that could be fatal to the narrative procedure. What is being held at bay here is any suggestion of full-scale Aristotelian *peripeteia*, in which a central situation is reversed into its flat opposite, as threatens to happen in the second novel, and which I think can be related to the self-reflexive ironies whereby Poe and Gaboriau sometimes question their own procedures. There are, of course, smaller *peripeteias* within each story, but the series format needs to prevent such local ironies from ever acquiring enough accumulated weight to suggest the inevitability of a final capping *peripeteia*.

The exception, which I should now like to consider briefly because it establishes an interesting set of contrasts, is Holmes's 'death' at Reichenbach Falls. This event, famously, was intended to mark the end of the canon and led to a public outcry which in turn led to Holmes's eventual rebirth as one of the immortals. 'The Final Problem', in which the death occurs, offers several features apart from the death itself which gesture towards resolution and summation and which could be described as capping *peripeteias* of the kind discussed above. The most important of these new features is Holmes's antagonist and *doppelgänger* Professor Moriarty, in whom, Holmes confesses, he has at last found his intellectual equal. This equality is brought out by a carefully orchestrated reprise, in the depiction of Moriarity and his organisation, of images and motifs earlier identified with Holmes himself.

Thus, whereas in 'The Cardboard Box' we are told that Holmes 'loved to lie in the very centre of five millions of people, with his filaments stretching out and running through them, responsive to every little rumour or suspicion of unsolved crime', it is now Moriarty who 'sits motionless, like a spider in the centre of its web, but that web has a thousand radiations, and he knows well every quiver of them' (Doyle, *Complete Adventures*, pp. 888, 471). But Moriarty's organisation also combines in itself the qualities, hitherto distinct, of the two main types of opponent that Holmes has confronted in the past: the indigenous criminal or small gang and the implacable, organised and faceless secret society. In Moriarty, 'cases of the most varying sorts – forgery cases, robberies, murders' – the source of all that disparate variety essential to our experience of the stories as a disjunctive series – become a single element, merely the 'veil' for 'some deep power behind the malefactor, some deep organising power' such as we have hitherto only found in such groups as the Avenging Angels or the Ku Klux Klan. Moriarty's own assurance to Holmes that 'you stand in the way not merely of an individual, but of a mighty organisation' reiterates the notion that this story will present a summation of previous motifs: not just John Clay or Grimesby Roylott, whom

Holmes has defeated with comparative ease, but also those vast and mysterious forces before which he has often previously been powerless. That earlier impotence, perhaps only experienced as a somewhat random 'win some, lose some' element at the time, now stands out in retrospect as a gnawing dissatisfaction or ironic and destabilising reversal of our expectations that builds up towards the need for a final capping *peripeteia*.

Another means by which Doyle shifts gear, as it were, from small- to large-scale reversal is by reversing the usual roles of detective and criminal so that for much of the story Moriarty is the pursuer and Holmes the pursued. This is accompanied by a further role-reversal whereby the secret society victim Holmes fails to save (such as John Openshaw in 'The Five Orange Pips') is himself; but at the same time, satisfyingly, the hand of Providence which avenges that victim at sea or in some foreign land is also his. Thus the various conceivable roles of the quintessential Holmes story are boiled down and concentrated in these two figures – both at once detective, murderer and victim – who then in turn merge together in death, leaving the only figure whose role could not be thus subsumed, Watson, to tell their story. In a final capping reversal it is precisely here, in his unassisted reading of the evidence of the footprints and so forth, that Watson shows his first and only sign of having learned his mentor's 'methods': in these last moments the Holmes–Watson split, like the hero–villain one, is obliterated.

Doyle's first response to the public demand for more Holmes stories was *The Hound of the Baskervilles*, which avoids the problem of the death by being set prior to it. Here, however, there seems to be a continuing trace of the idea of letting Watson go it alone in the long middle section where Holmes pretends to absent himself from the case. In further reprise of 'The Final Problem' considerable emotion accumulates both around the absence itself and around the mysterious figure on the moor taken by Watson for a Moriartyesque 'unseen force, a fine net drawn round us with infinite skill and delicacy, holding us so lightly that it was only at some supreme moment that one realised one was indeed entangled in its meshes' (p. 739). When this mysterious figure reveals himself as a Holmes who has never really been away, it is in a setting strikingly reminiscent of Christ's reappearance outside the empty tomb. And the feeling of resurrection is strengthened by a sense that this conversion of Moriarty back into Holmes reverses Holmes's earlier merging with a Moriarty whose name clearly connotes, above all, 'death'.

The resurrection and empty-tomb motifs of course recur more literally in the story where Doyle brings Holmes back from the dead, 'The Empty House'. In his idiosyncratic *Naked Is the Best Disguise*, Samuel Rosenberg points out a number of mythic-seeming elements which accompany the hero's return, the most striking being the name of the book which Watson accidentally knocks from the hands of an 'elderly deformed man' early in the story.[1] The elderly man is, of course, Holmes in disguise and the book is called *The Origin of Tree Worship*, a name which may recall the connection between resurrection myths and fertility cults explored in Frazer's recently-published *Golden Bough*. In similar almost playful allusion to the realms of myth and cult, Holmes now recounts his wanderings: in Tibet, where he 'spent most days with the head Lama'; Norway, traditionally associated with witchcraft; Mecca; and a Khartoum still strongly identified with the self-proclaimed Messiah or Mahdi (p. 488).

There is also a kind of half-resurrection of Moriarty in the person and name of his deputy, Moran. But this cheater-at-cards who can be arrested like any other solo crook while stalking a wax dummy with an airgun, as the chief survivor of the 'mighty organisation' of a man whose name his cuts in half, has all the qualities of a fear-exorcising parody. The wax dummy can itself be seen as a parody of the dead Holmes, the corpse that has usurped his place in the familiar position at the Baker Street window, Watson's description of which from the tomb-like empty house evokes earlier presentations of the same view – notably the opening of 'A Scandal in Bohemia'[2] – along with the intervening death and emptiness. The final triumphal entry into 221b, restored in every detail by Mycroft and Mrs Hudson, reverses another of the apparently terminal events of 'The Final Problem' when Moriarty set fire to the rooms, presumably on Doyle's own behalf and precisely to prevent such a return.

The stories surrounding Holmes's 'death', then, abound in elements of myth, irony and reversal. Some of these elements have doubtless been crucial in establishing the Holmes myth in another sense. The explanation of the continued existence of the Holmes cult is probably partly to be found in the filling-out and summing-up effect of these stories: to take one example, Moriarty's place as a key element in the myth, certainly not justified by number of appearances, clearly derives from his potential, as final antagonist, for disrupting the series formula. It is also here that Watson, by briefly becoming the protagonist of his own narrative, acquires an added apostolic dimension, and Mycroft and Mrs Hudson build themselves more firmly into the constellation by becoming the first Holmes museum curators. It is as if the cult, like most cults, has only discovered itself as a faith on the death, however temporary, of its founder.

In considering Doyle's debts to Gaboriau, we noted earlier that it is Tabaret who provides the text of Holmes's complaint that 'There are no crimes and no criminals in these days'. The corollary of that complaint, which is that the crime has to be imported from another time and often another place, is embodied in both *Monsieur Lecoq* and *A Study in Scarlet* in a very similar structure, whereby the antecedents of the crime are described in what amounts to another, historical, novel encased within the narrative of detection as pioneered by Poe.

In the heart of Paris, or London, a multiple murder is committed by a criminal who, once his identity is revealed, becomes the hero of this second novel, set in a comparatively primitive time and place and justifying his deeds in terms of the wrongs he has suffered. In a necessarily awkward conclusion, he is allowed to pass with honour from prison or from life while the reader's allegiance hangs unresolved between the two methods of narration that have been employed: the omniscient consciousness of the historical novel and the restricted consciousness of the modern detective story. The contrast between these two modes implies a further contrast of heroisms, heroic action and heroic perception: the 'fulness' of romance and the development of a single viewpoint characteristic of the early modernist text.

Sherlock Holmes only became the world's most famous detective when Doyle abandoned this mixed structure and allowed him to 'do it in twenty-four hours', within the concentrated form of the Poesque short story. But Doyle's later return to the mixed formula in *The Valley of Fear*, plus the fact that he saw Holmes as the opposite pole if not the actual enemy of the historical novels he wanted to be remembered for,[3] suggests an awareness that the winning formula was only attained at a coast. With the great crimes that are no longer committed nowadays we can equate a depth and breadth of action also no longer permitted. The omniscience of the detective superman transfers all significant action to the mind which from the start comprehends all but the final pieces of the jigsaw: any further movement is curtailed or vestigial and the past exists not as history but as pattern. Whereas in *Monsieur Lecoq* the site of heroic action is primarily distanced in time – the eras of revolution and restoration – in *A Study in Scarlet*, *The Sign of Four* and *The Valley of Fear* it is distanced in space – America or the Empire under the primitive conditions of settlement. (The fact that Doyle hardly distinguished them is attested to by Holmes's dream in 'The Noble Bachelor' of a 'world-wide country under a flag which shall be a quartering of the Union Jack with the Stars and Stripes' – Doyle, *Complete Adventures*, p. 300.) However awkward the structure, in both cases it seems clearly to have been adopted in order to assert links and connections, with the revolutionary past or with colonisation, to which the current metropolitan civilisation owes its strength and which it overlooks at its peril.

In the three Holmes novels one effect of the split plot is, as in Gaboriau, to assert simultaneously a difference and an equivalence between the two types of action depicted. The adventures in the 'primitive' worlds of America or India highlight the equivalent heroism of the modern and urban world Holmes shares with the reader; they also enact in their very position as captured or enclosed narratives their own subservience to and supersession by that modernity. In the first two novels the enclosed narratives are, exactly, those of captured men; in *The Valley of Fear*, rather more artfully, the enclosed novel has actually been written in a secret room hidden within the walls of the country house where the surrounding one takes place, and while it takes place.

Very briefly, the first part concerns Holmes's discovery that John Douglas, the apparently murdered squire of Birlstone Manor, has in fact killed a would-be assassin, dressed him in his own clothes, and hidden while his wife and friend assert that the body is his. In reality Douglas is the ex-Pinkerton agent Birdy Edwards, pursued by the sinister 'Scowrers' whose organisation he infiltrated and broke up in America twenty years earlier. On discovery, he hands over the story of his adventures, which he has just finished writing, in a grandly symbolic gesture to 'the historian of this bunch' Watson, who duly transcribes it as the second part of the novel we are reading (p. 812). There is, however, a third and final layer to the story, in which the Scowrers successfully contract out the killing of Edwards to Moriarty, whose restoration to undimmed power so late in the canon has led to endless speculation about dates among Holmes purists.

The enclosed narrative is in many ways similar to that in *A Study in Scarlet*: in both the tough conditions of settlement and survival in the United States have led to the formation of a powerful organisation whose public claim to protect the victims of oppression is belied by the oppression practised by its own secret arm. There is a documentary tinge to the presentation of both groups, but whereas the Mormon 'Avenging Angels' have a largely fictional source in the Stevensons' *The Dynamiter*,[4] *The Valley of Fear*'s Scowrers are undisguisedly based on a group of Pennsylvanian-Irish miners called the Molly Maguires who were believed to be the strike-enforcing terrorist wing of the more respectable Ancient Order of Hibernians (or 'Freemen' in Doyle's version). The source here was Allan J. Pinkerton's ghosted but purportedly factual *The Molly Maguires and the Detectives* (1877), describing the successful infiltration of the Maguires by the Pinkerton agent McParlan, whose testimony about their violent intimidation of strike-breakers, pit-managers and others led to a mass trial and the execution of ringleaders. The book's sympathies are made clear in the space it allots to the climactic courtroom oratory of the coal-baron Gowen, who initially hired the Pinkerton organisation to supplement his own private army of 'coal police'. Playing down the boss's role where possible, Doyle's version concentrates on the violence and sub-Masonic secrecy of the Scowrers, and the resourceful heroism of Edwards (that is, McParlan) who, like Jefferson Hope in *A Study in Scarlet*, is spurred on by his love for the allotted bride of one of the gang's thugs. Fleeing the vengeance of the surviving Scowrers, after leading the ringleaders into a police trap. Edwards has had time to make a fortune in California, before finally settling in England under the name of Douglas. In the Epilogue, Holmes's urgent advice to resume his travels fails to save Edwards from Moriarty, whose agents kill him en route to South Africa.

The incorporation of material from Pinkerton's self-advertising narrative creates several interesting links between *The Valley of Fear* (1915) and the beginnings, only a few years later, of the 'hardboiled' school of American detective fiction. Dashiell Hammett's first novel *Red Harvest* (1928), in particular, deals with the aftermath of a bloody conflict between miners and the owner's private army very similar to that on which Doyle's book is modelled. Hammett's later political radicalism, already discernible in *Red Harvest*, was fuelled by his experiences as a strike-breaking Pinkerton agent in mining communities like the Pottsville on which Doyle's Vermissa is based.[5] There is a considerable similarity of plot, in that Hammett's Continental Op and Edwards both infiltrate murderous gangs in order to destroy them. There is, however, a sharp difference of emphasis in that Doyle's gang consists of underpaid miners, whereas the several gangs of *Red Harvest* are the now-entrenched remnants of the strike-breaking army, and notably include the police. Hammett's 'Op' is, then, only infiltrating an earlier intake of people hired by the ruthless mine-owner Willsson on much the same basis as himself, which perhaps explains his growing and justified anxiety that he in turn is becoming 'blood simple'. Writers taking another view of the Molly Maguires case from Pinkerton and Doyle have argued that Gowen, the Pottsville mine-owner, mobilised a very similar alliance of private and public enforcement agencies, in an unscrupulous attempt to break the workforce by turning the 'Mollies' into scapegoats.[6]

Whatever the ideological divisions, the similarity between the two detective classics extends at times to the style:

> As he came forward his eyes fell upon the group, silent and motionless, under the engine-house. The men had drawn down their hats and turned up their collars to screen their faces. . . .
>
> 'Who are you?' he asked as he advanced. 'What are you loitering there for?'
>
> There was no answer; but the lad Andrews stepped forward and shot him in the stomach. The hundred waiting miners stood as motionless and helpless as if they were paralyzed. The manager clapped his two hands to the wound and doubled himself up. Then he staggered away; but another of the assassins fired, and he went down sideways, kicking and clawing among a heap of clinkers.   (Doyle, *Complete Adventures*, p. 850)

This is Doyle, not Hammett, but the short declarative sentences, as well as the use made of hats and collars, already seem to display hardboiled characteristics teetering on the edge of self-consciousness. The main difference lies in two sentences omitted from the above quotation: 'For a moment the presentiment of Death laid its cold hand upon the manager's heart. At the next he had shaken it off and saw only his duty towards intrusive strangers.' Such a translation of observable events into moral meanings is precisely what Hammett would have omitted, partly to accentuate the impact of the violence and partly because for him the division of the world into dutiful managers and intrusive strangers has become impossible.

The second section of *The Valley of Fear* is the only instance in the Holmes canon where Doyle deals with the industrial working class as such. For all the Scowrers' secret society paraphernalia, the nature of their activities is clearly determined by their class position, their consciousness of which is expressed in the rhetoric their leader McGinty uses towards the Captain of the Coal and Iron Police: 'What are you but the paid tool of men of capital, hired by them to club or to shoot your poorer fellow-citizens?' (p. 831). The book even makes some attempt to understand the forces the miners might really have been up against, in the warnings of the moderate Scowrer Morris, who argues that the society's activities are driving away the relatively impotent small employers only to see them replaced by big companies who, if they 'find that we stand between them and their profits, . . . will spare no pains and no expense to hunt us down and bring us to court' (p. 836). That this process is already in full swing is indicated by the presence of the Coal and Iron Police, 'a special body raised by the railways and colliery owners' (p. 831), as well as of the *agent provocateur* Birdy Edwards himself. Morris's suggestion that this has something to do with profits is hardly stressed in a narrative in which he becomes just 'one more' tragic victim, but is allowed to stand.

This, then, is the 'primitive' material encased in Holmes's investigation: as distant in space as Gaboriau's *'L'Honneur du nom'* is from *'L'Enquête'* in time and cultural experience. Where different but parallel types of romance-structure and approaches to the meaning of a name constituted a thematic link between the two parts of *Monsieur Lecoq*, here the link lies in the presentation of different but parallel types of detection. Though the encased narratives of Doyle's two earlier such novels involve their criminal protagonists in detection of a kind, Birdy Edwards is a professional whose triumph encourages us to compare his detective achievements directly with those of Holmes himself. As if to underscore the contrast, Holmes's investigation at Birlstone Manor is about as 'English' as it can be: in fact, it is closer to the deliberately nostalgic interwar country-house whodunnit than to the brisk contemporaneity of most earlier Holmes stories. Dennis Porter has drawn attention to the opposed 'landscapes of detection' in the novel: Birlstone with its time-eaten stonework and secret hiding-places, cut off from the world by a symbolic moat almost like Britain itself; and Vermissa, the allegorical hell down whose mean streets the isolated American hero must go (see Porter, p. 192).

The comparison between the two detectives is not entirely in Holmes's favour, as far as efficiency is concerned: indeed, the hitherto invulnerable Edwards is killed while fleeing the country specifically on his advice. None the less, the overall structure and rhetoric of the novel insist on the subordination of Edwards and his world of realistic-sounding American crime to Holmes and 'those rooms in Baker Street where this, like so many other wonderful happenings, will find its end' (Doyle, *Complete Adventures*, p. 815). Ironically, this subordination is only achieved by means of the third layer of narrative which encases the other two: the sharply separate introduction and epilogue concerning Moriarty, whose lack of plot-connection with the central story strongly suggests a more overriding thematic need for his presence.

The novel opens with Holmes's virtuoso decoding of a ciphered warning that Douglas/Edwards is in danger from Moriarty, and the ensuing news of Douglas's 'death' introduces a long discourse about Moriarty's powers. These include organisational abilities harking back to Jonathan Wild and forward, or at least across the Atlantic, to 'the American business principle' of 'paying for brains': his deputy Moran earns 'more than the Prime Minister' (p. 777). It is because of the Moriarty connection that Holmes involves himself in the case, and at the end we only have his word that Moriarty, not the Scowrers, is responsible for Edwards's death. The almost proprietorial tone of this assertion is interesting: 'There is a master hand here. It is no case of sawed-off shot-guns and clumsy six-shooters. You can tell an old master by the sweep of his brush. I can tell a Moriarty when I see one. This crime is from London, not from America.' The novel's adulatory final sentence, pregnant with the reader's knowledge of Moriarty's eventual fate, then elaborately transfers the colossal stature just attributed to 'this king-devil' back to Holmes himself: 'We all sat in silence for some minutes, while those fateful eyes still strained to pierce the veil' (p. 866).

Moriarty, then, is the agency whereby Holmes's grip on events is reasserted: a triumphant demonstration of Britain's ability to match American business principles and organisational enterprise, and go one better. The claim to superiority is confirmed by the relaxed 'consultant' status of the two imperial colossi as opposed to the crudely *ad hoc* methods of their American counterparts; and also, perhaps, less explicitly, by the fact that Holmes's one piece of advice as consultant delivers Edwards into Moriarty's hands. Holmes's removal of Edwards from British soil at once absolves us from further responsibility for his fate and enacts an unconscious revenge on this interloper who has tried to usurp the moated island home of Birlstone/Britain and turn it into an uncomfortable fortress within the alien world of six-shooters and sawed-off shotguns he himself has lured to its shores.

I began the discussion of this novel by suggesting that the America of the encased narrative represents a primitive, as opposed to Holmes's modern world. It also, however, represents the future, of detective fiction as well as of real patterns of crime. The fact that Holmes looks back to the eighteenth century of Jonathan Wild as well as forward to 'the American business principle' for models for the hallucinatory prospect of British organised crime confirms this double status. A similar doubleness is perhaps also evident in the Irish dimension of the American story: though Doyle tries to soften this, Pinkerton's account derives the Molly Maguires very directly from an Irish republican group of the same name. It is interesting that, except when Holmes himself plays the part of an Irish-American anti-British agent in 'His Last Bow', the canon does not refer to the Irish Independence agitation which created the most visible 'secret society'-type violence in what were still for most of this period 'the British Isles'. Then (as perhaps now?) Irish Republicanism may have seemed at once too 'primitive' and too insistent on a non-imperial future to be accommodated within the British self-image: treating it as a throwback to the alien past and shelving it indefinitely were perhaps the most comfortable responses, especially for determinedly anglicised Irishmen like Doyle. It is interesting, then, that when he deals with it at all he sets it in an American context where past and future also mingle in the harsh conditions of settlement and in forms of organisation in which Empire has no place.

Against this combination of the 'primitive' and the prospective stands the world of Holmes which is now also a world of growing nostalgia for the moated Birlstone, where tidy crimes committed by single individuals take place in ordered and beautiful settings. If this nostalgia also involves the fantasy of a renaissance of British crime incorporating the best of past and future practices, that is better than allowing ourselves to be taken over from without. But its shaky integration with the main plot and its metaphysical terminology indicate that it is still a fantasy, designed to bridge the gap between two worlds in a way which allows Holmes at least a vestigial relevance. On the surface, at any rate, he is still master of a present which is 'in England, now': but as the primitive future irrupts, it is a present beginning to slip irrevocably into the past.

7

Detective Fiction and Ideas

It is often said that British detective fiction deals in certainties whereas American detective fiction deals in uncertainties, and that therefore the English branch of the genre is socially uncritical while the American is critical.[1] Where Christie and Sayers are taken to epitomise the English school, and Hammett and Chandler the American, it is hard to disagree with this assessment, and indeed it does seem to hold for the 'Golden Age' between the World Wars and, often, since.

The domination of Sherlock Holmes, the upholder of high imperial normality, might suggest that the same is true of the period from 1890 to the First World War. This period was also, however, one in which many radical political and other ideas forced their way into literature. The authors to be discussed in this chapter, Israel Zangwill, Arthur Morrison, E. C. Bentley and G. K. Chesterton, all display loosely socialist sympathies, and the intended political edge of their writings is often linked to a drily paradoxical style owing something to the Aesthetic Movement. As with other writers of the period some of the socialism looks odd today (some being hard to distinguish from fascism), and some of the aesthetic concerns seem parochially class-based. The exact weight of the ideas is also hard to gauge from the cheerfully embraced 'lightness' of the detective form, verging in most cases on spoofery. In some ways, however, this very lightness makes the form particularly relevant to a period many of whose leading writers (Butler, Wilde, Shaw, Wells) use such abstract modes as the debate-play and science fiction in order to subject conventional attitudes to a series of intellectual *peripeteias*. Such *peripeteias* are certainly a staple of all the works to be discussed, whatever else one may wish to say about them. Though their aims and attitudes are very different, all these writers give the impression of having chosen detective fiction for more than purely commercial reasons; all were more notable (as Doyle would have liked to be) for literary and/or agitational work in other fields; all came to detective fiction with ideas to explore and axes to grind.[2]

Before setting Doyle aside, it is worth making a few further points about the novel which set up most of the 'Nineties' aspects of Holmes, *The Sign of Four*. Written under the influence of a meeting with Wilde (and commissioned alongside his *The Picture of Dorian Gray*), the novel presents in the figure of Thaddeus Sholto a deliberate and not unsympathetic portrait of the Wildean aesthete, and Holmes himself acquires traits often the opposite of those detailed in *A Study in Scarlet*: the cocaine-taking, the languid *ennui*, the sense of sexual isolation and the literary connoisseurship. He is, however, also in the grip of Winwood Reade's equally 'advanced' *Martyrdom of Man*, which leads fairly directly to agnostic neo-Darwinist speculations about whether or not the working classes have souls, and the discounting of such an idea in the case of the 'savage' Tonga.[3] Detached from the larger series, *The Sign of Four* could well stand as a novel which uses the detective formula to explore Ideas, and which is prepared to destroy or at least undermine that formula in an ending (the contrasting of Watson's marriage with Holmes's Goethean speculations on the divided soul) which gives those Ideas the last word.

ISRAEL ZANGWILL

In his life and work as a whole, Israel Zangwill (1864–1926) was very concretely involved in many of the issues and ideas of his time. A working-class Jew, he became best known for *Children of the Ghetto* and other social-protest novels on the one hand, and on the other for his agitational work within the nascent Zionist movement. His seminal detective novel, *The Big Bow Mystery* (1891), which preceded much of this activity, is sometimes nodded to in passing by histories of the genre for its innovatory treatment of the 'locked room' problem and for its highly ironic choice of culprit. Just as interesting, however, are the impoverished and politically conscious East End milieu to which all the main characters belong, and the relaxed assumption that the growing Labour movement is a natural and comprehensible setting for a work of this type. Reinforcing this relaxed posture is an epigrammatic tone which, while sometimes irritatingly self-conscious, just avoids condescension by not invoking any other specific milieu by which the norms of this one are to be judged. The aesthetic aspirations to which the style might be attributed, for instance, are placed firmly within the

East End itself in the person of the poetic hack, Denzil Cantercot (the rhythm of whose name, when you have got used to the slyly self-allusive style of the novel as a whole, perhaps very faintly hints at something like 'Zangwill cants a lot').

Arthur Constant, an idealistic young gentleman living in the East End as a gesture of Labourite solidarity, is discovered in bed with his throat cut; the discoverers being his landlady Mrs Drabdump and the eminent private detective, Grodman, whom she has summoned from across the street to break down the locked and bolted door. The absence of a weapon and the impossibility of egress from the room seem to rule out both suicide and murder, and the case accordingly becomes celebrated as 'The Big Bow Mystery'. The police detective, Wimp, attempts to put the blame on Constant's fellow lodger Mortlake, a rising labour leader, finally unearthing a motive in the story of an ex-fiancée of his who has received money from the murdered man. While Grodman gives out many enigmatic signs of working confidently on the mystery from another angle, Wimp makes his case stick in court, his explanation of how Mortlake *could* have rigged the door to seem internally bolted being one of the throwaway ingenuities which make this book a 'locked-room' classic. It is only a few hours before the execution that Grodman, acclaimed as a saviour by the crowd, bursts in on the Home Secretary to reveal the truth: that to confirm his artistry with a 'perfect crime' he himself cut Constant's throat, having drugged him the night before, while Mrs Drabdump predictably hid her face in horror. In a final twist, the Home Secretary reveals that Mortlake has already been reprieved following the last-minute reappearance of his missing fiancée, whereupon Grodman shoots himself.

Despite a heavily padded middle section, *The Big Bow Mystery* is worked out in meticulous detail, both as regards what really happened and what at various times is thought to have happened. Not only does Zangwill play the game fairly with the reader but he also gives in his preface one of the most succinct early accounts of what the game consists of: 'that it should be able and unable to be solved by the reader, and that the writer's solution should satisfy' (Bleiler, p. 201). Even more interesting is the way in which he involved readers as active partners in this game: a frenzied newspaper correspondence in the novel, in which Grodman takes a leading part, stimulated a similar real-life correspondence as to the culprit's identity in the *Star*, in which it was serialised. This then became the basis for a continuation of the game in which Zangwill claimed that he only fixed on the culprit at the last minute, when he discovered that Grodman alone remained unsuspected by readers. Though a later preface explains that this claim was a joke about the difficulty of mystery writing, it also gleefully confesses that the joke has backfired by still being currently believed. In all this working-up of reader-involvement Zangwill took the genre's 'least-likely-suspect' game-element to new heights, shadowing his anti-hero Grodman by using the techniques of detection to question detection itself.

Making Grodman the criminal clearly subverts two types of expectation at once: first, the popular hero-worship of real-life detectives, and secondly, the literary expectations fostered by the genre. To explore the social implications first, it is worth noting the extent to which Grodman's status as a kind of magical popular saviour ('Grodman' without the 'r'?) seems fully justified when contrasted with a police force whose motto is 'First catch your man, then cook the evidence' (p. 213), and whose chief representative, Wimp, has 'subverted' an 'intellect which might have served to unveil the secret workings of nature' to 'the protection of a capitalistic civilisation' (p. 243). Grodman, by contrast, is a local boy made good, who remains loyal to his Bow roots and sides emphatically with 'the people' when Wimp demonstrates his contempt for democratic institutions by launching a bloody police assault on a pro-Constant rally headed by Gladstone himself.

The whole theme of loyalty to roots is a major preoccupation throughout: witness the subplot concerning Mortlake's working-class fiancée, who absconds to Australia so as not to impede his political progress towards 'the "At Homes" of the aristocracy' (p. 245). Another figure who has in a sense betrayed his roots in an opposite direction, naïvely consuming Mrs Drabdump's dearly bought delicacies 'with the assurance that they were the artisan's appanage' (p. 207), is Constant. But the refreshing lack of inheritance-plots or whatever makes clear that his move to Bow was in the right direction, and in one sense the central struggle in the book is that between Grodman and Constant over the question of whether Bow is worth fighting for. Grodman hints at Constant's almost metaphysical fitness to be his victim in a concluding speech which recalls earlier literary monsters such as Iago, or Claggart in Melville's *Billy Budd*: 'I felt instinctively he would be the man. I loved to hear him speak enthusiastically of the Brotherhood of

Man – I, who knew the brotherhood of man was to the ape, the serpent, and the tiger' (p. 297). Like other 'perfect murder' stories (Gide's *Caves du Vatican*, Hitchcock's *Rope*), this one thus has a philosophical motivation, involving the opposition between Social Darwinist 'survival of the fittest' and ideas of collective advancement. From Grodman's point of view, his deed 'proves' the common assumption of Bow as a domain of 'mire, misery, and murder' which Constant has devoted himself to fighting (p. 231). For Constant, it is only at its worst that Bow confirms Schopenhauer's pessimistic view of man as a 'degraded monster' (p. 220); and it is perhaps significant that his murder depends on just such a hopeless pessimism on Mrs Drabdump's part, who hides her eyes at the crucial instant because she is convinced that the worst has already happened.

On a social level, then, *The Big Bow Mystery* undermines rosy fantasies about both the police and the Holmesian superman detective, hinting at the anti-democratic tendencies of both types of figure. At a more self-reflexively literary level, Grodman's crime also parodies Zangwill's own all-knowing role as the 'creator' of the puzzle, since his professional arrogance is also a literary arrogance: for him the murder follows on naturally enough from his bestselling memoir *Criminals I Have Caught*, to which, it is hinted, the present narrative is simply a posthumous appendix. Chesterton's later remark that 'the criminal is the creative artist; the detective only the critic' is in a sense the position both Grodman and Zangwill (or any detective writer) are trying to transcend: in so far as he claims to be an 'artist' the detective writer dangerously combines both roles in himself. Much of the book's subversive effect depends on the way Zangwill allows us complacently to accept Grodman as a critical champion of 'truth', only to reveal that his preoccupation with criminals has obsessed him with 'the terrible joys of their inner life' and the notion of the perfect crime as a 'work of art' (pp. 298, 300). The implied parallel between Grodman's self-admiration and Zangwill's own declaration that 'The only person who has ever solved *The Big Bow Mystery* is myself' playfully accuses a readership whose demand for evercleverer puzzles inevitably pushes detection towards just such criminal hubris (p. 201).

The conflict between truth and art embodied in Grodman is also present, whether fully intentionally or not, in the tension between realism and artful 'wit' which marks the novel's often irritatingly facetious style. (Julian Symons's dismissal of it as a 'somewhat uneasy' self-parody is understandable – see Symons, p. 87.) The tension is already evident in the opening treatment of the over-worked Mrs Drabdump, the comic overtones of whose name are only partly offset by some insistence on the real misery of her life. But the truth–art conflict has a more conscious manifestation in the comic subplot involving the opinions and antics of the would-be aesthete Denzil Cantercot and the utilitarian cobbler Peter Crowl. Their opening bout gives something of the prevalent facetious flavour:

> 'Yes, but what will become of the Beautiful?' said Denzil Cantercot.
> 'Hang the Beautiful!' said Peter Crowl, as if he were on the committee of the Academy. 'Give me the True.'
> Denzil did nothing of the sort. He didn't happen to have it about him.   (p. 232)

A page or so into the contest, its thematic relevance becomes clearer when Crowl's claims that 'The True is for all men' and 'The Good of Society is the only test of things' are countered by Denzil's argument that 'The Individual is before all. The mass must be sacrificed for the Great Man' (p. 234). Despite Crowl's many absurdities, the main butt of these scenes is Denzil's Nietzschean belief in the aesthetic superman, which throws a parodic light on Grodman's self-election to a similar status. The implicit link is underlined in Denzil's ghosting of *Criminals I Have Caught*, which Grodman sees as mere 'dressing' whereas Denzil claims to have 'idealised the bare facts and lifted them into the realm of poetry and literature' (p. 239). Lurking somewhere behind all this is De Quincey's 'Murder Considered as One of the Fine Arts', but despite Grodman's confidence in the self-sufficient perfection of crime he still appoints Denzil to 'work up' his final confession for the posthumous twenty-fifth edition 'with literary and dramatic touches after the model of the other chapters of my book' (p. 295). The obvious parallel between this worked-up confession and *The Big Bow Mystery* itself suggests that Denzil's labours are a direct parody of Zangwill's own pandering to the public thirst for the mythologised 'great detective'. In this context, Denzil's degrading hackwork for the bathetically named *New Pork Herald* perhaps has a special significance for the Jewish Zangwill, and the fact that he also supplies a tobacconist's shop with cheap 'plots' recalls Zangwill's account of how he 'stored' this particular plot in his mind for years before being able to sell it (p. 202). The literary/mercenary ambivalence of the word 'plot' is rammed home as Denzil's mind switches between selling another storyline to the tobacconist and giving 'a new significance' to the advertisement 'PLOTS FOR SALE' by unscrupulously selling evidence against the innocent Mortlake (p. 242). As with the parallels between himself and Grodman, Zangwill's second self-projection as Denzil is only a way of parodying the expectations of a readership whose fundamental demand is precisely to be made the *victim* of such 'plots'.

ARTHUR MORRISON

Grodman is not the only fictional detective of the Sherlock Holmes era with criminal tendencies. In so far as they detect at all (and they certainly do so, in stories closely modelled on Doyle's) the two most famous such figures are E. W. Hornung's Raffles and Maurice Leblanc's Arsène Lupin. These well-behaved 'rogues' are, however, clearly the heroes of their respective sagas and, once the initial inversion of roles is accepted, their non-homicidal adventures do not raise too many questions for the reader. More challenging, though less well known, are the 'bad' detectives Romney Pringle and Dorrington, created by R. Austin Freeman (under the pseudonym Clifford Ashdown) and Arthur Morrison respectively.[4] Both authors, as it happens, also created good detectives – Freeman's Dr Thorndike and Morrison's Martin Hewitt – who are far more celebrated and raise no problems as solid workmanlike investigators in the Holmes mould, with admiring Watson-like confidants. By contrast with such figures (and indeed with Raffles and Lupin, whose exploits are made acceptable largely through the use of admiring narrators), Pringle and Dorrington are sinister in part because they are solitaries, their actions and thoughts described in a cool third-person narration which only rarely comments on their immorality. A typical story will begin with one or the other uncovering evidence of a crime in approved detective fashion, but will end with the success, failure or (most often) partial success of his attempt to get his own hands on whatever booty may be in the offing, at whatever cost to anyone else.

Resembling Zangwill in this, Arthur Morrison is best known as the author of realistic social-protest fiction set in the East End: *Tales of Mean Streets*, *A Child of the Jago* and *The Hole in the Wall*. While not confined to the East End, his detective stories assume the normality of working-class and petty-bourgeois milieux, and his 'good' detective Martin Hewitt is refreshingly free from self-aggrandising mannerisms and clear that his job is a living rather than an amusement. Though hardly works of explicit protest, the Hewitt stories repeatedly make the point that 'there are many most respectable persons living in good style in the suburbs whose chief business lies in financing such ventures [as bank robbery] and taking the chief share of the proceeds' (Greene, p. 63).

Such links between crime and apparent respectability are far more pointedly explored in Morrison's Dorrington stories (and again we may note a rhythmic resemblance of names). In 'The Affair of the "Avalanche Bicycle and Tyre Co., Limited" ' (1897), the unscrupulous hero discovers that Mallows, the director of a respectable bicycle company – the 'Indestructible' – is augmenting his income by running a bogus 'rival' company called the 'Avalanche': an operation which involves sticking eye-catching transfers on to nondescript bicycles and crippling the 'Indestructible's' star cyclist in the middle of a race. Having deduced all this through an appropriately Holmesian clue – a thread from a piece of sticking plaster – Dorrington further discovers that each of the two factories named in the 'Avalanche' publicity deters curiosity by claiming that the other actually makes the bicycles. Running Mallows to earth in the otherwise deserted Birmingham branch he suavely extorts a half share of the proceeds in return for his silence. With the cheque in his pocket he then unwisely allows Mallows to lock him into an enamelling oven from which he only just escapes, releasing a wave of gas which blows up the factory, breaking Mallows's leg and exposing the real nature of the bogus company to the public gaze. After the discreet removal of Mallows from the board the 'Indestructible' continues to flourish, and although Dorrington keeps the hundred pound 'reward' cheekily extracted from Mallows for identifying him as the race saboteur, he cannot cash the far larger cheque for the 'Avalanche' proceeds since he himself has inadvertently caused the bogus firm to go bust.

Though the 'Ideas' implicit in this story are not underlined as self-consciously as those of *The Big Bow Mystery*, it is clearly if slyly constructed to highlight a broadly anti-capitalist position. Morrison ensures that the main points get made by putting them into the mouth of Dorrington, back to front as it were, in the scene where he couples his blackmail of Mallows with a wholehearted endorsement of his business methods. Though written in what was to become a rather conventional villainese, Dorrington's mock-kindly insistence on Mallows's blamelessness – 'But you mustn't look so ashamed of yourself, you know' – together with his constant repetition of the word 'business', invokes a universe in which the distinction between capitalist enterprise and robbery with violence has completely disappeared: 'Everybody does it' (p. 117).

Carefully preparing us for the central confrontation is a factual-sounding introduction describing the bicycle business as a classic boom industry. Its impact on the share market and on established advertising practices is sketched in, and then we are introduced to the gaudy 'Avalanche' publicity as the epitome of all this new activity. In apparent contrast, the well-established 'Indestructible' company affords Dorrington his entrée into the cycling world by hiring him to find out whether a previous patent exists for an invention which a less scrupulous firm would presumably market anyway. Its respectability is further established by its secretary Stedman, an honest cycling enthusiast who casts intelligent doubts on the 'Avalanche' as a viable company and later rightly suspects it of sabotaging the race. Having carefully set the contrast between the two companies against a background of rising business speculation, Morrison proceeds to confound it with the revelation that both are equally the creations of the same entrepreneur, who is at first chiefly characterised by his vociferous attacks on gambling.

Dorrington's attempt to insert himself into this nexus is initially seen as only an extension of the general public desire to make a killing, the ' "good thing" desired by all the greedy who flutter about at the outside edge of the stock and share market' (p. 99). As Mallows's greed has led him from reputable manufacture to fraud and then violence, Dorrington's leads him from the common quest for 'information, syndicate shares, directorships, anything' to frank extortion. This world of flimsy surfaces covering ugly realities is well symbolised by the fake transfers on the bicycles, the 'slight crêpe-hair whisker' Mallows adopts for his Birmingham identity and the sticking-plaster for a grazed finger which gives Dorrington the initial clue to his criminal activities. In tearing off such coverings, literally or symbolically, Dorrington performs half of his expected detective function but, as in *The Big Bow Mystery*, any reliance we may place on this function is then comprehensively challenged.

An important contrast with Zangwill's novel is that as a series-hero Dorrington has to escape from each adventure so that he can proceed to the next. He must also usually make some sort of profit, to preserve our belief in his abilities as such a hero, but also to demonstrate the corruption of a world which succumbs so easily to his predations. Countering this, however, is a need to communicate a feeling of crisis – a sense that things can't go on like this for much longer – which demands a picture of his kind of corruption as radically self-defeating. Some such tension seems to determine the account of the near-death in the gas-filled oven whereby it seems that his nefarious career can finally be summed up: 'It would seem that at last a horribly-fitting retribution had overtaken Dorrington in death by a mode parallel to that which he and his creatures had prepared for others' (p. 121). Since the series framework decrees his escape, however, the explosion of the bogus factory redirects the notion of a 'horribly-fitting retribution' on to Mallows: not only does his broken leg pay for the cyclist's broken arm, but his career, previously apparently as indestructible as Dorrington's, is appropriately buried by an avalanche as the crowd surveys 'the extrication of Mr Paul Mallows, managing director of the "Indestructible Bicycle Company", from the broken bricks, mortar, bicycles and transfers of the "Avalanche Bicycle and Tyre Company, Limited" ' (p. 122). The cathartic ironies of this scene, whereby 'the whole thing was thrown open to the general gaze', suggest a semi-apocalyptic feeling that 'the whole thing' will shortly self-destruct in a wider sense. But this is immediately damped down with the reminder that it is in everyone's interest to suppress the 'Avalanche' scandal as quickly as possible, retire Mallows, and ensure that the 'Indestructible' lives up to its name by detaching its fortunes from those of a single incompetent individual. Dorrington, meanwhile, escapes with the reward of his detection though not of his extortion, and his come-uppance is foreshadowed in the bald statement that Mallows's cheque for the latter 'was found among the notes and telegrams in this case in the Dorrington deed-box' (p. 123).

E. C. BENTLEY

The other two writers to be discussed are of a later generation, and as lifelong friends they had several attitudes in common. One of these shared attitudes is an occasionally anti-capitalist stance, but unlike the two works just considered G. K. Chesterton's Father Brown stories (1911–29) and E. C. Bentley's *Trent's Last Case* (1912)[5] tend to assume an alternative 'civilisation' upon which the workings of big business and the other attitudes being criticised are an alien intrusion. In their loving creation of this other world of real values, Chesterton and Bentley express a strong conservatism which sometimes interacts paradoxically with their determination to use detective fiction as a means of challenging received ideas and opening up new possibilities.

Though written shortly after the first Father Brown stories, it will be easiest to tackle *Trent's Last Case* first, since it operates at a somewhat simpler level and also, as another 'detective novel to end all detective novels', it offers some interesting parallels with *The Big Bow Mystery*. The irony on which it is based is not that the detective committed the crime, but that his conclusions are all completely wrong: another way of undermining the reader's faith in the infallible sleuth. Clustering round this departure from the norm are others, such as that he becomes emotionally involved with one of the chief suspects, that the technical culprit lacks all the attributes of villainy, and that the real culprit, technicalities apart, was at the time of writing a very novel choice of 'least likely suspect': the victim himself.

The American capitalist Sigsbee Manderson, vigorously denounced as a social menace in the first chapter, is found shot through the head in the grounds of his English mansion. The artist and journalist Philip Trent is sent to cover the case and then, thanks to his reputation as a sleuth, asked to investigate it by Manderson's widow, with whom he rapidly falls in love. He pieces together evidence – missed by the police, who suspect American trade unionists – suggesting that Manderson's English secretary, Marlowe, committed the crime because he too was in love with Mrs Manderson. Rather than learn more, Trent abandons the case and plunges himself into painting and foreign travel. Eventually, however, after much unravelling of misunderstandings, Mrs Manderson accepts his proposal of marriage and Marlowe explains that the suspicous rigging of alibis which Trent accurately deduced was the only way he could extricate himself from a fiendish plan whereby Manderson, unjustly suspecting him of having an affair with his wife, intended to shoot himself while framing Marlowe for the murder. Relieved to discover that the victim's guilt exonerates everyone else, Trent expatiates on the case to Mrs Manderson's uncle Cupples, an unworldly old gentleman who has been his confidant throughout. The second of what Frank Kermode calls the book's 'false bottoms' falls out when Cupples placidly announces that he was the real killer, although only in self-defence and after attempting to prevent Manderson's suicide. Stunned by all these revelations, Trent vows that he will 'never touch a crime-mystery again' (Bentley, p. 237).

Bentley's intention to undermine the detective genre, and the new elements he was perceived as introducing to it, are effectively characterised by Dorothy Sayers:

> The generally accepted legend, which I believe to be quite true, is that Mr Bentley wrote *Trent's Last Case* for a wager, at the instigation of Mr G. K. Chesterton. He was sick to death of the 'infallible sleuth' and meant to show him up for the humbug he was. The marvelous [*sic*] deductions might, he thought, easily go wrong from start to finish, their collapse providing the story with its magnificent 'surprise ending'. Mr Bentley did not altogether succeed in eliminating the 'infallible sleuth', though the wooden [*sic*: 'modern'?] detective does tend, perhaps as a result of this salutary warning, to be less bumptious and dogmatic than the old-fashioned kind. But the book was influential in a much wider and more important way, for it was the work of an educated man, with the whole tradition of European letters behind him, who was not ashamed to lay his gifts of culture at the feet of that Cinderella of literature, the mystery novel. (Bentley, pp. x–xi)

Sayers goes on to describe the book as a 'revolution', not least for its replacement of 'the old stock characters' by 'real flesh and blood': 'And even the love story, so often a weak sister, is, in this masterly book, made moving, credible and integral to the plot.'

It is not in fact hard to identify *Trent's Last Case* as an important influence on Sayers's own Lord Peter Wimsey novels, where the joke element is echoed in the hero's name, and the upgrading of the love interest in his romance with Harriet Vane. And, to digress further for a moment, it is also arguable that the self-doubting Philip Trent, emotionally involved with the chief female suspect and projecting his own feelings on to an *alter ego* named Marlowe, may have some bearing on the creation of an apparently very different type of detective, Raymond Chandler's Philip Marlowe. If any of this is so, it is interesting that for all three detectives the successful resolution of the love interest also marks the 'last case': *Trent* (though Bentley later wrote up earlier 'Investigations'), Sayers's *Gaudy Night* and Chandler's *Playback*. While such parallels go some way to support Sayers's claims for *Trent* as a 'liberating and inspiring influence', however, it is also important to remember that many of the most interesting earlier works in the genre – *L'Affaire Lerouge, The Moonstone, The Big Bow Mystery*, not to mention *Oedipus* – also feature deluded and emotionally over-involved detectives, together with no lack of love-interest or European culture. And in some ways the 'infallible sleuth' is enshrined as never before in the post-*Trent* work of Sayers herself and her contemporaries.

Trent's intention to question the genre is overlooked by Frank Kermode in an otherwise illuminating discussion of the book. Determined to describe it as a representative and therefore uncon-scious example of the 'hermeneutic' detective genre, Kermode shows that it is actually open to wider readings, so that 'the hermeneutic spawns the cultural' (Most and Stowe, p. 184). In particular, he explores its racist and élitist elements and the way in which at a symbolic level 'the myth is oedipal', with Manderson as a malevolent Laius, Trent and Marlowe as two variants of the supplanting rival-son, Mrs Manderson as Jocasta and Cupples ('a goodish name for Tiresias') as the old prophet who holds the true answer to the riddle. The argument is convincing on most counts, but overlooks the deliberate assault on generic convention that not only facilitates such wider readings (though Bentley might not have relished these particular ones), but actually demands them.

The 'ideas' Bentley himself seems most concerned to explore are unmissably introduced in the opening chapter, which virtually constitutes a detachable essay on the evils of American-style capitalism. Thus Manderson's death is presented to us, on one hand, in the context of its shattering effect on Wall Street and world markets and, on the other, in terms of its total lack of effect at any 'real' level, either that of personal relationships ('nobody loved him') or that of the real basis of the economy, in production rather than exchange: 'To all mankind save a million or two of half-crazed gamblers, blind to all reality, the death of Manderson meant nothing; the life and work of the world went on' (Bentley, p. 9). There is a vivid picture of a Wall Street Crash eerily prefiguring those of 1929 (the mass suicides) and 1987 (the arrest of a corrupt Boesky-like figure leads to a scare which only fully erupts, on a Monday, some time later). But it is important to Bentley's argument that the market quickly recovers, so that only financiers 'blind to all reality' suffer real damage. The archetypes of crash – 'In Paris a well-known banker walked quietly out of the Bourse and fell dead upon the broad steps among the raving crowd of Jews, a phial crushed in his hand' (p. 16) – are not followed by the archetypes of Depression: 'Nothing in the texture of the general life had changed' (p. 9).

The sense of a contrast between the unreal world of finance and 'the general life' has been variously articulated in this century. The Russian Revolution was only a war away when Bentley wrote this; but the fascist movements of only a few years later also drew (to different effect) on long-established images of international capital as an alien conspiracy sapping the national roots, at least until they acquired the power to manipulate big business for themselves. Bentley displays a mixture of such impulses, with attacks on capital repeatedly merging into racial paranoia. Though there are no more references to the 'raving crowd of Jews', Manderson's twisted nature is first ascribed to 'the Forty-Niner and financial buccaneer, his forebear', and then to the fact that 'most of the very rich men . . . in America had become so by virtue of abnormal greed, or abnormal industry, or abnormal personal force, or abnormal luck' (pp. 4, 186). But then such vague anti-American gesturings are suddenly focused, as Kermode points out, in a lengthy passage specifically attributing Manderson's 'mixed mind' to a 'strain of Indian blood' (p. 187). (At a less serious level of xenophobia, the book also offers a siren-like maid – 'What sort of a woman is she?' 'She's French, sir' (p. 70) – whose gabbling advances it takes all Trent's grasp of 'European letters' to fend off.)

A further point is worth making briefly about the negative portrayal of Manderson and the world he represents. To help the condemnation of him as a capitalist there is at least some mention of his victims in the American working class. Interestingly, the Pennsylvania miners' organisation chiefly suspected of his murder somewhat resembles the Molly Maguires on whom Doyle based the Scowrers of *The Valley of Fear* (actually published three years after *Trent*, though Pinkerton's account had been published long before). For Bentley's 'Tiresias' Cupples, Manderson seems to have imitated the Pottsville magnate Gowen in abusing 'the proper relationship of the capitalist to the employee' during 'the trouble in the Pennsylvania coal-fields' (p. 29). Cupples's benevolent humanism is not, however, developed too far, perhaps for fear of undermining the claim of the opening chapter that Manderson and his ilk are simply *irrelevant* to 'the general life'.

The values to be contrasted to Manderson's are gradually uncovered in the working out of the story as a whole, but an early indication of them is given at the very end of the first chapter, where the lack of mourners at his grave is contrasted with all those 'who flock round the tomb of Keats' (p. 10). If the values of high art, also represented in Trent's painting and Mrs Manderson's love of opera, are one part of the positive pole, the others are such things as delicacy of feeling, wit, and the ability to form relationships. In other words, virtually the values of E. M. Forster's *Howards End*, written two years earlier: 'art and personal relationships' versus 'telegrams and anger'. And the Forsterian motto 'only connect', which could easily be applied to all detective novels, is particularly apt to this one.

A failure to connect on a personal level is the cause not only of Manderson's death, in that he never discusses his jealous suspicions either with Marlowe or his wife, but also of Trent's chief error in that he suppresses similar suspicions until very late in the case. His secondary error, the failure to suspect Cupples, is more understandable, but in his final revelations Cupples makes it clear that he has never actively lied and has indeed dropped repeated hints as to the truth. 'Connecting' in one sense is of course what Trent's detective activity ought to be all about, but with his collapse as a detective the alternative human possibility emerges that the need for such a figure would disappear if everyone simply communicated more openly with everyone else. Manderson has been from the start the chief block to 'connection' in this sense, his habitual chilly distance from his wife shading naturally into his misreading of her purely platonic friendship with Marlowe. It is Manderson's refusal to communicate his suspicions that leads to all the other concealments in the case, beginning with those of Mrs Manderson herself, who later tells Trent that 'I swore to myself on the spot that I would never show by any word or sign that I was conscious of his having such a thought about me' (p. 166). As more and more of the miasma of concealment and suspicion is tracked back to Manderson, his death seems increasingly to represent a sacrifical purging of all that prevents society from realising its best potential.

It is one of the main ironies of the book that the hero's own suspicions precisely replace those which led to the crime he is investigating. This theme of replacement brings us back to Kermode's suggestion that 'the myth is oedipal', which it will now be useful to follow up in rather more detail before returning to what the book seems to be trying to say on more conscious levels. Trent's reduplication of Manderson is expressed most graphically in his choice of the same person, Marlowe, as a scapegoat for his own wishes, and in the gradual development of an early preoccupation with Mrs Manderson's sleeping arrangements into full-blown sexual jealousy. In the early part of his investigation he concludes, correctly as far as this goes, that Marlowe impersonated Manderson after his death by wearing his clothes and imitating his voice in order to establish an alibi. The most daring part of this impersonation involved talking to Mrs Manderson from the adjacent conjugal bedroom and then creeping through her room when she was asleep in order to escape through her window. This is what actually happened, but Trent's further suspicion of collusion between the two throws a different light on all this bedroom business which as a gentleman he would rather abandon his calling than inquire into. There are several teasing parallels here, in that Manderson sacrificed his life (and, incidentally, the whole of world capitalism) from similar fears of Marlowe's youthful, ingenuity; while at the same time the 'insider' Marlowe is clearly attracting from Trent the resentment really owed to the patriarchal Manderson.

Earlier, before developing such qualms, Trent explores Mrs Manderson's bedroom in a purely sleuthing capacity (the chapter is titled 'Poking About') and lies down 'with deliberation on the bed' (p. 69). Such mysterious actions are part of any great detective's job, and we later learn that this was justified in terms of eyelines and so forth, but the act also mimes out what is to become Trent's growing obsession with the mysteries of Mrs Manderson's sex-life. At the height of this obsession, during his self-exile, we are later told that though 'broken to the realities of sex, he was still troubled by its inscrutable history. He went through life full of a strange respect for certain feminine weakness and a very simple terror of certain feminine strength'. This terror is explicitly linked to his first sight of Mrs Manderson when, unaware of his observation, she reached out her arms in a 'great gesture of passionate joy in her new liberty', a gesture which he immediately connects 'in the unconscious depths of his mind' with his first impression of Marlowe as attracting women with his 'looks and manners', and doubtless also 'obsessed by passion like himself' (pp. 147–8). However unintentional, Trent's inaugural bit of spying mirrors the snooping on which Manderson's evil suspicions were founded, especially when conjoined with his wife's praise of Marlowe for 'his manners' (p. 163).

Marlowe, the scapegoat of all their worst suspicions, is clearly a kind of two-way substitute figure for criminal and detective alike. Not only does he literally put himself in the dead man's shoes (the strain on which provides Trent with his first real clue), but he also lies in his bed, to 'tumble it' (p. 214), while Mrs Manderson sleeps in the next room, thus perhaps underlining the fact that his real resemblance to Manderson is not his equal access to his wife's favours but his equal exclusion from them. This bit of symbolism, taken in conjunction with the earlier image of Trent lying on Mrs Manderson's bed, points us towards the dominant substitution in the book, whereby it is Trent, the supposedly uninvolved detective, who finally replaces both his real and his imagined precursor in Mrs Manderson's affections. The Oedipal dimensions of all this emerge further in the way that Mrs Manderson, though by no means old enough to be their mother, refers to both Marlowe and Trent as 'boys' (pp. 163, 176), and that just as Laius fails to destroy his feared supplanter, Manderson's attempt to frame his imagined rival–son Marlowe leads directly to his actual supplanting by Trent. Such a reading links *Trent* to 'The Purloined Letter' as analysed by Lacan, where similar acts of Oedipal substitution are seen as exemplifying the master-thesis that 'the unconscious is the discourse of the other', so that each character in displacing another repeats and 'relays' that other person's motivations and wishes. Oddly enough, Cupples (Kermode's Tiresias) comes up with a similar suggestion just before revealing his own unsuspected place in the chain of events. Talking of Marlowe's continuing ignorance of the sexual suspicions he has aroused, Cupples tells Trent that 'Nearly all of us, I venture to think, move unconsciously among a network of opinions, often quite erroneous, which other people entertain about us' (p. 226).

The exploration of the theme of reduplication I have just been conducting has taken us some way from the earlier discussion of the book's conscious ideas and 'values', and it is important to remind ourselves that the fact that you can 'do' a narratological or Oedipal or whatever reading of a text does not necessarily mean that these things are incorporated at the level of ideas. But nor does it mean that they are not, as Kermode rather implies, and I think some of the passages just quoted indicate a reasonably sophisticated awareness of the relevance of such readings, particularly the last one. Cupples's remark can be applied to almost every character in the book and particularly Trent, whose surrounding network of opinions is supplied by us, the gullible readers trained to assume he will always be right.

Apart from Trent, the book's other main detective has been Manderson, whose 'poking about' has led to so much suffering and destruction. The good things that happen are not the results of detection but of honest expressions of feeling and impulse. Ironically, this includes the actual 'crime' itself, since Cupples's shooting of Manderson, which is never remotely condemned, was motivated by the simple impulse of self-defence. Cupples has, moreover, also been the only person to express to Manderson's face the conviction already instilled in us from the start that 'such men as he were unfit to live' (p. 32). Elsewhere there are suggestions that Marlowe really *should* have committed the murder in defiance of the 'modern feebleness of impulse in the comfortable classes, and their respect for the modern apparatus of detection' (p. 149), and that 'the law certainly does not shine when it comes to a case requiring much delicacy of perception' (p. 232).

In the Forsterian terms invoked above, then, detection and the law belong very clearly with Manderson in the realm of 'telegrams and anger', at least where the anger is bitter and suppressed. On the other side are the human values of strong impulse (Mrs Manderson's gesture of freedom, Trent's passion for her) and delicacy of perception (art, opera, the knowledge that platonic relationships are possible). Trent's movement from one to the other is, like many rites of passage, also a sexual initiation, in which he overcomes his 'simple terror of certain feminine strength', and it is made possible because, unlike Manderson, he ignores evidence and relies on feeling. Certainly, the book encourages us as well-trained detective readers to follow the evidence, whose laws it scrupulously observes, but the implication is that this will not equip us to confront the real problems of life and that, however much we have learnt, this should be for us, as for Trent, the last case.

Put thus it sounds very admirable, but it should also be pointed out that the human values applauded depend very strongly on a very limited social support system. One of the most striking examples of a 'human' response which puts the evidence in doubt is Trent's immediate recognition of Marlowe as an Oxford Man with 'that air of clean living and inward health that is the peculiar glory of his social type' (p. 41). And, though she apparently has Spanish blood, Mrs Manderson is also vouched for from the first by her uncle Cupples (Trent's 'best of friends') and by the fact that she has 'lived mostly among people of artistic or literary propensities' (p. 34). These pointers, combined with the unremitting condemnation of Manderson in the first chapter, strongly suggest from the start what the final distribution of innocence and guilt will be, so that the book's eventual 'discovery' of the real human truth behind the mystery is only a reaffirmation of the rigid assumptions about social 'types' with which it opened.

G. K. CHESTERTON

As a detective writer, G. K. Chesterton combines several of the concerns of the other writers in this chapter while clearly having many further axes of his own to grind. In his best novel, the early *The Man Who Was Thursday* (1905), he effortlessly deconstructs the whole notion of detection by showing how an apparently diabolical conspiracy might consist entirely of the quasi-divine detectives bent on exposing it. A similar double insistence on the absolute distinction between good and evil, and on their mirror-like resemblance, runs throughout his work, and helps to explain why he turned so frequently to detective formulae to express theological concerns. The *doppelgänger* motif is everywhere, corresponding at the level of action to the 'paradoxical' mannerisms for which Chesterton is notorious at the level of style.

Apart from his religious concerns Chesterton also used detective fiction to attack inequalities of class and wealth. While allotting the poor a rather token number of appearances, he frequently uses the 'overlooked details' fundamental to the genre as a basis from which to satirise the shortsighted presumptions of the rich. Such refreshing radicalism does not, however, always sit comfortably with the numerous doctrinal, racial and cultural xenophobias exhibited in a story such as 'The Wrong Shape', where a murder committed by a utilitarian atheist is linked through a network of suggestions with the aesthetic 'wrongness' surrounding an Indian mystic whose 'queer, crooked Oriental knife' gives the story its title: 'It's the wrong shape in the abstract. Don't you ever feel that about Eastern art? . . . I have seen wicked things in a Turkey carpet' (Chesterton, *Complete Father Brown*, p. 92). Such nonsensical conflations of one thing with another are only a short step from the Bellocian crypto-fascism of later years. But the preoccupation with aesthetic judgement is also part of a wider ambivalence about 'art', to which we shall return.

The last introductory point to be briefly made involves the character of Chesterton's dumpy clerical detective, Father Brown. The archetypal 'unimpressive' detective, he is passed over in story after story not only by the other characters but also, apparently, by the narrative itself: hence often making the same kind of social point as the 'overlooked detail' with which he has a special kinship. But the great array of devices for making him look small, stupid-as-the-world-sees-it and so forth, do not ultimately disguise the authority he embodies. It is one of the repeated paradoxes of the series that he never solves a case through divine inspiration but only through reason or the confessional-derived empathy with the criminal mind which enables him to claim that 'it was I who killed all those people' (p. 464). None the less, he invariably emerges from a carefully arranged obscurity into a blaze of something like glory, as in the annunciatory 'Blue Cross'. The paradox of power-in-humility is of course central to Christianity, and Chesterton did not need to invent the black cassock which at once shrouds and proclaims its wearer. But it will be easiest to explore the further paradoxes inscribed in this figure by turning to the first four stories from *The Innocence of Father Brown*, which establish a kind of opening movement for the series as a whole.

The first story, 'The Blue Cross', describes the hunt by the star French detective, Valentin, for the master-criminal Flambeau, who is thought to have fled to London disguised as one of the clerical guests of a major 'Eucharistic Congress'. Unable to find him, Valentin acts on 'the paradox of Poe' that 'wisdom should reckon on the **unforeseen**' (p. 11) and starts his quest at random in a coffee-shop where, it turns out, one of a pair of harmless-looking priests has recently put salt in the sugar-bowl and then thrown soup at a wall.[6] Via a trail of similar small outrages – upset apples, broken windows, and so on – Valentin trails the priests to Hampstead Heath, and recognises one as Flambeau and the other as Father Brown, a genuine priest carrying a jewelled cross to the Congress, whom he has met earlier on the train from Harwich. As Valentin and his police reinforcements listen from their bushes, Flambeau breaks off a theological debate and demands the cross, only to learn that Father Brown, suspecting his 'bad theology' from the start, has posted it to safety after much switching of brown-paper parcels, and left a trail of clues which he knows the police must have followed. Valentin emerges and arrests Flambeau, but both acknowledge that they have met their master in Father Brown.

The story inaugurates the series effectively in a number of ways. It is, first of all, typical of many subsequent stories in that it initially focuses attention on a figure other than Father Brown himself, allowing us plenty of time and scope to sympathise with this apparent protagonist and to take in the specific atmosphere of the setting – here, the loose and attenuated links between one part of London and another – through his eyes. As with most subsequent stories, the nature of this setting proves to be connected in a kind of symbolic unity with the problem being investigated: thus here the attenuation of the London suburbs, 'like passing through thirteen separate vulgar cities all just touching each other', mirrors the tenuousness of the trail Valentin is following, along with the crudeness of the clues which provide the links (pp. 15–16). The story is also typical in that the real hero Father Brown, after first being elaborately overlooked by the narrative voice, provides the solution through a mixture of empathy with the criminal and a nose for theological or other kinds of deviation, which allows Chesterton to foreground some cherished tenet in the same breath as solving the mystery.

The story is atypical, however, in not really being a detective story at all. The systematic following-up of logical clues on which the genre normally depends is replaced by an equally systematic dependence on wild coincidence. Clearly Father Brown has no realistic way of knowing that Valentin will stumble into all the right restaurants and sweet-shops, and few real detectives, however French, would adopt a 'paradox of Poe' as a serious *modus operandi*. The flouting of conventions is carried through in the fact that

Father Brown himself occupies the structural space that would belong to the criminal in a normal detective story: not only does his knowledge of thieves' tricks such as the spiked bracelet match Flambeau's, but he is also responsible for the trail of mayhem followed by the apparent 'hero', Valentin.

But these distortions of the convention help to open up some of the ideas, particularly about the genre itself, that Chesterton is concerned to establish. The wild chase through central and suburban London in search of 'any sort of queer thing' acts as a programmatic example of the 'realisation of the poetry of London' (or of 'modern life') which he had earlier described as the genre's main achievement in 'A Defence of Detective Stories'. In striking anticipation of modern semiotics, he points out there that a city is 'more poetic even than a countryside, for while nature is a chaos of unconscious forces, a city is a chaos of conscious ones . . . there is no stone in the street and no brick in the wall that is not actually a deliberate symbol – a message from some man, as much as if it were a telegram or a post card' (Chesterton, *Defendant*, p. 159). In reading the 'deliberate symbols' left by Father Brown and following them up with the aid of his own 'romantic fancy', Valentin initiates himself and us into the specific imaginative world of tenuous connections and significant disruptions which Chesterton calls the 'romance of detail in civilisation'.

The other programmatic idea which the reversal of conventions helps us to explore is succinctly conveyed in Valentin's aphorism that 'The criminal is the creative artist; the detective only the critic' (Chesterton, *Complete Father Brown*, p. 12). Great play is made here and elsewhere with Flambeau's 'artistic' genius as a criminal: indeed, his most dramatic exploits seem to have involved playful transformations of the urban scene, such as switching the milk-cans on people's doorsteps and repainting all the numbers in a street (p. 10), of which Father Brown's similar disruptions are clearly an echo. Hence we might say that whereas Valentin does play an almost purely 'critical' role in his pursuit of the symbolic trail, Father Brown shows a more inwardly 'artistic' grasp of Flambeau's creativity, so that the final tableau in which detective-critic and criminal-artist both acknowledge his supremacy comes to seem symmetrical and appropriate.

Coming on the heels of another reference to Poe, Valentin's aphorism looks back fairly directly to the speculations on the 'creative and resolvent' duality in 'Rue Morgue'. But if it is important for Chesterton to demonstrate Father Brown's 'creative' equality with figures like Dupin, it is also important to show that he is indeed a critic: not only of the criminal's creation but also, more ambivalently, of the author's. Thus in the theological disputation near the end, the still-disguised Flambeau seems to voice the whole spirit of irrational serendipity on which the story so far (including Brown) has relied, when he speculates on 'wonderful universes above us where reason is utterly unreasonable'; to which Father Brown retorts that 'On plains of opal, under cliffs cut out of pearl, you would still find a notice-board, "Thou shalt not steal" ' (p. 20). In pitting the plain noticeboard of 'reason and justice of conduct' against the criminal's world of aesthetic freedom Father Brown is performing the militantly 'critical' role also symbolised by his cloth. Of course, such criticism of the criminal's defiance of order is natural enough in a detective as well as a priest, and in his 'Defence' Chesterton sees detection as a 'successful knight-errantry', more 'original and poetic' than the role of the criminals who are 'merely placid old cosmic conservatives, happy in the immemorial respectability of apes and wolves' (Chesterton, *Defendant*, p. 161). None the less, there is something puzzling in the way that, here and elsewhere, he not only creates but also revels in an imaginative congruence between the nature of the crime or criminal and the atmospherics of the setting, only to bring both crashing down together at the point of Father Brown's lance. In a single story this has an interesting self-reflexive effect, informing the reader of the artifice on which his or her pleasure has been based; but as the series elongates it begins to produce the effect of an irreconcilable split in the author himself.

The ending of this particular story, at any rate, clearly signals Father Brown's role as someone who unites creative and critical impulses by transcending the restrictions of both, in line with his priestly calling:

> 'Do not bow to me, *mon ami*,' said Valentin, with silver clearness [to Flambeau]. 'Let us both bow to our master.'
> And they both stood an instant uncovered, while the little Essex priest blinked about for his umbrella.   (Chesterton, *Complete Father Brown*, p. 23)

The image of two geniuses acknowledging their intellectual master is cleverly merged with the traditional gesture of reverence before

God; in neither joining in this gesture nor acknowledging that it is directed at him, Father Brown fulfils his sacramental role as a kind of unscathable lightning-conductor for the praise man owes his Maker. The humility which floods back into the scene as he blinks for his umbrella at once prepares us for the insignificance he is to reassume at the start of each new story, and attests to his professional acceptance of the role of intermediary.

If 'The Blue Cross' deliberately challenges detective conventions, the next story, 'The Secret Garden', redresses the balance in being a highly ingenious and well-clued puzzle, with a satisfyingly unlikely culprit. Valentin, now chief of the Paris police, gives a dinner party whose guests include the once again inconspicuous Father Brown, an aristocratic couple and their daughter, a dashing Irish officer and an American millionaire given to subsidising fringe religions. Enough is made of the fact that the garden is totally inaccessible except through the house, whose front door is continually guarded, to render the discovery of a beheaded stranger in the garden virtually inexplicable. The fact that the officer's sword is missing makes him the clearest suspect until the aristocratic daughter gives him an alibi; suspicion then falls on the millionaire, who has gone missing but apparently left the bloodstained sword and a second severed head just outside the garden walls in his flight. Finally, Father Brown demonstrates that this second head actually belongs to the millionaire himself, the rest of whose corpse is lying in the garden, fitted out with the head of a recently-executed stranger. Only Valentin, who presides at executions, had access to such a head; as a freethinker he was violently opposed to the millionaire's plans for subsidising the Catholic Church; his suicide proclaims his guilt.

This bald outline of the story does no justice to the ingenuity with which it dovetails subsidiary clues, red herrings and alibis, or its efficient coverage of movements and motives in what is an unusually large cast of suspects for a short story. Making the great detective the murderer gives us a legitimate least-likely-suspect shock which gains a boost from the expectation fostered in the preceding story that Valentin will settle into the role of a faithful Watson: an expectation further bolstered by presenting the opening of this story too through his eyes. The final revelation has some of the same effect as that of Grodman's guilt in *The Big Bow Mystery*, and there is also some of the same feeling of a philosophical battle between detective reason and unreasonable philanthropy. The subversive effect is more muted here, however, or rather, it is channelled to enhance the greater glory of Father Brown, the difference of whose faith in reason from that of Valentin can now be clarified.

The philosophical position Valentin represents is only briefly sketched in, and the only polemical hint of it before very near the end is an early statement that 'He was one of the great humanitarian French freethinkers; and the only thing wrong with them is that they make mercy even colder than justice' (p. 24). Made in the context of praise for his 'honourable' efforts towards 'the mitigation of sentences and the purification of prisons', this remains a somewhat puzzling remark even when we see that we are meant to link it to the later revelation that 'He would do anything, *anything*, to break what he calls the superstition of the cross' (p. 38). The inference is clearly that freethinking leads to murder, even though this may be complicated by wider musings on 'that great brutality of the intellect which belongs only to France' (p. 34), whereby the Catholic Nationalists betray a similar bloodlust to Valentin's in publishing a gory cartoon calling for his head. This further image of decapitation helps to underline the symbolic appropriateness of the motif in a story depicting a battle of dehumanised minds. The murdered millionaire, all too appropriately called Brayne, also illustrates the theme in that he uses his 'crazy millions' as an indiscriminate ideological weapon, and even Father Brown describes his drift to Rome (in a scarcely sympathetic pun, since his head has just been thrown over a wall) as 'scatterbrained' (p. 38).

In a context where 'brutality of intellect' is chiefly a French aberration, and with his hands full with the case, Father Brown hardly needs to stress his own ideological stance, beyond pointing out that rationalists can be mad. The alternative to excessive rationalism is conveyed more fully in the responses of the Irish officer O'Brien. It is through his revulsion at the cartoon that we receive the message about brutality of intellect, and it is through 'the ancient mirror of his Irish soul' that we perceive 'the shameful symbolic shapes' that the mysterious garden subconsciously evokes: 'A voice older than his first fathers seemed saying in his ear: "Keep out of the monstrous garden where grows the tree with double fruit. Avoid the evil garden where died the man with two heads" ' (p. 37). Apart from their specific meanings, these evocations of nameless horror are important to the effect of the story in showing us how the deeds of intellect border on irrational diablerie. But the archetypal imagery, evoking the apple of knowledge and the division of consciousness itself, also hints that the 'secret' garden is something like Valentin's unconscious mind, rendered monstrous by his refusal to admit any influences other than through the 'conscious' of the house. In being open however 'shamefully' to other voices O'Brien demonstrates the human sanity, including the recognition of insanity, unattainable to the closed mind of Valentin.

Valentin's earlier picture of detectives as critics is ironically echoed here: it is pre-eminently as a critic of 'the superstition of the cross' that he here transgresses and dies. In committing his one murder he becomes in a sense the 'creative artist' of the story; but by pitting him against the Catholic imaginativeness of O'Brien as well as Brown, Chesterton preserves the negative, limiting meanings of 'critic' in a specific association with atheistic rationalism.

The next story, 'The Queer Feet', concerns Father Brown's detection of a robbery simply from the sound a pair of feet make in a hotel corridor. The alternation of the footsteps from those of a lounging gentleman to those of a hurrying waiter informs him that their owner is passing himself off as a diner to the waiters and as a waiter to the diners. Knowing that the latter were using some specially valuable cutlery, he retrieves it from the thief, who turns out to be a Flambeau one step further on the road to repentance. The relative simplicity of the plot allows Chesterton plenty of time to comment on the absurdity of English social divisions, whereby the distinction between identically dressed gentlemen and waiters depends entirely on attitude and deportment.

The story is one of Chesterton's most effective social parables, and uses Father Brown's class-transcending function to good finger-wagging purpose: 'it is immeasurably unlikely that you . . . will ever sink low enough among slums and criminals to find Father Brown'; but 'There is in this world a very aged rioter and demagogue who breaks into the most refined retreats with the dreadful information that all men are brothers, and wherever this leveller went on his pale horse it was Father Brown's trade to follow' (pp. 39, 41). As earlier pointed out, 'we' do not sink very far among slums and habitual criminals, partly because Chesterton does not take us there. But the suggestion of an alliance between Brown the priest and the 'Death the Leveller' of Shirley's poem reminds us of how detective fiction too is specially empowered to 'break into the most refined retreats'.

The confounding of social distinctions normally taken to be paramount is a recurrent motif throughout. Paradoxically, a part of this confounding is apparent in the contradictory nature of the 'refined retreat' of the hotel itself, which is sought after by the ruling class in direct proportion to its pokiness and inconvenience. And as represented by the diners' club, 'The Twelve True Fishermen', the ruling class partakes of further absurd contradictions, such as revering politicians while being appalled at any suggestion 'that there is some difference between a Liberal and a Conservative'. A Cobbett-like note creeps into the satirical portrait of the club president who with no outstanding abilities – 'He was simply in the thing; and there was an end of it' – represents 'a kind of symbol of all that phantasmal and yet fixed society' (pp. 45–6).

What is most phantasmal about these people, then, is that while so firmly assuming the distinction of class which permits Flambeau to steal the silver from under their noses, they are themselves oblivious to the distinctions – in ideology or achievement – on which their power claims to rest. Even their snobbery is revealed as half-hearted in a brilliantly conveyed moment when a (genuine) waiter stops dead in his tracks on seeing that the precious cutlery is missing. At this disruption of routine they feel neither aristocratic anger nor democratic concern but 'merely a dull, hot embarrassment. They did not want to be brutal, and they dreaded the need to be benevolent. They wanted the thing, whatever it was, to be over' (p. 47). In moments like this Chesterton effectively conveys a genuinely radical picture of a whole order trembling in the balance, sensing but not yet acknowledging the contradictions by which it deserves to be destroyed. Standing on the sidelines of this world, Father Brown and Flambeau are united rather than divided in their grasp of the necessity of overthrowing its absurd distinctions by insisting on certain simple class-transcending uniformities.

The political issues raised by this story are perhaps best explained in terms of Chesterton's own political position. He did in fact advocate revolution, violent if necessary. His political philosophy, to which he increasingly devoted his energies using Father Brown as a prime source of funds, was a socialist–conservative hybrid called Distributism, partly inspired by the theories of Pope Leo XIII, which advocated a pure form of what is now much too unproblematically termed a 'property-owning democracy'.[7] To understand how this position may have had even a passing radical legitimacy, it is essential to understand how much was still politically up for grabs in the 1910s – *before* not only the Russian Revolution, but also the clear emergence of the Labour Party in Britain. There is also no need to doubt that Chesterton's anti-imperialism, however warped by Little-England nationalism, was partly based on such serious diagnoses of ruling interests as displayed in 'The Queer Feet'. It is then very depressing to find him revisiting similar territory from a clearly proto-fascist standpoint in the 1922 series *The Man Who Knew Too Much*, where a terminally disillusioned member of Cobbett's 'thing' apocalyptically uses detection to ascribe its decline to foreign influences (and where an early mild obsession with the name 'Fis(c)her' emerges as the secret language of a gnashing anti-Semitism).

Some of the themes of 'The Queer Feet' are taken up in the next story, 'The Flying Stars', where they are neatly entwined with the more aesthetic issues concerning crime and detection raised in 'The Blue Cross'. A suburban Christmas party includes the householder and his daughter and visiting Canadian brother-in-law, a young socialist, a financier called Fischer and, with the inevitable insignificance, Father Brown. An apparently aimless political discussion leads to the Canadian's proposal to stage an impromptu pantomime in which, as Harlequin, he fits a tail on to the financier and later wrestles with a policeman played, as he claims, by an actor-friend he has invited to join the fun. When the financier discovers that the diamonds he intended to give to the daughter are missing from his pocket, Father Brown rapidly establishes that the still-inert 'policeman' is actually a real policeman, chloroformed, and that no one can personally vouch for the Canadian, who has now disappeared. Following him into the garden, where he is escaping by swinging through the trees, Father Brown once more recognises Flambeau and delivers a homily which again makes him surrender the loot and this time ultimately converts him for good.

This story provides perhaps the best illustration of the often-stressed parallel between crime and art. It begins with the reformed Flambeau describing the robbery as 'the most beautiful crime I ever committed' because 'as an artist I have always attempted to provide crimes suitable to the special season or landscape in which I found myself, choosing this or that terrace or garden for a catastrophe, as if for a statuary group' (p. 54). Flambeau here slyly speaks for Chesterton's own perennial effort to invest his settings with symbolic and imaginative significance so that truly to understand their 'meaning' – or the meaning of the feelings we have about them – is also to be on the way to understanding the nature of the crime itself. Other good examples are 'The Sins of Prince Saradine', where the 'looking-glass' atmosphere of the Norfolk Broads accurately reflects the ensnaring of one brother by another in an endlessly repetitive terrain of mirrors, reeds, rapiers and spear-like oars; and 'The Yellow Bird', where a poet-detective deduces the manic state of a libertarian psychologist from the sight of a yellow canary in a wood.[8] Here, at any rate, much of the enjoyment comes from the very precise matching of festive Christmas elements to the details of the robbery. Thus the traditional 'feast of fools' license of the pantomime allows Flambeau, as Harlequin, to perform in play those very assaults on authority-figures – the financier and the policeman – which he is also performing in earnest. Furthermore, the tinsel of his costume provides camouflage for the diamonds which he pins to it in full view, and the moonlit garden into which he escapes to great applause through wide open doors has been integrated into the play from the first, as an appropriately seasonal backdrop.

Other aspects of the match between crime and setting are, however, less in Flambeau's control. Father Brown reminds him, as he swings glittering through the trees, that though the diamonds are called 'The Flying Stars', 'that always means a Falling Star at last' (p. 63). Citing other 'star' criminals with romantic beginnings who have then fallen into meanness and ignominy, he goes on to round out the imagery of winter trees which is an integral part of Flambeau's scenario: 'You will sit in your tree-forest cold at heart and close to death, and the tree-tops will be very bare' (p. 64). Here, as so often, Father Brown is playing critic to the criminal's artist, entering with gusto into the symbolic resonances created by the crime, but then taking their implications back into his own world of values.

Artist and critic, then, continue their duel unabated in 'The Flying Stars', although the growing improbability of Flambeau's remaining unrecognised means that he now surrenders the 'artistic' baton (and perhaps, in following Father Brown into detection, suggests that the division can be transcended). But the story also includes some of the political polemic of 'The Queer Feet', and in some ways takes it further. The discussion which leads into the proposal of a pantomime consists chiefly of an argument between the young socialist, Crook, and Sir Leopold Fischer, the financier: beginning with the injustice of Fischer's having the diamonds in the first place and the hypothetical justice of stealing them, Crook goes on to say that rather than wanting to embrace chimney-sweeps he wants them properly paid. At this point Father Brown interjects that everyone should own their soot (presumably a 'Distributist' position) and adds that it is useful for blacking one's face with at Christmas parties. It is this hint which leads into the pantomime proposal, which Flambeau flamboyantly supports after receiving a telephone message that the police are after him, and presumably hatching his whole subsequent scheme on the spot. References to pantomime characters sitting on top hats lead to cracks about Fischer letting his top hat sit on him, and mention of another traditional gag prompts Crook to call turning policemen into sausages 'a better definition of Socialism than some recently given' (p. 58).

Flambeau's promotion of the required anarchic pantomime atmosphere, then, evolves almost imperceptibly out of Crook's revolutionary rhetoric, as well as Father Brown's ideas on soot, and this loose alliance of forces is maintained in the gusto with which Brown changes a pillow into a baby and endures a donkey's head, as well as in Crook's inspirational piano accompaniment to Flambeau's frenzied antics. Father Brown's approximate empathy with Crook is also apparent when he later defends him from Fischer's suspicions by affirming that 'That Socialist would no more steal a diamond than a Pyramid' (p. 62). There is at least an association of ideas between the pantomime, with its licensed assaults on authority and its wild inventiveness inspired by 'the very tameness of the *bourgeois* conventions from which it had to create' (p. 59), and the revolution which Crook recommends and Father Brown himself seems partly to endorse.

Detective writing from the 1890s to the 1910s was, then, capable of handling current ideas with some sophistication. Chesterton's may have been the most sophisticated, but in all the instances considered in this chapter, 'ideas' of some kind determine some of the fundamentals of plot and theme, as well as providing matter for more occasional discussion. After the First World War the politically questioning edge seems largely to disappear, as I shall demonstrate in a later chapter. First, it will be useful to remain for a little longer in the Holmes era, to explore rather more thoroughly the 'aesthetic' issues raised by several of these texts; and, more generally, the relationship between the detective fiction and the important 'high' literature of this period.

8

'A Little Art Jargon'

This chapter will attempt to relate some of the formal concerns of detective writing to those of the early modernism with which its heyday clearly overlapped. What 'modernism' consists or consisted of is a large topic: I am perhaps extending it somewhat to include works written in and even shortly before the 1890s by Oscar Wilde, Henry James and Joseph Conrad. While some critics would put the birth of modernism as late as 1910, the 'aesthetic' and other movements of the 1890s clearly marked a reformulation of literary theory and practice continued in later more overtly experimental work, and it will be mainly the radical aspects of the writers named that I shall be discussing.[1]

Out of chronological order but in line with my sub-title, I shall begin by looking at some connections between the crudities of detective fiction and the subtleties of Henry James's long short-story, 'The Figure *in* the Carpet' (1896; my italics). The eponymous 'complex figure in a Persian carpet' is one of a series of metaphors for the key to the works of the great novelist Vereker, which he also calls 'my little secret' and 'the very string . . . my pearls are strung on' (Henry James, pp. 161–2). The nature of this 'figure' is the object of a futile quest by the slightly obtuse critic who narrates, but the story also refuses to tell even the canniest reader what this figure of a figure is actually supposed to stand for. This very refusal, however, makes it a classic of the 'symbolist' phase of modernist development which relies on an intensification of metaphor wherein the referent or tenor – the thing the metaphor is meant to evoke – can theoretically never be given.[2] To this extent 'The Figure in the Carpet' can be seen as a kind of supreme anti-detective story: deliberately teasing us with an intellectual quest-structure which implies a solution, it makes its point by frustrating the expectations it has deliberately aroused.

My subtitle can perhaps be extended to include the idea of the reader as a baffled figure standing on a carpet which is about to be pulled from under his or her feet: if so, James's story is a good example of such a narrative. Detective stories also go as far as they can to pull the carpet from under our feet, however: if we never receive the shock of no answer we actually expect to receive an answer which makes us re-examine the ground we thought we were standing on. And it is arguable that detective fiction also gives the kind of priority to form which can be compared to what James argues for in the short story: 'the forms of wrought things, in this order, *were*, all exquisitely and effectively, the things; . . . [they] might, that is, in the given case, have an inevitability, a marked felicity' (Henry James, p. 9). Leaving aside the specific issue of the short story (whose English development actually owed a great deal to Doyle at precisely this period), this could virtually describe Poe's detective genre where form, inevitability, and the 'felicity' of fitting surprise are all paramount over any mimetic function.

The *chief* meaning of my 'figure *on* the carpet' subtitle in this context is, accordingly, that in detective fiction crime, as represented as blatantly and unsubtly as possible by the figure of the corpse splayed in the drawing-room, none the less has some of the same unifying effect as James's more intricately inwoven 'figure'. Lapsing into what he calls 'a little art jargon', Sherlock Holmes himself remarks in *A Study in Scarlet* that 'There's the scarlet thread of murder running through the colourless skein of life, and our duty is to unravel it, and isolate it, and expose every inch of it' (Doyle, *Complete Adventures*, p. 36). While Vereker's 'string my pearls are strung on' may call equally for exposure, it stays firmly threaded; whereas in detective fiction the intertexture of mystery eventually falls away and leaves the completed 'figure' (or 'study'!) ritually exposed to view.

I propose to begin exploring James's story more closely in terms of its approach to the question of consciousness. It is notorious that early modernism suffers from, or glories in, an acute awareness of the relativity of consciousness, whereby any given reality can only be mediated through the subjective impressions of a specific individual mind. James was a pioneering figure in putting this awareness to use as a fictional method: typically, his narratives focus on the consciousness of a single character attempting to plumb the mystery of other consciousnesses. This is very much the case with the narrator of 'The Figure' who is confronted, not only with the mystery of the great Vereker, but also with that of other characters whom he believes to be further ahead in his quest than himself.

This can be made clearer by a brief account of the plot. Alerted to the existence of a key to Vereker's works by the great man himself, the narrator joins forces with the much abler critic Corvick and his fiancée Miss Erme to find out what it is. While away in India Corvick hits on the answer and has it confirmed by Vereker, who shortly after dies, as does his wife. The narrator is himself abroad when Corvick returns and marries Miss Erme, only to be killed in an accident during the honeymoon; though he revealed the secret to his bride on their wedding-night, the narrator returns to discover that she now guards it as a sacred trust. Years later, after she has remarried and then died in her turn, the narrator confronts the widower, yet another critic named Deane, only to discover that he knows nothing of the secret, though now he likewise becomes obsessed by it so that 'as victims of unappeased desire' there is finally nothing to choose between the two surviving critics.

Certain detective parallels are reasonably obvious even from this outline. Not only does the secret quested for control every detail of the plot and seem, at least, connected with four deaths, but also the story is so manipulated that we as readers are kept, as it were, on the outer rim of a concentric series of consciousnesses with Vereker's secret at the centre. This can be compared quite closely to a Sherlock Holmes story in which our awareness of what is going on is directed through the garrulous Watson inwards by way of Holmes's much more gnomic utterances towards the silent centre occupied by the consciousness of the criminal.

While nowhere linking Vereker's 'little secret' with crime as such, the story does link it firmly with the comparable taboo areas of death and sex. The actual sequence of the four deaths gives the secret itself a more than passing resemblance either to a fatal disease or to one of Doyle's more ruthless secret societies. The equally powerful sexual association is most clearly underlined when Vereker hints that Corvick's and Miss Erme's quest will be best aided by their marriage (p. 162). This event is endlessly postponed by Miss Erme's soi-disant 'dying' mother until Corvick's departure abroad which, as for the heroes of *The Moonstone* and *Trent's Last Case* under similar combinations of sexual and detective frustration, can easily be seen as a metaphor for becoming 'broken to the realities of sex', as Bentley gracefully puts it. The suggestion is strengthened when Corvick dies on his honeymoon having communicated the secret discovered in India only to his bride. The virginal narrator's own experience negatively confirms the same ideas: *his* sojourn abroad has been in respectable Germany rather than the Paris seen by his respectable relations as 'the school of evil, the abyss' (p. 172), and from where he could have visited Vereker and the initiated Corvick at Rapallo. Uninterested sexually in Miss Erme, he none the less half-flippantly contemplates marrying her for her secret, and his closing words on having convinced her second husband that he too has missed true initiation – 'I feel it to be quite my revenge' – suggest that like many Jamesian heroes he is awaking too late to the sexual opportunity he has foregone (p. 184).[3]

Early on he begs Vereker to initiate him, only to be asked 'What else in heaven's name is criticism supposed to be?', a charge which makes him first blush then determine 'to do or die' (pp. 156–7). In the sex-and-death context just discussed, this last phrase is particularly ironic in that the narrator's final survival of everyone except the equally uninitiated Deane suggests that he cannot die because he has never 'done'. But Vereker's point about criticism confirms that however important the sex-and-death undertones may be, the chief intended contrast is that between the richness of art and the impoverishment of criticism as practised by the narrator. In his Preface, certainly, James insists that 'the issue of the affair, can be but whether the very secret of perception hasn't been lost' (p. 16). This secret of perception, bridging the gulf between critic and artist, implies a shared arcane knowledge of which sex and death are perhaps only the symbols rather than the content.

As a hero of critical perception it is Corvick who most resembles the great detective, and his sharing of the secrets of art with the practitioner Vereker can be compared with the kind of *doppelgänger*ism between detective and criminal often noted elsewhere in this study. The most dramatic outward signs of the detective calling – Holmes's opium-den disguise, Father Brown's familiarity with spiked bracelets – confirm our sense that their detective powers spring from an initiation into the ways of crime which can be traced back to the origin of detection in such thieves turned thief-taker as Vidocq. And of course the element of initiation in the true detective is emphasised by his contrast with the false or inadequate detective, the policeman or Watson, who looks on at his activities with the same bafflement as that with which he himself at first regards the criminal. Returning to our earlier image of concentric circles, the detective is not only our means of access to the criminal's secret knowledge, he also reduplicates and relays its *mystery* to the Watson or narrator who can then convey only a 'weak' idea of it to the reader on the outer rim. The significance of Corvick's glimpse, accompanied as it is by a Reichenbach-like merging-in-death with Vereker, is relayed to us through a much more intricate series of refracting circles due to the sexual dance involving his wife and then Deane; but the basic concentric pattern is the same.

The crucial difference is, of course, that in James's story, owing to the deaths of its initiates and the inadequacy of the narrator, we never do learn the secret. This distinction brings us back to the importance of symbol and metaphor in the early modernist text. Through the vaguely grasped image of the 'complex figure in a Persian carpet', and a comparatively clear if unstated parallel with the complex and interwoven nature of the story itself, we are teased and challenged by James, as the narrator is by Vereker, to set out on our own quest for the literal meaning of this 'figure'. Attempts to suggest that the figure 'is' sex or death, or simply a more general 'experience' embracing the two, though possibly moves in the right direction, finally seem inadequate in the artistic context in which we are supposed to be searching, so that we are thrown back on the 'figure' itself or, more precisely, on the fact that the story is controlled by the figure of a figure, as the answer to the riddle. We are led into such convolutions as that the mystery the figure of a figure represents is itself the controlling figure, both as transcendent image and as active patterning force. The fact that at this kind of stage words either fail us or we start sounding like Henry James ourselves is perhaps part of the point that, like Corvick's, an appropriately active criticism must start to flounder into the realms of art. Less flippantly, we could argue that the failure of words to capture transcendent realities except through images and metaphors is a vital plank in an early modernist project of which this story is a classic example.

While being another highly developed instance of the 'concentric circles' technique, Conrad's 'Heart of Darkness' (1899) resembles a detective story more clearly in continuing to move towards rather than away from its goal, and in apparently having something specific, however mysterious, at its centre. But we are warned early on that the narrative will not be a conventional yarn, in that to Marlow, the main narrator, 'the meaning of an episode was not inside like a kernel but outside, enveloping the tale which brought it out only as a glow brings out a haze' (Conrad, p. 30). The direction of movement, then, is outwards rather than inwards, or to be more exact we might say that the meaning moves outwards while the action moves inwards.

Thus at the level of narrated action we move 'in' on a group of men on a Thames yawl, including the nominal narrator, who are listening to Marlow's account of his journey into the heart of Africa, which ultimately becomes an attempt to plumb the mind and motives of a figure who has penetrated furthest into that heart, the ivory hunter Kurtz. It is, in particular, Marlow's attempt to disentangle the truth about Kurtz from a series of further, conflicting, accounts that gives the story an explicitly 'detective' dimension. But it finally emerges clearly that Kurtz's pursuit of the imperial dream has led to an ultimate confrontation with Africa and himself 'summed up', as Marlow tells us, in his dying cry, 'The horror! The horror!' (p. 111). This constant moving in of the narrative is accompanied by other movements in on many levels: from solid London to dubious Brussels and then to the increasingly monstrous Congo trading-stations; from the reader's armchair security to the listeners' half-exposure on the Thames to Marlow's fuller exposure to threats from without and within, and then to Kurtz's climactic disintegration and self-confrontation; more brutally, from comfortable reliance on Empire to the real 'robbery with violence' at its base, and from a confident belief in civilisation to Kurtz's genocidal self-apotheosis. But countering this inward movement of the action there is a corresponding outward movement of meanings, from Kurtz to us, all tending finally to confirm Marlow's first remark that London also 'has been one of the dark places on the earth' (p. 29). The heart of darkness is as much in ourselves and what we allow others to confront on our behalf as at 'the uttermost ends of the earth' where the maps conveniently locate it (p. 121).

Conrad's story clearly contains far more than a self-reflexive exploration of the relativity of consciousnesses; none the less, it does contain such an exploration. As with James, each outer ring tries to comprehend those inside, only to find itself comprehended by them: the final such 'comprehension' being perhaps that Kurtz seems 'bigger' than the rest of us in having allowed his civilised consciousness to disintegrate even more completely. And Conrad also relies on metaphor to express what is otherwise incommunicable. Kurtz's final cry is the only response he can give to what

the story can only describe as 'some image, . . . some vision':
like James's 'figure', this 'image' (of which Kurtz's cry and the
more general surrounding 'darkness' are only further relaying
images) controls every aspect of the story's meaning by remaining
unspecified.

Despite this final reluctance to specify what lies at the 'heart'
of the mystery, the narrator/detective/criminal pattern is clearly
evident in Conrad's story, and in this case the central motivations
uncovered are indeed criminal. The fundamental difference from
a detective story is that Marlow is more concerned to relay Kurtz's
disintegration back up the line of communication than to shield
his listeners from it, and this involves him in taking some of its
'meaning' on himself. Instead of being the tower of strength his
own narrative partly allows him to be, he resigns himself (Buddha-
like?) to only being one link in the chain relaying that meaning all
the way back from Kurtz's monstrosities to the fatal innocence
represented by his European 'intended' and then to the listeners
on the Thames yawl.

Returning once more to literary-critical ground, Oscar Wilde's
earlier 'The Portrait of Mr W. H.' (1889) can, like James's 'Figure',
be described as a deliberately organised anti-detective story. Essentially a close reading of Shakespeare's Sonnets for evidence of his
relationship with the young man to whom they might have been
dedicated, the story also demonstrates the flimsiness of all such
attempts to combine literary criticism with 'objective' biography.
This demonstration is conducted by encasing the central inquiry
within a fictional framework once again involving a series of
concentric circles. Thus the unnamed narrator is introduced by a
second critic to the theory of a third that the Sonnets were
addressed to Willie Hughes, a young actor for whom Shakespeare
also wrote his leading female parts. The main 'evidence' is a
portrait of the actor which is in fact a fake, but this knowledge
does not prevent each critic in turn from passionately supporting
the theory, its first propounder killing himself to defend it, and
the other two alternating successively between overwhelming
commitment and world-weary apostasy. The obsessed second critic
finally also dies, of natural causes but after faking a suicide-
confession in order to reconvert the recently disabused narrator,
who ends up pensively contemplating the forged portrait and the
'truth' it may still none the less convey.

As in the other stories we have looked at, the detective parallels are reasonably obvious, although the repeated swapping of positions between the three critics sometimes makes the distribution of criminal/detective/Watson roles a little more problematic. The central mystery is clearly Shakespeare's real intentions, although in the discussion of the Sonnets themselves we can see him too as a kind of detective, trying to discern the true feelings of Willie Hughes. Graham, the critic who first propounds the theory, in many ways fills the 'great detective' position, except that his faking of the portrait and subsequent suicide are crimes which leave his friend Erskine and the narrator with the job of plumbing *his* intentions. Both take on the responsibility of writing the theory up as Watson-like scribes at different times, but although the narrator begins on the outer rim of awareness it is his inquiry that constitutes the critical core of the book; and when Erskine resorts to the 'crime' of faking his own suicide we feel finally that it is impossible to come any closer to the truth than the half-belief implied in the narrator's continued perusal of the fake portrait.

As in James, however, the thwarted quest for literal verification seems to be accompanied by a broader inquiry into sexuality, for which death sometimes acts as a metaphor. Central to the discussion of the Sonnets, whether Willie Hughes existed or not, is a carefully researched argument about Shakespeare's possible homosexuality; it seems to be its highlighting of this more general argument that makes the Willie Hughes theory so fatally attractive to the three critics, whose passionate involvements with each other provide many echoes of the relationship they are trying to reconstruct. The dying crimes committed by two of them in the name of the theory hint that their artistic insight is in itself somehow criminal; and it is not hard to connect this criminal aura with the still-illegalised homosexuality for which Wilde himself was later to be imprisoned.

There is, at any rate, a recurrent connection between art and crime in Wilde's work, extending from general remarks such as 'All art is immoral' (Wilde, p. 1039) and 'Crime . . . created individualism' (p. 1090) to more specific explorations such as 'Pen, Pencil and Poison: a Study in Green', describing the career of the artist and poisoner Thomas Wainewright, and copying its subtitle from *A Study in Scarlet*, written two years earlier. *The Picture of Dorian Gray*, in which a work of art is in a sense the criminal, is perhaps the most famous articulation of this theme.

If art can be persistently equated with crime in Wilde's work, his approach to criticism sometimes shares a common language with the claims made elsewhere for detection. In 'The Critic as Artist' (1890), his spokesman Gilbert explains to the Watsonesque Ernest that 'it is only by intensifying his own personality that the critic can interpret the personality and work of others' (Wilde, p. 1033); which can be compared to the 'strong exertion of intellect' by which the Dupinesque analyst 'throws himself into the spirit of his opponent' (Poe, p. 316). The insistence that, as 'the thread that is to guide us across the wearisome labyrinth', criticism 'can recreate the past for us from the very smallest fragment of language or art, just as surely as the man of science can from some tiny bone, or the mere impress of a foot upon a rock, recreate for us the winged dragon or Titan lizard' (Wilde, p. 1056) closely recalls *A Study in Scarlet*'s talk of scarlet threads and deducing Niagara from waterdrops, the latter borrowed in turn from Tabaret's famed ability to 'reconstruct all the scenes of an assassination, as a savant who from a single bone reconstructs an antediluvian animal' (Gaboriau, *Lerouge*, p. 27). And Chesterton's ironic pronouncement that 'the criminal is the creative artist; the detective only the critic', and earlier definition of detection as 'the most romantic of rebellions', with criminals as merely 'placid old cosmic conservatives', sound like a kind of double ricochet from Gilbert's claim here that 'it is the critical faculty that invents fresh forms. The tendency of creation is to repeat itself' (Wilde, p. 1021). Finally, Wilde's notion that criticism is 'more creative than creation', because 'the critic deals with materials that others have, as it were, purified for him', fits well with the formal 'purity' of the detective genre whereby the hero is always at one remove from the sordid concerns of life which specifically constitute the criminal's 'material' (p. 1027).

All the texts examined in this chapter, including 'The Critic as Artist', seem repeatedly to assert two positions. The first is that consciousness is subjective, and that the comprehension of one consciousness by another is at once the most urgent of tasks and apparently impossible. The other is that through symbols and metaphors, which may give others the same feelings as they give us, some relaying of awareness may be possible, but only as long as the symbols and metaphors are not pinned down to a single 'meaning'.

Detective fiction may not insist that consciousness is subjective, but none the less it adopts very similar strategies for demonstrating that consciousnesses are in fact separate. And it may prefer specific meanings to elusive metaphors, but it also adopts similar strategies for ensuring that the 'shape' of the central mystery is relayed through a layering of consciousnesses corresponding to a similar layering of narratives. Underlying this adoption of similar strategies in two apparently different forms of writing, we might identify a common preoccupation with the notions of the 'Self', or isolated free-standing individual, and the 'Other', the mysterious realm occupied by consciousnesses different from that self.

The quests for what we may call 'The Other' in the modernist works discussed are not quests for direct communal or person-to-person contact, the possibility of which seems denied, but quests to find the Self reflected in the Other. The fact that the Self is only one in a chain of seekers of the Other (for the other members of which the Self is in turn an Other) asserts a kind of community in isolation in which meanings are not shared in common but passed on down the line in what is not quite a hierarchy but not a fully interactive community either. Hence the towering central figures – Vereker, Kurtz, Shakespeare and 'The Artist' – dominate the pattern with meanings that can only be relayed symbolically by the successful seekers – Corvick, Marlow, Graham and 'The Critic' – who thereupon take on some of their mystery. The listener or looker-on, the unnamed Self of the narrative, in turn relays the symbols, with some of their dimly grasped meanings still attached, to the ultimate Self of the reader.

At the fringes of these texts there is the further suggestion that the chain of Otherness can be extended equally in both directions. With varying degrees of emphasis it is implied that Vereker, Shakespeare and Kurtz find their own Others through sex: Vereker's wife, Shakespeare's Willy Hughes and Kurtz's white and black 'Intendeds' have inspired their work, as The Artist is inspired by 'life' as embodied in such a figure as the original Mona Lisa. That such further figures in the chain are often left largely 'out of it', as Marlow says of the Intended (Conrad, p. 84), is partly a way of making the chain itself the thing rather than of indicating an end-point. If anything it indicates a circle, in that these further figures are, like us, comparatively 'ordinary'.

In detective fiction there is also a 'chain of command'. No one except the central Other, the criminal, knows the truth, or can do so until it is relayed back by the successful seeker, the detective. In his concluding narration of the criminal's deeds he takes his

Otherness on himself and relays it out to us by way of the Self of the narrative, the Watson. What does not happen, however, or is not supposed to happen, is any relaying back down the line of the specific quality, or 'meaning', of the criminal's Otherness: his criminality. The 'towering figure' becomes the detective, who is now placed at the head of the chain of command: unlike the towering Others of modernism, the criminal recedes into insignificance. Thus, rather than offering us a theoretically endless chain of Selves and Others, the detective story offers us a way of breaking such chains, whereby the Self of the detective triumphs over the Other of the criminal. In so far as we play a well-rehearsed game, we too have been drawn into attempting a similar triumph on our own accounts: a triumph over Watson, over the detective, and even over the author if we can spot the answer first and thus tell the story ourselves. If the story goes according to plan, it is the detective who triumphs: none the less, he is only anticipating us in a project we have also undertaken. In short, the triumphant Self of the detective, though 'other' in being beyond us, is also an unambiguously positive role model for our Selves, just as he clearly is for Watson's. Following many other critics, I would suggest that the model of Selfhood offered by the great detective is that of the bourgeois ideal of the free-standing, destiny-creating Individual.[4]

As such an Individual, he teaches us to know both ourselves and the world. We know, for instance, that it proceeds according to the laws of cause and effect, in which free-standing individual phenomena affect other such phenomena to produce certain results. We know that a wife doesn't love her husband if she doesn't brush his hat, since we know that the dramatic or *outré* exception, far from symbolising anything or indicating any permanent disturbance in the order of things, exists only to be referred back to the rule which it really proves. The fact that we still have, as it were, to queue up behind the exemplary detective, does, however, suggest that this free-standing sense of knowing the world is in urgent need of repeated reinforcement.

It is arguable that the forms of both modernist and detective works can be related to a crisis of confidence in the isolated individual consciousness. Whereas modernism reflects the crisis directly, detective fiction gives us the initial experience of isolation but firmly places us in a hierarchically arranged community of the like-minded, with the challenging 'Other' safely on the other side of the fence. The sense of hierarchy partly depends on the careful handling of the detective's *doppelgänger* relationship to the criminal: too much, and the detective himself becomes deconstructed to form only one more link in an endless chain (a possibility always present in his descent from Vidocq, and exploited in such interesting throwbacks as Dorrington); too little, and the detective loses that magic 'specialness' which constitutes him in particular the sought-after role-model.

The similar strategies adopted by modernist and detective works might, then, be attributed to a common concern with 'Individualism', which Wilde indeed maintained was created by crime but perfected by art (Wilde, p. 1090). The problem with the notion of Individualism is that it can be identified as a 'new' motivating force from the sixteenth century onwards, responsible in turn for Shakespeare (Hamlet and/or Iago), the novel (Robinson Crusoe and Pamela) and Romanticism. It would probably be more accurate to say that the late nineteenth century was reeling from a series of *assaults* on the bourgeois idea of the free-standing, destiny-creating Individual. In the world of ideas, at any rate, the quaternity Marx, Darwin, Nietzsche and Freud all suggested or were about to suggest that our destiny was created by forces outside ourselves but operating through our Selves. The notion of profound ideological, genetic, Dionysian or unconscious forces at work within the individual's personality made that individual at once more isolated and less independent. The needed connection with others was then not by way of direct communication, whose real motivations could no longer be trusted, but by a series of intense individual efforts to grasp or to overwhelm these 'other' forces.

But change does not live by ideas alone, and I shall conclude with a somewhat broader attempt, which cannot hope to be exhaustive, to relate the forms and ideas just discussed to the changing circumstances of literary production. An initial problem is posed by the fact that many of the postulates of modernism as well as of detective fiction seem to have their origin in Poe, who in turn takes us back to his precursors in Romanticism. One of these, De Quincey, clearly writes as though the aestheticising of crime has already happened; others, from Coleridge to Byron, assume a corresponding criminalisation of the aesthetic. Surely the Romantics, with their opium and albatrosses, were already isolated consciousnesses at once seeking and threatened by the Other?

The Romantics' position has been explained at a sociological level in terms of the trauma whereby the writer, torn from the shelter of patronage, is thrown on to the open market.[5] Instead of voicing communal truths, the ideal writer must now seek the ideal reader by an intensification rather than a transcendence of a particular style and a particular 'self', or selves. We have seen how in Poe this becomes a selfconscious quest for specific 'effects': the periodical short story becoming a vehicle at once for the pleasure of the specialising reader and for the efficient packaging and retailing of Poe's own fragmented personae. The 'isolation' which Roderick Usher and Dupin have in common can in part be seen as mirroring the isolation of the author, but it also clearly separates them from each other in line with the separation of horror from ratiocination on which the unities of their respective tales depend. The horrors which they confront, Madeline or the ape, can then be seen as the Others they have cut themselves off from through their respective specialisations. The modernist/detective divisions between the relaying of Otherness down the line through a series of symbolic projections and the offering of role-models to defeat or exclude the Other are already in operation.

How do we explain the separation in time between the Romantic and Modern manifestations of similar tendencies? The nature of the intervening period is clearly relevant here. For Britain the Victorian period witnessed the assimilation, with apparent success, of the revolutions in social organisation which Romanticism expressed. The open market, in publishing as well as in industry more generally, seemed to offer its own kind of stability after the earlier traumas. The new kind of self-marketing writer returned to a powerful position in society: witness the later Wordsworth and the ennobling of Tennyson. In the novel the special effect and the specialised 'character' could be successfully combined with other such effects and characters in a form that could thereby claim to give a comprehensive overview of society, comprehending peculiarity and isolation but also incorporating them in a larger picture and retailing them to a mass market. In the work of Dickens and Collins the particular interest of detective fiction becomes only one of many interests. Thus in *The Moonstone* the idiosyncrasies of Gabriel Betteredge and Miss Clack, as well as the romantic isolation of Rosanna Spearman and Ezra Jennings, are permitted to amuse or move in their own right while still contributing to the central investigation. Through such incorporations Collins's novel – with its overlapping narratives – offers a model of a diverse but connected society where the central unifying figure of the great detective is rendered unnecessary.

Very broad generalisations are needed, in a study of this compass, to explain the shift that took place towards the end of the century. Malcolm Bradbury suggests that from about 1870 the literary world at least had

> its confidence and unity shaken not simply by Darwin and the growing bulk of social and political problems attendant on expansion and industrialism, but by the capacity of growth potentially to outrun control in thought and art as well as in culture and society. . . . The cultural dialogue begins to pluralize and lose its centre, producing a marked specialization and professionalization in writers and artists, and a withdrawal from the larger social life. The cultural hierarchy increasingly begins to divide into fairly sharp levels which are 'stabilized' by the multiplication of the media which arose in increasing numbers and types both to define them and to serve them.   (Bradbury, p. 41)

The return to the specialisation of literature to which Poe was responding is accompanied by the appearance in England of the short-story form which he pioneered in America. New, specialising periodicals were very important in this development: the impetus to James's 'Figure' was given by the commissioning of similar self-reflexive works by the leading 'aesthetic' periodical, *The Yellow Book*, whose editors shared the American James's enthusiasm for 'our ideal, the beautiful and blest *nouvelle*' (Henry James, p. 9). The *nouvelle*, or novella, is of course the long short-story form also used in 'Mr W. H.' and 'Heart of Darkness', both first published in periodicals. The use made of the form by early modernist writers coincides closely with Doyle's virtual reinvention of the Poesque short-story series, in the *Strand*. Holmes's two first appearances in short-novel form were also in periodicals, and it is arguable that their awkwardnesses spring more from difficulties with the slightly extended novella length than from the legacy of the confidently expansive Gaboriau.[6]

All these discoveries of new short forms can be related to the moribundity of the once-popular Victorian novel, whose periodical serialisation depended on a very stable readership and whose subsequent three-volume publication depended on expensive circulating libraries. Cheaper periodicals, cheaper libraries and indeed much cheaper books meant that the readership need not confine itself to a single work for so long at a stretch. The falling price of books and periodicals, both welcomed and deplored by writers, again implied a multiplication and differentiation of the market, enabling publishers to aim with less capital investment at smaller areas while simultaneously in quest of rapidly repeatable blockbusting formulae (see Bradbury, pp. 204–8). Sherlock Holmes can of course be attributed to this latter quest, but the detective explosion he brought about can be seen as just an aspect of the sharpening and specialisation of interest represented in other ways by the high art of early modernism.

This rapid expansion of the market, together with the breakdown of a 'cultural centre', led to an outbreak of 'isms' which, as with the Romantics from Wordsworth to Poe, also involved an outbreak of literary manifestoes: it is significant that the three modernists discussed all routinely introduced their works with manifesto-like prefaces, as well as engaging in other critical activity. The slimming down of fictional forms, accompanied by a beefing-up by James and others of critical reflection on the results, put fiction under the microscope in new ways. The work, then, had to be mediated to the new readerships by further work and this can in turn, perhaps, be related to the growing importance of mediation in the literary works themselves. The constant removal in these texts of the thing-to-be-explained from the final recipients of the explanation can then be seen as reflecting the constant sifting process whereby writers find readers and readers find writers through intervening forms of mediation.

Detective fiction has its own form of framing critical apparatus in the ritualised opening homily in which Holmes instructs the reader, through Watson, in the principles according to which the ensuing narrative is to be read. Paradoxically, then, as the different literary forms and formulae became more widely separate from each other, they also came to resemble each other in mirroring that separateness in their style and content. Just as the specialist – Holmes, Corvick, Marlow, Graham or The Critic – knows that 'by curious inversion, it is only by intensifying his own personality' (Wilde, p. 1033) that he can hope to grasp those of others, so these characters' respective creators know that their readerships (as well as their 'meanings') can only be grasped through parallel intensifications of style and literary form.

9

A Version of Pastoral

For most of this chapter I shall discuss the kind of British detective writing which became established between the World Wars: what Colin Watson and Julian Symons call its 'Golden Age'. In evoking a separate realm of literary innocence, the phrase chimes in well with W. H. Auden's 'Great Good Place', C. Day Lewis's 'fairytale', and George Orwell's game of cricket; as well as with William Empson's account of popular literature generally in this period as a 'version of pastoral'.[1]

Before looking at particular texts, a few generalisations about the genre's altered relationship with 'serious' literature may be useful. All the writers and critics just named belong roughly to the generation which came into its own in the 1930s, and their similar approach suggests a particular mixture of pastoralising nostalgia for the social innocence lost in that turbulent decade, with a then-radical resolve to 'place' popular literary forms in sociological terms. With hindsight, however, much of this exploration can be seen as simply exemplifying the open secret that literary intellectuals in this period were engaged *en masse* in a love-affair with the form, part of whose spice depended on a pretence of secrecy: as witnessed by the pseudonyms adopted by such intellectual/detective writers as J. I. M. Stewart (Michael Innes) and Day Lewis himself (Nicholas Blake). As early as 1929, Marjorie Nicolson argued that 'the detective story . . . is escape not from life, but from literature': an escape, that is, into order and objectivity from the subjective streams-of-consciousness and cloudy symbols of modernism (Haycraft, p. 113).

This argument has more recently been taken further by Michael Holquist, who argues that 'what the structural and philosophical presuppositions of myth and depth psychology were to modernism (Mann, Joyce, Woolf, and so forth), the detective story is to postmodernism': the symbolic possibilities Homer offers Joyce are replaced by 'the ambiguous events, the psychologically flat and therefore mysterious world which Holmes and Poirot make available to Robbe-Grillet and Borges' (Most and Stowe, pp. 150, 165).

In a nutshell, the belief in order and objectivity welcomed by Nicolson gives the relentlessly ironic postmodernist masters a classic model to be ironic about.

The psychological flatness and rejection of symbolism on which Nicolson and Holquist would however agree is well exemplified in Agatha Christie's *Death on the Nile*, where Simon's desertion of Jacqueline for Linnet is described by both erstwhile lovers as like the fading of 'the moon when the sun comes out'. But what sounds at first like a significant metaphor emerges instead as a clue, a metonymic sign that the pair have concocted this account of their estrangement in preparation for the murder of Linnet. As in Dupin's inaugurally metonymic mindreading in 'Rue Morgue', 'the figure' – or at least the figurative figure of speech known as metaphor – is still firmly 'on the carpet' in the Golden Age.

The mystery which, for Holquist, detective fiction offers for further postmodernist deconstruction resides instead in a sense of 'the ambiguity of events'; and it is arguable that the Golden Age has its own pre-postmodernist awareness of all this. The outstanding example is Christie's *The Murder of Roger Ackroyd*, whose technically unimpeachable narrator–murderer turns numerous assumptions about the reliability of narrative on their heads.[2] But almost as sly are such virtually routine remarks as Miss Marple's 'I know that in books it is always the most unlikely person. But I never find that rule applies in real life. There it is so often the obvious that is true' (Christie, *Vicarage*, p. 179). In the context of the recurrent 'least-likely-because-most-likely' formula, such moments of scrupulously pretended realism simply aggravate the pastoral remoteness of the form from real 'real life'.

Having made these very brief opening points, it is time to turn to the more concrete characteristics of the Golden Age, with particular reference to its most successful performer, Agatha Christie. Because of the repetitive formula of the short story series, and a genuine diversity of locales and concerns, the Holmesian hero was the focus of a wide range of interests, and though doubtless many specific class attitudes were present they tended to be aspirational rather than settled. In the Golden Age the weight of the form shifts on to the novel, where a specific 'world' is more fully evoked, and the detective becomes a more abstract, often much more skimpily visualised figure. The genre becomes much more of a puzzle addressed directly to the reader, with the novel form permitting many more game-like permutations on one hand

and much less prodigality with basic plot-ideas on the other. The authors tend to be more leisured, either through inherited wealth or an academic profession; accordingly, the parallel between detection and hack-work implicit in Doyle, Zangwill and Morrison is replaced by an implicit parallel between detection and household or institutional management. We can summarise that an ordinary Golden Age reader is assumed (or encouraged!) to have a far more restricted range of aspirations than the reader of Holmes: basically the aspiration to 'belong', especially to the landed and cultured classes. The fact that this aspiration could be so thoroughly and correctly assumed in such a wide readership was perhaps initially a response to the destabilising effects of the First World War: thereafter it simply seems to denote a settled nostalgia for the *ancien régime*.

Raymond Williams has suggested that in this period detective fiction became the fitting 'true fate of the country-house novel'. The two forms have clearly been at home with each other since Collins, though books like *The Moonstone* carry far more sense of the specific gravity of an actual community than, say, Christie does. It is, however, possible to mount a critique of the country-house form itself, even as far back as Jane Austen, in terms of its idealisation of a very particular type of community as if it represented 'community' in a wider sense. Williams argues that from its first literary envisaging this particular image of order and stability was always something of a façade for a series of invisible commercial connections, but that in this century the façade is all that is left: the country house is the place where, in the occasional weekend gathering, the rich meet and make deals. (The idea could easily be extended to the idea of itself as a whole which Britain has so successfully sold worldwide, along with its 'Cluedo'/'Masterpiece Theater' vision of criminality.)[3] Perhaps the attraction of Christie in particular is her instinctive ability to express the two aspects of this façade-structure simultaneously: the notion of a community, even a home, to be run with dedication and efficiency; and the simultaneous knowledge that the dedication is to a morally empty world where 'events prepared elsewhere, continued elsewhere, transiently and intricately occur' (Williams, pp. 298–9).

As Stephen Knight has pointed out, it is more appropriate to talk about Christie's 'world' than about her heroes' adventures, since she is far less interested in her detectives than predecessors such as Doyle or Chesterton: the authority they do have derives from generally applicable methods rather than special knowledge or techniques, and they are not objects of strong fantasy-identification.[4] Interesting things can indeed be said about the Herculean buffoon Hercule Poirot, the insider–outsider inspired by 'gallant little Belgium', or the more usefully choric Miss Marple. But our attention is directed more strongly in each given case to the stereotyped group of suspects whose settled existence is suddenly threatened by the irruption of murder. The fact that the crime now always *is* murder, rather than one of the far less predictable situations handled by Holmes or Father Brown, may partly be a function of the shifting of weight to the novel, where a sense of exceptional disaster is needed to hold our attention. But murder also serves more satisfactorily than any other crime to freeze a given circle of suspects in a given place for a given period of time.

The social range of this circle is more or less confined to the upper-middle class, and one of the subliminal effects of the crime is to focus our attention exclusively on this particular group. Though the existence of the world outside is routinely invoked by babble of an 'intruder' as the culprit, this possibility is always finally denied. If not initially: challenged with the theory of 'some wandering lunatic with homicidal mania' in *Peril at End House*, Poirot confidently asserts on no evidence at all that 'the culprit is someone in Madamoiselle's own circle' (Christie, *End House*, p. 78). Equally firmly repudiated is the involvement of servants: though sometimes nominally suspect because unavoidably on the scene, and a specific focus of fear where blackmail is concerned (as with Parker in *Ackroyd*), they are routinely eliminated early on. Hence, even when investigating a series of crudely botched murder attempts, Poirot can exonerate the capable housekeeper since the 'general mentality of the crime seems above her level' (ibid., p. 85). Apart from blackmail, servants may evoke some interest if secretly well-born or through a disreputable contact (Ursula and Miss Russell in *Ackroyd*), but even in such cases the old adage that 'the butler did it' is never true in Christie.

In ten representative texts (*The Mysterious Affair at Styles*, *The Murder of Roger Ackroyd*, *The Murder at the Vicarage*, *Peril at End House*, *Death on the Nile*, *One, Two, Buckle My Shoe*, *Towards Zero*, *The Hollow*, *A Murder is Announced*, *Ordeal by Innocence*) eight types of serious suspect and/or victim recur repeatedly: property-owner, English rose, 'weak' young man, siren-with-a-past, respectable wife, tongue-tied colonial, attendant professional (lawyer, doctor or vicar), and female dependant. The dominant property-owner is often the victim, and very often female. As Knight points out, such powerful women are usually presented more sympathetically than their male counterparts, though with a similar stifling effect on their dependants: the Oedipal pattern so frequent in the genre seems to address itself particularly to the strong mother-figure.[5] Where the powerful figure is the murderer, it is to preserve the status quo by suppressing knowledge of a past crime. The English rose is rarely guilty, since the book's happy ending depends on her marriage: if she is, a hitherto suspected or overlooked character emerges as the 'real' rose in her place. The weak young man is often a leading suspect because of sexual and/or financial entanglements, or ridiculous left-wing views. As a suspect he often focuses fears of Oedipal revolt against the parental order: where these are borne out there is, however, a defusing twist whereby the parent-figure he murders is not actually a blood-relative (*Zero, Innocence*). He is more likely to be involved with a secretly forceful woman in one of the *folie à deux* spouse-murders particularly favoured by Christie.

The obvious siren is rarely guilty, though often involved with the suspicious outsider: drug-addiction and the horrible face at the window frequently symbolise the nemesis of her 'past'. Of the remaining types, wives can kill from jealousy, but colonials are usually the reassuring figures they seem, as are attendant professionals, though *Ackroyd* provides a startling exception. The female dependant or 'companion' is a more interesting figure: if we stretch the category to include such 'gossips' as Caroline Shepherd and Miss Marple herself, she appears prominently in all ten books, being murdered in two, a murderess in three, and a strong focus of narrative sympathy in four. The unattached but secretly observant and/or sexual woman, whom everyone overlooks but to whom attention is then dramatically drawn, provides a significant Cinderella-like focus of interest, whether positively or negatively.

The central motives are of three main types: money, fear of exposure, and sexual jealousy. (A wider sample of novels would turn up a few other motives, such as revenge – *Murder on the Orient Express*; a perverted sense of justice – *Ten Little Niggers*; or indiscriminate malice – *Curtain*; but the three just outlined probably cover most instances.) Whereas a naked desire for more money or property is generally condemned and leads to the swift removal of the culprit, murder to preserve the status quo, either because of jealousy or fear of exposure for past misdeeds, receives more indulgence in that such murderers are often permitted their 'say' at the end. Notable instances are Dr Sheppard in *Ackroyd* and the plutocratic triple murderer in *One, Two, Buckle My Shoe*, who is permitted to argue at length with Poirot about the need to subordinate justice to the political status quo he represents: arguments which Poirot at least considers.

It is possible to argue that some of the types and motives discussed have a special significance for Christie, brought up as she was in a similarly confined if privileged world. Her own strong dependence on her mother and grandmother, following her father's early death, may account for the ambivalent attitude to the powerful female victims of many novels; her desertion by her first husband for a younger woman may lie behind the clandestine couples and jealous wives of some later books; a real sense of solidarity with exploited or patronised women emerges at times in her Cinderella-like 'companions'.[6] But such individual elements do not finally seem as significant as the overall assumption that this world of country house-parties is the only world that matters. At a stretch it may also include a semi-feudal village, an exclusive dentist's patient-list, an archaeological dig, a pleasure cruise or a group of hotel guests. But it is fitting that in *Curtain*, where the scene of Poirot's first case, Styles, has been turned into a guest-house, this sad sign of the times is accompanied by an apocalypse in which Poirot first kills the unprosecutable murderer and then himself.

It would be very easy to continue to deconstruct Christie in terms of her class attitudes, with occasional sideswipes at her undeveloped novelistic style.[7] The first line of defence against such commentary is, presumably, that she is only nominally writing novels at all, for the sake of the puzzle; rather more interesting is the way in which the puzzles help to bring out some elements inherent in the traditional form which, however nominally, she does adopt. I propose now to follow up my suggestion that while professional hackwork was the model for detective writing before the First World War, the chief model now becomes household management. Whereas much of the humour, both intentional and unintentional, of Poe, Gaboriau, Zangwill, Morrison and Doyle alludes to the humiliations of putting a talent for perception on to the open market, so a great deal of Agatha Christie's spoken or unspoken humour alludes to the problems and intricacies of organising social gatherings.

The detective-less *Ten Little Niggers*[8] provides a particularly clear illustration, allowing Christie to play around with the idea of plot-creating murderer and invisible host as joint creators of the basic *mise en scène*. The mysterious U. N. Owen ('Unknown'), who invites nine ill-assorted guests to the house-party on Nigger Island and murders them all one by one, displays the even distribution of attention to each guest in turn that is one of the ideals both of a good party and of the Golden Age detective novel itself. The signature of the killer's real name at the very end of the book neatly identifies him both with the hitherto nameless host and with the 'author' of the story we have just finished reading.

In another novel without a star detective, *Towards Zero*, the connections between crime, house-party management and authorship also emerge particularly clearly. We are given a very early hint that 'the murder is the *end*. The story begins . . . with all the causes and events that bring certain people to a certain place at a certain time on a certain day' (Christie, *Zero*, p. 9), and accordingly the first section describes the build-up to a two-week house-party at the isolated 'Gull's Point' in carefully dated diary form. The implicit link between author and murderer is highlighted by an early description of the latter, unidentified as yet, drawing up the same list of dates: 'There was only one person in the room and the only sound to be heard was the scratching of that person's pen as it traced line after line across the paper' (p. 15). In his greater meticulousness of planning, the killer has already usurped the function of the hostess, the bedridden Lady Tressilian, and it is fitting that his scheme involves murdering her, exactly halfway through the book, in a way which ensures that the gathering over which she has tried to preside morally from her bed will continue on his terms: that is, frozen in the potentially endless 'party' of a police inquiry.

The central awkwardness of the guest-list is the convergence of the tennis star Nevile Strange, his present wife Kay, and his apparently jilted first wife, Audrey: a *fait accompli* everyone's good breeding forces them to accept without knowing who initiated it. Though proposed by Nevile, it is generally read as a mark of his capitulation to one more of Audrey's jealous demands, so that when Lady Tressilian is murdered in a way clearly designed to frame him, Audrey is the obvious suspect. The concluding double twist is that it was in fact she who ditched him, on discovering his sadistic character, and that he committed the murder in such a way as to frame her for trying to frame him (the ingenious double trail of clues including his use of his famous tennis backhand for the fatal blow, in imitation of her well-known left-handedness). The true crime indicated by the 'zero' of the title was not the murder itself, but Audrey's intended execution.

Since the murder occurs relatively late, much of the book consists of scannings of the social horizon, by the characters and by ourselves, for all and any omens of disaster. One focus for this is provided by the old lawyer Treves, who dies in suspicious circumstances after indicating that one of the group, whom he recognises because of a minor disfigurement, committed a murder as a child. By remaining largely silent about all this until the end, Christie cunningly involves us as readers in the horizon-scanning, whetting our appetites by revealing minor deformities in every member of the party without explicit further comment. The significant defect, a short finger, is cleverly introduced in a context of palm-reading which makes it the hardest of all to spot. But whatever the answer, our carefully stimulated quest for it aligns us symbolically with the screening-out of pariahs on which, as we have already seen in Lady Tressilian's thwarted efforts, a harmonious social gathering ought to depend.

The general level of social tension is well illustrated by an incident when Nevile brings a requested magazine to the terrace where his past and present wives are sitting:

> Then two things happened at precisely the same minute.
> Kay said: 'Oh good, give it to me,' and Audrey, without moving her head, held out her hand almost absent-mindedly.
> Nevile had stopped half-way between the two women.   (p. 54)

Audrey's gesture, which really denotes her reluctance to look at Nevile, appears to the jealous eyes of Kay and Audrey's stolid admirer Royde as an attempt to reassert dominance, while Nevile's final bestowal of the magazine on her shows that it is a dominance he unconsciously accepts.

In a key scene – typically witnessed by three other characters, including Treves – Nevile is about to speak to Audrey when she exclaims that she has lost her earring; they both bend to look for it and his cuff button gets caught in her hair, pulling some of it out by the roots, a situation from which they both emerge 'trembling'

(p. 70). At the social level this re-entanglement of the divorced couple, with its attendant emotional tension, is an effective image of what everyone has been trying to prevent. At a 'red-herring' level, Audrey's apparent anxiety about her earring (actually an impulse to counter Nevile's attempt at intimacy) draws attention to the permanently scarred ear which apparently launches Treves's story about the disfigured killer. At the 'real' plot-level, it hints at Nevile's concealed sadism as well as enabling him to get hold of some incriminating hairs for later use in his complex double frame-up.

The further we get into such social detail, the more 'novelistic', despite certain very apparent stylistic differences, Christie comes after all to seem. In Jane Austen's *Emma*, the disastrous 'alphabets' party encodes Frank Churchill's secret marriage to Jane Fairfax in actions which rather similarly speak louder than words: 'Mr Knightley's eyes had preceded Miss Bates's in a glance at Jane. From Frank Churchill's face, where he thought he saw confusion suppressed or laughed away, he had involuntarily turned to hers; but she was indeed behind, and too busy with her shawl' (Austen, p. 346). There are many differences too obvious to discuss, but the 'world' of Jane Austen, with its 'three or four families in a country village', all acting as 'a neighbourhood of voluntary spies' on each other, is very recognisably one ancestor of Christie's.[9]

Though Austen's mysteries concern love affairs rather than murders, in many of Christie's best-known novels from *Styles* to *Nile*, an *Emma*-like reversal of the presumed emotional pattern is crucial, and in *Ackroyd* a precise reprise of the Frank Churchill situation provides the leading red herring. And while generally touting a 'least-likely-suspect' formula, Christie often falls in with much older patterns of suspicion in the 'least-likely-because-most-likely' technique whereby the socially and/or sexually obnoxious first suspect proves guilty after all. In numerous books from *Styles* onwards (for example, *Vicarage*, *Nile*, *Innocence*, *Prosecution*), a lover-accomplice has helped to rig the evidence; in others, such as *Zero* and *Hollow*, a deservedly jilted character rigs it on his or her own. Hence in *Styles* the general instinctive dislike of Alfred Inglethorp ('an absolute outsider . . . a great black beard and wears patent leather boots' – Christie, *Styles*, p. 7) is fully vindicated, and in the more stylistically ambitious *Hollow* the general pitying contempt for Gerda Christow, expressed at an 'artistic' level in Henrietta Savernake's derisive sculpture of her, is proved right in a way which suggests that social unimpressiveness is a serious moral failing.

To round off, it is important to restore the perspective whereby these are, after all, detective stories. The detective is perhaps the final avatar of the host. Poirot's, Miss Marple's or Inspector Battle's remorseless occupation of the premises and climactic invitation to the drawing-room assert a restorative right to do the final 'honours': in the frequent cases where the original host or hostess is the victim, a right often wrested directly from the usurping murderer. To return to Williams's view of the country house as offering a stable façade for an increasingly transient population, this crowning seizure of the property (which, as indeed in Austen, is largely what the various other battles of love, morals and money are really about) by the most transient figure of all, seems appropriate.

The house-party has continued, in the hands of such writers as Dorothy Sayers, John Dickson Carr, Michael Innes, Margery Allingham and Ngaio Marsh. All of these can claim to be better 'writers' than Christie although none has sold quite as well. Far more than Christie, they all consciously address a readership that aspires to be intellectual as well as one that aspires to know its way around the upper classes. In this connection Christie's professed belief that the snobbery of birth is 'more palatable' than intellectual snobbery, but that one shouldn't talk about it too much, brings out her differences from them very effectively (Christie, *Autobiography*, pp. 45, 124). In contrast to her somewhat passive acceptance of her world, further muted by the marginal character of her detectives Poirot and Miss Marple, these writers actively assert their worlds by making their detectives cultural insiders, and through an aggressively confident jocularity of style.

George Grella's perception that 'English' detective fiction derives from traditions of stage comedy is far better borne out by these writers than by Christie; they also inherit some of the generosity of that tradition in such democratic gestures as a concern to get accents right (Innes's various Scots dialects), and generally comradely relations between the well-born detectives, their comic manservants, and the plebeian police officers who are now more often archly respected friends than moronic rivals.[10] This can be linked with a more general search for 'broad' characters, which goes hand in hand with the search for new and interesting milieux. As well as the persistent comedy, these writers also incline to the Gothic: there is more use of London as a sinister labyrinth, especially in Carr and Allingham, and where a country house is the main setting (as it still usually is), its imposing or daunting qualities are more likely to be stressed. (In the case of Innes, its architectural peculiarities will also be described in intimidating scholarly detail.) Again there is a contrast with Christie, who tends to take her rural settings for granted: these writers express a more urban and touristic fascination with the rural order they so energetically celebrate.

The deliberately comic and Gothic elements are part of a more general project to assert the values of the 'literary', which emerges in slightly different ways in each of them. Lord Peter Wimsey, with his endless quotations, is clearly a walking cultural as well as social fantasy. John Dickson Carr's Dr Gideon Fell is closely modelled on G. K. Chesterton, and his exclusive commitment to 'locked-room' puzzles constitutes a lifelong homage to the Poe of 'Rue Morgue'. Of all these writers, Carr seems to have the most conscious inkling of being a 'pre-postmodernist', asserting the value of detective fiction as an autonomous alternative tradition and delighting, like his two chief models, in the artifice of the form. A trick like the use of mirrors in *The Hollow Man* (borrowed from Chesterton's 'The Man in the Passage') plays with notions of illusion and reality at the very edge of the possible, and is accompanied by a lecture on locked-room puzzles introduced by Fell's pre-postmodernist remark that 'we're in a detective story, and we don't fool the reader by pretending that we're not' (Carr, p. 186).

A different kind of literary cross-reference appears in Michael Innes's *Lament for a Maker*, where the multiple-narrative technique of *The Moonstone* is married to the surprise ending of *Trent's Last Case*. The book's further attempt to link lonely-tower Gothic with the bedroom-farce methods needed to introduce the required plethora of suspects works rather less well. In general Innes uses the detective form as a clothes-horse on which to hang a silky literary style replete with wit and cultural information, whose promise of balanced restraint typically breaks down under the weight of the frenzied conclusions required by his ultimately farcical piling of one mystery on another. In Margery Allingham's *More Work for the Undertaker* two members of the Palinode family communicate entirely through recondite literary allusions and the murderer is called Henry James: a type of nudge repeated from an earlier short story, 'The Hat Trick', where the main characters are called Burns, Herrick, Whitman and of course (Allingham's customary detective) Campion.[11] Ngaio Marsh's titles usually contain a heavily significant pun (*Died in the Wool*, *Grave Mistake*), and she habitually links crime to art through the choice of a theatrical background (Marsh's own milieu) or through the involvement of her detective Alleyn's painter-wife Troy. Marsh writes best when able to establish such milieux at length: the reluctant changes of gear after the crime (when, in later books, Troy's observations yield to her husband's deductions) well illustrate what Auden called the clash between the 'aesthetic' and the 'ethical'.[12]

For all their frequent condescension, the writers just discussed invoke the literary and aesthetic very largely in the name of enjoyment. Something slightly different seems to be at work in the writer who has comparatively recently ushered in a resurgence of the traditional whodunnit: P. D. James. Often acclaimed as a serious writer, James certainly replaces the ingrained jocularity of her predecessors (even including Christie) with something far more earnest. Before examining one of her books, *Shroud for a Nightingale*, in some detail, it will be useful to return one more time to Raymond Williams's commentary on detective fiction as the 'fitting end' of the country-house novel:

> the country-house could be made the place of isolated assembly of a group of people whose immediate and transient relations were decipherable by an abstract mode of detection rather than by the full and connected analysis of any more general understanding. . . . The real houses can be anything from schools and colleges and hospitals to business retreats, estate offices and subsidized museums. In the same way, emotionally, they can be the centres of isolated power, graft or intrigue . . . . It is not a sad end; it is a fitting end.   (Williams, p. 299)

Several of P. D. James's novels are set in just such 'indifferently functioning' country houses, for example the forensic laboratory and nursing home of *Death of an Expert Witness* and *The Black Tower*. In *Shroud for a Nightingale* the maladaptation of the Victorian-Gothic Nightingale House to its present function as a hospital teaching wing and nurses' residence is repeatedly stressed: 'Most of the rooms would be far too large'; 'The iron staples, driven brutally into the woodwork, . . . were in incongruous contrast to the row of elegant light fittings' (P. D. James, *Shroud*, pp. 17, 58). This stress on the incongruity of setting to function has a self-reflexive significance in a novel which imports a number of apparently earnest 'modern' concerns into the timeworn structure of the Golden Age whodunnit.

To take that whodunnit side first: investigating two murders, James's series-hero Adam Dalgleish interviews everyone concerned and comes up with a fairly unsurprising solution, although a purist could claim that until the end we are given too little information to make a guess at it. Particularly unconvincing is Dalgleish's climactic identification of the matron rather than the sister as the ex-death-camp nurse who has been recognised by a patient, solely on the grounds that only she has 'a face so beautiful and so individual that it can be recognized even in a fleeting glance' (p. 281). But among the more 'serious' concerns overshadowing this comparatively simple plot are Lesbian sexuality, the inheritance of the Nazi extermination camps and, at a more allegorical level, the replacement of Victorian privilege and privacy by the communal institutions of the Welfare State.

Inextricably linked with the solemnity of James's concerns is a style devoted to the expertly 'placing' judgement. Thus the narration of the first murder is presented through the eyes of a Training Inspector, Miss Beale, whose evidence has no bearing on the case and who subsequently disappears until the end, but whose judgements on the setting, the students and the discipline have the right stamp of experienced authority. Even her own Gothic premonitions on entering the grounds are handled with an appropriately 'balanced' firmness: 'It was only a second's folly and she quickly shook it off. . . . But it had been an odd and disconcerting experience' (p. 16). Much of the rest of the book is seen through the eyes of another kind of 'inspector', Chief Superintendent Dalgleish, whose visits to the private rooms of the various victims and suspects permit some of the book's most bravura displays of expert assessment. Dalgleish's sideline as a poet ensures that he is as reliable on aesthetic taste as on clues: this translates as 'a sense of waste, of a personal, irrational loss' on surveying the second victim's 'nicely balanced' taste in books, which include not only 'Greene, Waugh, Compton Burnett, Hartley, Powell, Cary', but also 'modern poetry, his own last volume included' (p. 55). Other visits to other rooms supply much of the interest of the case: Walter Benjamin's point that detective fiction starts from an obsession with other people's 'private' spaces receives massive confirmation here (perhaps particularly in a context where the private is so clearly delved out of the public).[13] The inner dynamic of the book revolves not around who did what, but around what each character *is* – in two favourite words – 'fundamentally', or 'essentially'. As already indicated, the case culminates in Dalgleish's essentialist distinction between the 'plain, ordinary, inconspicuous' Sister Brumfett and the beautiful if murderous Matron Mary Taylor, to whom he explains that 'she was essentially a stupid and dull woman and you are not' (p. 284).

Admittedly, the detective urge to 'know' others also enters the criminal plot as the blackmail appropriate to a community where 'there's no real privacy' (p. 124). Two symbolically named characters who use such placing knowledge as a basis of personal power, the blackmailing Nurse Pearce and the sadistic Sergeant Masterson, are presented very negatively, while Dalgleish himself has frequent doubts about his job and carefully reminds himself that there is no 'identikit for the human mind' (p. 164). Furthermore, if the book has a moral, it is one of indulgence towards human frailty, especially the search for sexual solace in a context of daily medical knowledge of 'what the body can suffer in agony and degradation' (p. 206). Still, however, the placing judgements pile up until it seems that there is no other way of looking at things, just as there is virtually no tension between, or need to cross-check, the perspectives of Miss Beale, Dalgleish, or the more virtuous and hard-working nurses who carry most of the rest of the narrative. The one sustained attempt to convey a less virtuous perspective, through the eyes of the sadistic Masterson, seems to belong to a different novel, both in its sleazy setting and its grotesque improbability. The weight of all these discriminations has little to do with the solution of the crime, though such a tie-up seems promised: in fact, Mary Taylor's guilt does not really affect her status as a focus of adoration both for the book and for Dalgleish – largely, perhaps, because she closely resembles him in her normally benign use of institutional power. This benignity includes the same kind of omniscient blind eye to minor peccadilloes which he habitually turns: both bear the sins of the world on their weary shoulders while inwardly acknowledging that 'We are all alone, all of us from the moment of birth until we die' (p. 83).

The parallels between the institutions of policing and health to which Doyle **was so** alert are very explicit in James, and at one point here both are also fleetingly linked with the 'orders' of the Nazi camps. The challenge of the comparison is, however, greatly weakened when the Jewish chairman of the Health Authority is experienced as more of a threat to the former death-camp nurse Mary Taylor than might ever have been true the other way round. In so far as James is 'up-to-date' she is so in acknowledging that such communal state institutions as health and policing have taken over some of the representative centrality claimed by Christie's private country houses. Her actual vision of communal working life is, however, deeply regressive: not only is Nightingale House (as its name implies) a very Victorian institution, with its antiquated muslin headdresses and rigid hierarchies, but it seems to be deeply cherished as such, founded as it is on the conviction of original sin which is the prevailing note of the novel. It is more like a girls' boarding school than a workplace (indeed, we hardly ever see a patient), and it is this repressive 'hothouse' atmosphere that then provides all the illustrations of human depravity which validate the 'placing' authority of Miss Beale, Dalgleish and Matron herself. The back-biting power-structure surrounding and sustained by Matron is a major cause of her downfall, but this downfall is then seen primarily as a tragic demonstration of the burdens of office in a context of universal sin. Her secret philosophy that 'we are all alone', powerfully endorsed by Dalgleish's solitary musings, constitutes in fact a denial of the idea of community they are both supposed to be trying to sustain. The notion that the reactionary world of Nightingale House may be at fault is hinted at in a Gothic subplot whereby the ghost of a murdered Victorian maid is exorcised by a fire which clears the ground for rebuilding. In the closing paragraphs, however, a Miss Beale hastily resurrected to represent the claims of common sense ('normality, sanity') experiences an 'emotion, suspiciously like regret, at witnessing the violent destruction of Nightingale House' (p. 300).

The literary claims made by James's style are very much those of the traditionalist mid-century English novel, as represented by the writers on the victim's bookshelf (Greene, Waugh, Compton Burnett, Hartley, Powell, Cary), in which a fastidious literateness constitutes the outward sign of a kind of cosmic disapproval, and the 'discriminations' of the English class and educational system are presented as necessary bastions against the endemic chaos and sinfulness of ordinary life. The writer on the list who did most to import this outlook into crime writing was Graham Greene who, for all his interest in the 'common' world, still approached it with his handkerchief to his nose and, in books like *Brighton Rock* and *A Gun for Sale*, used thriller formulae to help him do so. In *Nightingale* the incongruous episodes involving Masterson, whose sadistic contempt for the sleazy Mrs Dettinger clearly reflects something of the author's own, are straight out of Greene. My aim here is not to smear Greene or the other writers on the shelf by association but to notice how, in James, detective fiction has offered to re-house a tradition which if offered as innovatory novel-writing would already, in 1971, have looked fairly moribund.

Yet James is increasingly seen as a serious and innovative writer: her recent novel, *A Taste for Death*, was nominated for the 1987 Booker Prize and implicitly establishes some such claim in its very length of over 500 pages. Again, the actual identity of the murderer is a matter of comparative indifference in what the reviews on the cover claim as 'An astonishing novel of range and complexity' (*The Times*), 'A major and magisterial book' (*Daily Telegraph*), 'meticulous in detail and nuance' (*Observer*), and the work of 'a wonderful stylist' (Peter Levi, *Today*). The 'range' is perhaps there in the treatments of abortion, radical leftists, high politics, abandoned children, mugger-threatened old Londoners, and an ambitious policewoman's struggles with her job and her background. All this 'teeming' contemporary life is, however, carefully arranged round the two central locations of ancestral mansion and church, the twin pillars of the rural order transposed (as an Author's Note admits) to inauthentic London addresses. In a familiar pattern, house and church are presented as not allied but opposed, the two alternatives of 'life', and the exalted victim's choice of the latter constitutes an awe-inducing central mystery clearly designed to transcend the book's more earthbound detective dimension. This dimension, however, establishes through a familiar Christie-like scramble for inheritance that the doings in the great house are what the novel is really about. The book *is* well-written in its way, but it is a way that makes us want to ask why. In trying to elide the mysteries of detection with those of religious conversion, James gestures towards a transcendence of her chosen form. Yet without the kind of preservation order that form slaps on a certain way of ordering experience, it is hard to see how she could write at all. The reviewers quoted suggest an abiding (perhaps, in the Tory 1980s, growing) urge to find the meticulous and wonderfully styled in modern writing: maybe James's discovery is that these needs are far more important than content, and that the fundamentally indifferent content of her detective plots none the less offers her (and hence us) endless new things to be meticulous *about*.

Few of the above criticisms apply to James's 1972 book *An Unsuitable Job for a Woman*, featuring a female private eye. Perhaps because her situation makes Cordelia Gray interesting as a person and not just as a persona, and perhaps because the Chandleresque mode implies a less authoritarian, more tentative perspective, the tone of this book is relatively free of the burdens of literary office. Cordelia Gray's vulnerability, not just as a woman but also as a solitary in the field, aligns the book in sympathy with the young victim's similar vulnerability rather than in weary contempt for the world in general. The book's acclaim as a thoughtful blow for feminism when it first came out was justified, and later writers such as Sarah Paretsky and Gillian Slovo took over its female private-eye formula to good effect.[14] It is, however, significant that Cordelia finally surrenders the case to the fatherly Dalgleish; especially given that the victim, who has become a kind of *alter ego*, was murdered by *his* father. Although Cordelia reappears once more in the conventionally Gothic *The Skull Beneath the Skin*, the question behind this title seems, ultimately, to get an affirmative answer: detection *is* an unsuitable job for a woman.

This brings me to an aspect of 'Golden Age' detection which deserves much more attention than I've given it, but with which I shall conclude this chapter (to pick it up in slightly different terms a little later). This is the fact that it is a branch of writing in which women have reigned supreme (indeed in a continuous succession of 'Queens of Crime'), but also one which seems highly resistant to any specifically feminist interpretation. In a long perspective it is arguable that this is a form which speaks of confinement and restriction: the formula that 'a woman's place is in the home' doubtless has applied, within given periods and outlooks, to the attention to minutiae of social arrangement, the cross-checking of details which familiarises a particular domestic space, out of which the 'classic' form has been constructed. There is a certain continuity from the place-names of nineteenth-century fiction – Mansfield Park, Middlemarch, Wuthering Heights – to those of Christie – Styles, The Vicarage, End House. But, compared to their nineteenth-century ancestors, there has been little attempt by women detective writers to explore this restriction *as* restriction by, for instance, allowing female characters to act very far outside the terms of their allotted place.

Such a rare Golden Age female detective as Miss Marple does, at least implicitly, assert that her expert knowledge of this overlooked terrain constitutes a kind of power which should have its due. But Miss Marple, and even the later and very different Cordelia Gray, are rare phenomena compared to their counterparts in Victorian and Edwardian detective fiction where, as Michele B. Slung has demonstrated, the female detective, ladylike but tough and resourceful, was a fixture from the moment the genre became popular, if not before.[15] Generally, after the First World War, the powers of a Loveday Brooke or a Lady Molly of Scotland Yard were conceded unresistingly to Poirot, Wimsey, Campion, Alleyn and Dalgleish. There were, doubtless, popular prejudices to be assuaged (as Ellis Bell and 'George' Eliot had also found, much earlier), but together these writers had at least enough clout to make the detective anyone they wished.

Perhaps it's not irrelevant that it was only at the height of her confidence and fame that Christie created Miss Marple out of such early silly gossips as Caroline Sheppard.[16] Perhaps also the Golden Age male detective, authoritative but sexually rather blank, is already a kind of neutral space on to which writers and readers of either sex can most conveniently project the notion of social/domestic insight as power. The fact remains that because of the profound conservatism of all these writers, it is very hard to discern any awareness of the contradictions involved: the more apparently alert the writer, the more the difference between 'we' who know (how to behave properly, have to read a coffee-table, how to cap a French quotation) and 'they' who don't takes priority over questions of who is really in power. Tentatively, we might conclude that, in the area of gender as well as in most other areas, the innovating and aspiratory potential which detective writing embodied before the First World War was replaced after it by an acceptance of the rewards to be won by allowing unlimited ingenuity to flicker over an order deliberately conceived as unchanging and unchangeable.

10

The Hardboiled Heritage

THE AMERICAN HARDBOILED

In this final chapter, I shall not be attempting to do justice to the American hardboiled school. To confine the book within manageable bounds I shall instead emphasise the impact of the hardboiled on various kinds of recent British writing. To justify this procedure, I would point to the debatable emphasis on 'national' characteristics which tends to come into play over this issue in many studies. In Dennis Porter's *The Pursuit of Crime*, for instance, a somewhat complacent contrasting of English snobbery with American individualism hardly scratches the surface of the heavyweight European Marxist theory (Gramsci, Benjamin, Althusser, Foucault) adduced to demonstrate the impact of social factors on literary forms.[1] There are indeed reasons why it was America that produced the hardboiled mode, but once produced it provided a vocabulary for the expression of a wide range of concerns in many Western societies including the British.

The loose idea of 'pastoral' invoked in the last chapter can perhaps be applied to the particular awareness of transatlantic relationships which the detective genre seems to call into play. In discussions with both English and American students and friends, I have found that each nationality tends to dislike the clichés of its own branch of the genre while admiring the literary qualities of the other. This seems to reflect an ongoing transatlantic relationship whereby, for instance, Poe creates the 'classic' form from European models such as Godwin and Vidocq, only to have it reassimilated in France by Gaboriau and in England by Doyle. Doyle, in turn, shows repeated interest in American patterns of crime and detection from his first Holmes novel to his last, *The Valley of Fear*, where an American private-eye story constitutes a pastoral excursion within a Golden Age country-house mystery. America remains the heartland of the Holmes cult, and also responded eagerly to dime-novel transpositions of Gaboriau, whose guilty magnates, brutal interrogations and over-involved detectives may have influenced the hardboiled form as much as the indigenous romance tradition of Twain and Fenimore Cooper.[2] The more recent 'procedural' form of Ed McBain and *Hill Street Blues* also owes a great deal both to Gaboriau and his successor Simenon. The purest practitioner of the English puzzle-form was the American-born John Dickson Carr; Agatha Christie's father was half-American; Raymond Chandler was educated at an English public school and first acclaimed as a serious writer by English rather than American intellectuals. Leaving aside a further Australasian dimension which links some of Doyle's cases with the bestselling 'gold-boom' thrillers of Fergus Hume and perhaps the subsequent success of Ngaio Marsh, and the important transformations of the genre effected by European writers such as Leonardo Sciascia and Friedrich Dürrenmatt, it seems reasonable to summarise that the three leading nations in the game, America, Britain and France, tend to find in each other's detective writing satisfyingly distanced reflections of their own concerns which can well be described by Empson's formula for pastoral: 'putting the complex into the simple'.[3]

But before considering some recent British uses of the hardboiled mode as just such a form of pastoral, some brief points about the mode itself do need to be made. For brevity I shall concentrate on Raymond Chandler, although Hammett's *Red Harvest* (already briefly discussed) can claim to be the most radical instance of the genre which it virtually founds, at least as far as the novel is concerned. In a very different way from the English whodunnit, the American hardboiled novel can also be seen as a version of pastoral. The sense of division from other books and other lives is enforced by the specialisation of the private eye's work: in this one perspective, from this one point of view, the complex life outside looks simpler and clearer. It is not, as in the English whodunnit, that a microcosmic society has been carefully sealed off from the larger one (although in some cases the 'underworld', with its colourful characters, does constitute a kind of *Beggar's Opera* microcosm) but that a sprawling and threatening world is made manageable by being seen in terms of a deliberately limited range of issues.

But if the limitation of the private eye's perspective constitutes a necessary means of keeping this world under control, it has also often provided a highly effective means of evoking a world where such control seems impossible. For writers like Hammett, Chandler and Macdonald, this is done by repeated apparent transgressions of the nominal barrier separating the detective from the world he investigates: he covers up crimes, gets sexually involved with suspects, and ritually fights against the only two legitimate sources of his authority, the client and the police. None the less, the barrier is finally just maintained (with the hero's final lonely exit), and hence Auden's dismissal of Chandler to the realms of 'art', on the grounds that he fully enters the milieu he describes, is overstated.[4] However, a constant straining at the leash to leap the fence seems to be a leading characteristic of the hardboiled form.

In the case of the most famous hardboiled hero, Chandler's Philip Marlowe, this edgy, ambivalent relationship with the 'world' as represented by the affairs of his clients permeates the style as well as the content. Critics have often drawn attention to the *noli me tangere* attitude to women, homosexuals, clients and police which is expressed in a literary style bristling with rejection, refusal and summary judgement. There is, however, another side to it: for Marlowe, even more than for the less realised but more comfortably 'placed' detectives of the English school, the world opened up to him by his clients is simply all there is. The fact that he has no other existence gives a self-contradictory resonance to the recurrent skirmishes in which he attempts to reject his clients' money while demanding instead more information about their lives and motives.

Thus in *The Little Sister*, where as usual the client turns out to be one of the guilty parties, Marlowe's contradictory motives are clearly indicated: ' "I think you're a fascinating little liar. You don't think I'm doing this for any twenty bucks, do you?" . . . I didn't have the heart to tell her I was just plain bored with doing nothing. Perhaps it *was* the spring, too. And something in her eyes that was much older than Manhattan, Kansas' (Chandler, *The Little Sister*, p. 18). His later attempts to return the money ('I didn't even bruise it' (p. 38)) further underscore his rejection of the financial contract, while his repeated requests for more information insist equally strongly on his insatiable need for access to that 'real' human world to which the client, however unwillingly, offers an introduction. The fact that the introduction ritually leads, through a maze of connections, back to the client, provides a retrospective validation for this compulsive behaviour.

Marlowe's put-downs define by negation a whole realm of dependence, sarcastically projecting it as childishness ('I'm all

grown up. I go to the bathroom alone and everything') or effemin-
acy ('I'm kind of cute sometimes') (Chandler, *Farewell, My Lovely*,
pp. 10, 19). This dread of dependence has been well analysed by
John G. Cawelti as an expression of the 'other-directed' personality
which unsuccessfully seeks its sense of identity in peer-groups
rather than the family, and hence divides its attacks between
successful role-models (the rich) and reminders of the need for
dependence (women and 'weak' men) (see Cawelti, pp. 158–9).
The sense of deliberate self-exclusion from a distrusted but richer
world can perhaps be further related to Chandler's own edgy
attitude to the relations between his chosen form and 'serious'
literature, claiming 'to have taken a cheap, shoddy, and utterly
lost kind of writing and have made of it something intellectuals
claw each other about', while not caring 'a button about the
detective story as a form. All I'm looking for is an excuse for certain
experiments in dramatic dialogue' (Chandler, *Raymond Chandler
Speaking*, pp. 74, 219). The story is hence what F. R. Jameson calls
a 'pretext': at once an excuse for writing and an indifferent initial
text over which a 'richer' literary text can finally be draped (see
Most and Stowe, p. 215).

Jameson further argues that Chandler's own richness of observation depends very largely on its continually tangential nature.
Since modern urban experience ensures that much of what we
perceive is perceived instrumentally, en route to something else,
Chandler's abruptly described and dismissed scenes and encounters convey the experience of modern life particularly well. His use
of the story as a 'pretext' for the construction of this richness of
tangents is illustrated in his tendency to 'cannibalise' his early
short stories, written for *The Black Mask* and other pulp magazines,
and incorporate them wholesale in his novels.

To illustrate this point further, I propose to examine in some
detail the relationship between two early stories, 'Killer in the Rain'
and 'The Curtain',[5] and his first full-length novel *The Big Sleep*. In
this as in all his novels there is a noticeable tendency to swing
quite wildly from one case and set of preoccupations to another,
while all the time giving the impression that there must be
some as-yet-unexplained link, whether of meaning or of precise
interconnection, between them. This tendency is already present
in the short stories, but these also display certain simple kinds of
thematic unity; the very roughness with which Chandler stitches
them together in the novel disperses the notion of a unifying theme

while highlighting the sense of everything being tangential to something else, and open in fresh ways to Chandler/Marlowe's skills as a writer/observer.

'Killer in the Rain' already presents us with a series of loosely interconnected plots, but, through the sexual involvement of all the leading male figures with the same woman, at least a kind of significant pattern emerges. The narrator (a prototype for Marlowe) is hired by the wealthy roughneck Dravec to warn off a blackmailing pornographer from paying attentions to Carmen, the adoptive daughter whom Dravec sentimentally hopes to marry. Exactly as in *The Big Sleep*, the detective finds Carmen drugged and naked at the house of the pornographer, who has been murdered. In search of the photographs for which she was posing, he discovers that an ex-lover of hers, Joe Marty, has taken over the pornographer's racket and that another ex-lover, the chauffeur Carl Owen, has been found drowned in Dravec's car. In the climax Dravec trails Carmen to Marty's apartment, where she has gone to demand the photographs at gunpoint following a hint from the detective, and there is a shoot-out in which Marty and Dravec kill each other. In a final clearing-up session, it emerges that the pornographer was killed by the jealous Owen, who was then slugged by Marty for the photo-plates but revived sufficiently to drown himself. The urbane gangster Slade, who earlier warned the detective off the case, is only tangentially involved as the pornographer's 'protection'; Carmen survives, blankly chewing her thumb.

The plot of 'The Curtain' can be briefly outlined as follows. General Winslow hires the detective Carmady to find his missing son-in-law Dud O'Mara, though Carmady already suspects he was killed by the gangster Joe Mesarvy and his sidekick Lash Yeager. At the centre of the mystery is Mesarvy's vanished wife Mona, whose previous lovers include O'Mara, with whom she is thought to have eloped, and Carmady's friend Batzel, who is killed near the beginning of the story for knowing too much. Carmady eventually finds Mona hiding out in a house guarded by Yeager, whom he kills in a shoot-out. It turns out that O'Mara was killed by his twisted young stepson Dade, whose mother somehow (apparently by presenting a good target for subsequent blackmail) pressured the gangsters into hiding Mona Mesarvy so as to confirm the rumour of elopement. Carmady persuades Mrs O'Mara to have her son committed to an asylum in return for his silence.

In *The Big Sleep* these two plots become further complicated by being interwoven with each other. General Winslow changes his name to Sternwood and also takes over Dravec's function as grieving father, and Carmen adds Dade's psychopathic nature to her well-established depravity. Slade and Mesarvy are merged in the composite Eddie Mars. The main differences include the building-up of Mrs O'Mara into the central siren-figure Vivian Regan (now covering up for her sister Carmen rather than her son), and the inclusion of the pornographer Geiger's homosexual lover Carl Lundgren to replace the now-discarded Dravec as the killer of Brody (Marty). The character of Batzel is also dropped, to reappear as Terry Lennox in *The Long Goodbye*, and the fuel for Marlowe's hatred of Lash Canino (Yeager) is now provided by his murder of the pathetic Jones, using a trick unsuccessfully attempted on Carmady in the original story. But despite the impression of labyrinthine complexity given by the fusing of the two cases, the join between them (after the solution of the Geiger murder) is very clearly discernible: Chandler has just stuck the stories end to end, the glue being provided chiefly by the attempts of the two sirens, Carmen and Vivian, to seduce Marlowe. It is true that General Sternwood hints at both cases at the beginning, but for Marlowe, as for us, the Regan commission remains tantalisingly unfocused until the Geiger plot is over.

There are, certainly, three factors making for a thematic overlap between the two plots: the promiscuous woman whose affairs provide the link between disparate social milieux, and whose offer of intimacy starts to draw the detective into the web; the idea of the culpably spoiled child; and the pervasion of the background by the smoothly civilised gangster Slade/Mesarvy/Mars, whose silky diplomacy comes increasingly under scrutiny as the violence with which it is linked becomes clearer. But an enhanced sense of *dis*unity – of apparently important figures, settings and emotions appearing as if from nowhere or vanishing without trace – is the main effect of Chandler's 'cannibalisation'. The replacement of the Geiger plot by the Regan one halfway through enhances the sense of a linear journey in which Marlowe, rather than any given criminal or even crime, is the unifying factor. This is further reflected in the fact that the sirens who occupy the magnetic centre of the stories without involving the detective very directly, now arrange themselves linearly along Marlowe's path as so many potential but discarded sexual partners. Vivian, who combines some of the opposed qualities of Carmen and Mona (she is

Carmen's sister and was inevitably combined with Mona to create the Lauren Bacall role in the movie version) holds a central position to some extent, but is largely discarded, both sexually and structurally, as the second plot gets under way. And Mona, the subject of the identical last sentences of 'The Curtain' and *The Big Sleep* ('All they did was make me think of Silver-Wig, and I never saw her again') loses her previous centrality and becomes simply the last woman encountered on the path. (This is specially so since the removal of one ex-lover, Batzel, makes her less of a universal *femme fatale*, and hence her husband's concealment of her becomes even less clearly motivated.)

The plot elements of *The Big Sleep*, then, now constitute chiefly a kind of emotional paintbox, supplying a range of strong contrasts for the writing to play with as vividly as possible, rather than a firmly anchored pattern. Though there are now new elements of build-up – the 'heart of darkness' discovery of the real characters of Carmen and Eddie Mars and the slow approach to the fate of Rusty Regan who, as a man involved with the same three women (he was shot because, like Marlowe, he turned Carmen down), becomes more clearly an *alter ego* for Marlowe – the sheer complication of other plot elements ensures that these remain diffused and, once again, always at a tangent to something else.

The same jerky effect is if anything even more marked in Chandler's second novel, *Farewell, My Lovely*. Here Marlowe's boarding of the gambling-ship *Montecito*, whose intense build-up is transposed with only slight elaboration from the climax of 'The Man Who Liked Dogs', yields only meagre results in plot terms (the confrontation with the amicable Brunette, who agrees to pass a message to Malloy), but remains a bravura passage in 'emotional paintbox' terms. The effect of all this decentring of the plot is to make Marlowe's own attitudes and responses the key to everything: 'He is the hero, he is everything', as Chandler wrote in 'The Simple Art of Murder'.[6]

This concentration on Marlowe himself has been firmly deconstructed by Stephen Knight, who sees him as simply a disguised projection of the alienated intellectual: the convoluted plots are little more than repeated opportunities for Marlowe to express his verbal skills and his dislike of being touched by other people, in contexts where he significantly only usually confronts them one at a time. The fact that the central criminal is almost always a woman vividly enacts this dread, and while his narrating voice expresses the cultivated individual sensibility of the Dulwich College-educated Chandler, his speaking voice expresses a uniformly childish rejection of personal contact. The apparent challenging of social corruption (which Knight concedes to other hard-boiled writers such as Hammett) is simply an excuse for a nakedly bourgeois and élitist individualism.

Knight considerably softens this polemic in a later article,[7] but one of his arguments does seem to me very important in understanding not only the hard-boiled tradition but also the legacy it bequeaths to later writers. He points out that though Chandler may seem to be a social realist, the 'outer' plot concerned with corrupt links between respectable and criminal worlds always gives way (often via a moment when the main gangster turns out to be a kind of gentleman) to an 'inner' purely private plot where a woman threatens Marlowe and then kills or turns out to have killed the male *alter ego* he is seeking: Regan, Malloy, Quest, Lennox. Parts of Knight's argument about public and private plots and the hero's quest for an *alter ego* can, I think, be usefully applied to a wide range of modern writing, including the British reworkings of the hardboiled formula I shall shortly be discussing.

Though the threat from the *femme fatale* is common, the really fundamental elements of the formula are the missing *alter ego* and the fact that the doings of the (usually rich) family with which the hero has become involved are offered as providing at an emotional level the 'answer' to the problems of the outer plot concerning public corruption. In this recurrent formula the example of a later hardboiled author, Ross Macdonald, is also important. Writing somewhat after the hard-boiled heyday, from the 1950s to the 1970s, Macdonald takes the form's critical view of an increasingly acquisitive society as a starting point, but focuses most of his narrative ingenuity on the uncovering of buried family traumas which tend, in works like *The Chill* and *The Underground Man*, to be overwhelmingly Oedipal. 'Crazy mixed-up kids' are also prevalent in Chandler, from 'Killer in the Rain' and 'The Curtain' to *The Little Sister* and *The High Window*, but whereas these tend to be either vicious or pathetic, in Macdonald's more youth-worshipping Dr-Spock-influenced world they tend to be perceived as creative symbols of hope, their very confusions the key to a better future. Precisely as such symbols, they also tend to be missing for much of the story, thereby providing an idealistic space into which the otherwise disillusioned detective, Lew Archer, can insert himself. As a highly self-aware writer, Macdonald has written at length on his detective as a self-projection,[8] and perhaps the same could be said of the lost kid whose idealism and turmoil so often seem to reflect Archer's own. The other type of person who recurrently goes missing in Macdonald is the artist, such as Chantry in *The Blue Hammer*, who clearly enough speaks for another of the author's aspirations.

Before turning to British uses of such formulae, a few more comments on American crime-writing since the hardboiled heyday may be useful. It is arguable (and has been argued by Julian Symons)[9] that since then the genre has split into two. On one hand there is the crime-thriller, presented through the eyes of the criminal without recourse to the moral safety-net of detection, whose best representative is Patricia Highsmith; and on the other there is the 'police-procedural' of writers like Ed McBain, where the solitary detective is replaced by a police team, and the project of realism is sustained by a balance of losses and gains at the end (though generally more of the latter). Neither of these forms is totally new: crime-thrillers are in a sense as old as *Macbeth* (and for all her avowed amoralism Highsmith comes as close to the tragic pattern of personal nemesis as any twentieth-century writer);[10] and in Gaboriau's *Monsieur Lecoq* police procedure is presented as being just as important as the solution of the particular case. None the less, the recent mass adoption of both these forms seems to respond to a common feeling that crime is no longer rationally explicable, or at least soluble through explanation. In her meticulous demonstrations of murder as an extension of ordinary motivations and behaviour, Highsmith dissolves the barriers by which we normally hold it at bay and challenges us to accept it as endemic, while the police procedural seeks among other things to contain the 'wandering homicidal lunatic' so firmly debarred by Poirot within the partial reassurance of a workaday pattern.

One of the best current American crime-writers, Elmore Leonard, often combines the two approaches by dividing his narrative between an unnervingly empathised portrayal of the thoughts of a serial murderer and a more reassuring narrative featuring a courageous but hamstrung cop, whose 'aesthetic' interest is vouched for through the eyes of a girlfriend, and who finally bests the villain in something resembling a wild-West shoot-out. (Leonard began by writing Westerns, and the subtitle of his later *City Primeval: High Noon in Detroit* brings out his continuing debt to the form.) Although an excellent and sensitive writer, Leonard's formula expresses some of the vigilante fever of films like *Death Wish* and *Dirty Harry*, in which the forms of liberal society are held to have broken down and atavistic feelings about 'us and them' demand only that the hero (whether or not nominally a cop) know how to use a gun. But the various forms just discussed all in a sense feed into the anti-liberalism at present very current in the United States, whereby the ills of an increasingly acquisitive society are no longer to be accounted for in terms of its structure but of inherent human evil. Against this background the hardboiled quest to make sense of a largely senseless world by understanding its connections comes to seem heroically outdated.

The breakdown of this quest, in a context which still admires its nobility, is the starting-point for the frequent use of hardboiled formulae in self-consciously postmodernist 'high' literature. Though the arguments of Michael Holquist mentioned in the previous chapter largely relate to uses of Golden Age formulae, those of the hardboiled school have often been even more eagerly played with: a clear recent example being Paul Auster's *New York Trilogy*. Here, in three thematically linked novellas, the commitment of the private-eye-like hero to his case is repeatedly made to overshoot any chance of his making sense of it, in ways which demonstrate the existential absurdity of all such tasks and commitments. In the most schematic story, 'Ghosts', the private eye Blue is hired by the obviously disguised White to spy on Black from a window across the street. Losing his fiancée early in the process, Blue himself becomes lost in a maze of mirrors in which the obvious conclusion that Black is really White and spying on Blue for *doppelgänger*istic reasons ceases to seem very important. Laced with knowing references to Borges, Poe (especially the quintessential *doppelgänger* story 'William Wilson') and most of the rest of the American literary tradition, *The New York Trilogy* is really a state-of-the-art self-refraction on writing as a quest for meaning. While very enjoyable as such it also, however, loudly declares not only that the world outside makes no sense but also that (despite the loving detailing of New York as a network of remembered tangential connections) there is no world out there to make sense of.

BRITISH USES OF THE HARDBOILED

Of the British works I shall consider, four are 'quality' dramas which make conscious use of hardboiled methods for specific purposes, and two are novels marketed as crime fiction, but also 'using' hardboiled formulae to express specific views and ideas. The first of the novels, William McIlvanney's *The Papers of Tony Veitch* (1983), is technically a police-procedural which, like McBain or Leonard, offers a range of narrative points of view, including those of very violent criminals. The choice of Police Inspector Laidlaw as hero logically admits that the Glasgow underworld has no need of undercover 'private' investigations to expose its endemic criminality.

None the less, McIlvanney uses many hardboiled conventions on which to hang his powerful denotations of Glasgow life. Though ostensibly part of a team, Laidlaw operates above all as a loner, and his doing so is constantly validated for us by the intensity of his feelings: 'he so obviously cared about people, was so unmistakably hurt by what happened to them, sometimes through his doing, that he would have put a stone under pressure to feel things' (McIlvanney, p. 130). This account, framed in the mind of his admiring sidekick Harkness, is typical of the upward-looking view in which Laidlaw is habitually presented to us as a sensitive outsider. Without this heroic gift of sympathy, he would hardly spend the police time he does in following up the last ramblings of the wino Auld Eck, which lead him into a case involving street-gangs at the bottom and aristocrats at the top of society. As a further index of his special status, Laidlaw is a martyr both to a confining marriage and to guilt at having a mistress, a martyrdom which helps to define a private-'I'-like identification with the existential demands of his job. And though he may have his acolytes in the force, he is typically pitted against more workaday policemen such as the corrupt Ernie Milligan.

The most effective parts of the book are the depictions of the habitual criminals, through the eyes of one of whom we are given our introduction to Glasgow, 'the city of the stare'. The discovery that our perceptive guide through this opening section, Mickey Ballater, is at once thoroughly human and a thoroughgoing sexual sadist is only the first of the jolts the novel is concerned to deliver to our expectations. Others lie in such intimate evocations of a whole shame-culture as another gangster's slow and careful pouring of a pint of beer over the head of a youth who has stepped out of line: an act 'far more sadistic than striking him would have been' (p. 33).

Against this background Laidlaw's 'solution' to the case, when it comes, is rightly thrown in almost for nothing:

> Tony Veitch went into hiding from Paddy Collins. Paddy Collins beat up Lynsey Farren to find where Tony was. Dave McMaster killed Paddy Collins because he beat up Lynsey Farren. Dave McMaster killed Eck Adamson because he knew about Paddy Collins. Dave McMaster killed Tony Veitch because he needed a scapegoat. Mickey Ballater was a makeweight, although he didn't know it. So were Cam and John, although they didn't know it. As always, it was meaner than you would imagine.   (p. 224)

While nodding gruffly to our possible expectations of a more significant resolution, the last sentence reminds us that disappointment is the real essence of this whole violent world, as well as of the genre which looks for answers within it.

So far, so police-procedural. But there is also the dimension of Laidlaw's lonely personal quest for 'meaning' in a wider sense, which leads him from his more-than-policemanlike concern for the derelict Eck into an obsessive search for the missing young intellectual Tony Veitch. As the above resumé suggests, Veitch is first a scapegoat but then a victim in the main murder case: he also, however, provides Laidlaw himself with a very recognisable kind of *alter ego*. The Oedipally-estranged son of a rich father, whose Pollokshields house we explore with a familiar fascinated disgust, he is also, like Rusty Regan in *The Big Sleep* and numerous Macdonald kids, missing. In this absence, which is itself an accusation of his corrupt family, he becomes the central figure in Laidlaw's quest for a wider meaning to it all. Not only does he link all the book's disparate worlds together, but the outpourings of literate disgust in his eponymous 'papers', most of which have been destroyed, come to stand as a kind of authentic lost text lying beyond the impure text we are reading. Rather as with the murdered newspaper editor Donald Willsson in Hammett's *Red Harvest* (and the literary *alter egos* of Auster's *New York Trilogy*), Veitch's lost writings constitute the missing answer to the city's mysteries, although in fact their 'need to connect' and 'terrible attempt at an uninhabitable compassion' (p. 224) are exactly the values aimed at in McIlvanney's own writing.

The emotional commitment of the writing, then, is validated in terms of another piece of writing of which we only catch glimpses. But this clever playing on the notion of absence is only part of the Oedipal 'private plot' which, as in so much hardboiled fiction, comes to replace the standing public scandal of poverty and violence we have been confronted with from the start. Accordingly, the aspect of McIlvanney's novel which seems most formulaic is the lack of real connecting substance between the thwarting parent of the private plot, Tony's father Milton Veitch, and an underworld apparently subsisting sheerly on its own vitality. Despite such gestural remarks as 'the wealth of the few had become the poverty of the many', Milton Veitch is so clearly there just to *represent* the rich few that the actual source of his wealth is never specified. Instead, his role as the real villain of the piece is defined in exclusively Oedipal terms. His most apparent crime is to have a mistress, Alma, whom one of Tony's extant letters pruriently compares to a deluded acolyte of his father's priestlike certitudes, the crunch being that 'under his cassock, he is masturbating' (p. 173). This, like the further remark that his father could 'only make love to a woman with a dildo made of tenners', notionally accounts for his wilderness quest for authenticity in the mean streets of Glasgow. But we can add as a footnote that the person-to-person linking of the few with the many that is admirable when Tony does it, is bad and corrupt when performed by the slumming *femme fatale* Lady Lynsey Farren, whose various love affairs are the real key to the case.

If it were not for the ghettoisation of detective from 'serious' fiction, *The Papers of Tony Veitch* and its predecessor *Laidlaw* would and should be seen as important novels of the 1970s and 1980s. In the posing, in depth, of a problem and the crying out, in fantasy, for a solution to do with more compassion and understanding, the hardboiled convention serves McIlvanney far better than would a doggedly procedural realism which did not even look for answers, or a postmodernist playing around with fictionality which did not really consider the questions. At the same time, the convention offers its benefits at a price: that of the sly replacement of social issues by middle-class Oedipal ones, and the corresponding transference of protesting action to protesting male sensibility.

Gillian Slovo's *Death Comes Staccato* makes fewer literary claims, but is a far more explicit attempt to rework the hardboiled formula for 'alternative' ends, using it to present a feminist, socialist and anti-racist perspective on the Britain of the 1980s. The cult of macho solitude tacitly endorsed by McIlvanney is theoretically undermined from the start by making the detective a woman, Kate Baeier, who runs an agency committed to fighting discrimination and derives support and solidarity from her black assistant, Carmen, and devotedly uncompetitive boyfriend, Sam. In Carmen's occasional prickliness about her sidekick role and Kate's doubts about moving in with Sam questions about racial and sexual independence are efficiently raised, and the main breaks in the case are provided by an injured black worker and an exploited maid, each of whom is politicised by the experience. We might, then, expect to see some more of the genre's conventions enjoyably reversed, such as the preoccupation with the lifestyles of the rich, and the search for the *femme fatale*.

But what is striking about this novel is how closely it adheres to the Raymond Chandler formula it seems to set out to question. Thus the social plot, concerning the criminal negligence of a radio-parts firm, progressively yields emotional precedence to the private plot concerning the Oedipal imbroglios of the wealthy Weatherby family. While the industrial plot is largely hived off to Carmen (in ways the book has the grace to admit are indicative), Kate pursues the private case by steps taken straight from *The Big Sleep*. Thus on the one hand, the decor of Mrs Weatherby's 'ice palace' (Slovo, p. 2) reduplicates Vivian Regan's domain of mirrors and snow-white carpets, but on the other, Kate identifies immediately with the household's one vulnerable member. Hired to investigate a relatively trivial harassment, she tampers with murder evidence to protect the client's daughter, stumbles on a drug racket, gets brutally assaulted by corrupt cops, resists the client's attempts to buy her off, rejects the advances of a high-class seducer, and finally tracks the case back to the obvious *femme fatale*, Mrs Weatherby herself.

As in Chandler, the combination of private and public plots presents a kind of rough approximation to the complexity of the 'world' against which the detective has to define her integrity. The conventions of the form are so well established in this respect that only relatively few links at plot level are necessary to give the impression that somehow their vividly contrasted milieux are really one, or at least linked far more closely than we at first suspected.

Here the linkage is established more through parallellism than through direct interconnection, the only clear overlap being Mrs Weatherby's involvement with one of the radio firm's fat cats. But in both cases an initial wall of silence is gradually broken down to reveal a traumatic crime buried in the past: the sexual abuse of Alicia by her apparent father being matched by the death and maiming of workers in a fire resulting from the radio firm's evasion of safety regulations. To further the sense of labyrinthine complexity both plots twist away from their most clearly signalled conclusions, though not in essentials: thus while the firm is not as directly racist as at first suspected it has still maimed its black workers and, while the child-molesting Weatherby is not the central murderer, another paternal figure linked to Mrs Weatherby is.

In broad outline, the 'inner' plot very clearly follows the contours of a wish-fulfilling Freudian romance, in which the mentally crippled Alicia is saved from the technical guilt of incest by a last-minute substitution of fathers. This basic emotional alignment is confirmed by Kate's growing identification with Alicia, whose expressive powers as a musician recall those of Tony Veitch as a writer, and who like him goes missing for much of the book. Her talent provides a somewhat fairytale-like clue to the identity of the brilliant 'real' father whom Kate wishes were also hers (and who shares her own Lithuanian ancestry). In the climax Kate performs for Alicia the task of challenging the ice-mother Mrs Weatherby, the revelation of whose plethora of lovers is the cathartic beginning of Alicia's cure. Meanwhile Alicia's paternally derived mid-European musical genius constitutes the book's cultured middle-class version of royal blood. The fact that the private trauma (as in *The Big Sleep, The High Window, Playback* and much of Macdonald) is of a quasi-Freudian kind where articulation is the first step towards a larger cure suggests by a kind of osmosis that the 'public' troubles will also somehow be cured through the book's attempts to articulate them. It is a fundamentally liberal formula, with the crucial changes taking place in the hearts of middle-class families, and then in the hearts and minds of readers.

McIlvanney and Slovo are both writers with other strings to their bows, and both use the detective form to express longstanding radical commitments – McIlvanney's moulded by a powerful Glasgow tradition, and Slovo's by a family history in the forefront of the South African anti-apartheid movement. Neither of the detective novels discussed is a first stab: Laidlaw and Kate had both appeared in previous books. As I hope I have shown, the attempt to push the form beyond what it usually says is only partly successful (though more so than I may have suggested in the case of *Tony Veitch*): without turning wilfully postmodernist, the conventions can perhaps only be altered up to a certain point within the detective novel itself. In the rest of this chapter I shall look at comparable attempts in recent 'serious drama', which, because not so closely identified with the conventions, has felt freer to exploit them on one hand and expose their limitations as part of the problem on the other.

The political playwrights David Hare and Howard Brenton have often used detective conventions to expand and question the English dramatic vocabulary. The *anagnorisis* of something fishy going on in the Establishment is repeated in many plays including their two collaborations *Brassneck* and *Pravda*. But while the un-Dixon-like British bobby is virtually a fixture in Brenton's early work, the first play by either to exploit specifically hardboiled conventions is Hare's *Knuckle*, written in 1973 in acknowledged homage to Ross Macdonald (with further nods to John Dickson Carr and Patricia Highsmith in a more recent preface).[11]

A successful gun-runner, Curly Delafield, returns to his hometown of Guildford in quest of the truth behind the apparent suicide of his sister Sarah, whose abandoned coat has been discovered on the beach at Eastbourne, containing two return train tickets which suggest that she may have been murdered. Curly's main contacts are Sarah's glamorous friend Jenny, whose 'Shadow of the Moon' nightclub is one of the play's chief settings, and his wealthy merchant-banker father Patrick from whom he, like Sarah, has long been estranged. It finally emerges, through a series of confrontations, that the idealistic Sarah was driven to desperation on learning of her father's involvement with a property company which has robbed a sick old woman of her home and set a dog on her son, with whom Sarah was having an affair. The climax comes when the urbane Patrick's mask finally cracks, as he describes his last meeting with Sarah on the beach. In the ironic conclusion, Curly, having forced his father to this cathartic confession, decides to let sleeping dogs lie and return to the business opportunities his silence will open up for him; while Jenny, who has actually uncovered most of the evidence, reveals that Sarah is still alive, having faked her death in a way designed to throw a lifelong burden of guilt on her father.

Though the ending emphasises his virtual irrelevance to the real scenario, Curly is strongly established, through soliloquy and his forceful conduct in the major confrontations, as the central 'I' of the investigation. We are made to invest strongly in his fearless bearding of his fat-cat father and the inauthentic lefty Max Dupree, whose sadistic treatment of Jenny and subsequent force-feeding with booze and cigarettes by the abstemious Curly provide the play's most dramatic scenes of threat. But while the alienated cynicism expressed by Curly's choice of profession enables the attitudes of a middle-class Sixties drop-out to express themselves in convincingly hardboiled terms, it also makes him thoroughly dislikable in line with the play's general project to turn the hardboiled form on its head. In fact, however, his final return to his guns, leaving a Jenny who is neither the expected sidekick nor *femme fatale* to carry on the good fight, is a closing irony which perhaps ignores or perhaps admits the extent to which the well-concerted cover-up is already a standing motif of the hardboiled form.

Knuckle clearly contains many similar elements to the two (later) novels just discussed. Like Tony and Alicia, the missing Sarah is young, mixed-up and gifted: here with a radical anger that far outstrips her brother's, and a power of expressing it which makes the letter/poem received from her at the end an incisive summary of what the play itself is trying to say: 'Forbid ignorance. . . . Insist on decay' (Hare, p. 86). Unsurprisingly, her confusions are largely Oedipal, and by making the detective her brother Hare simply expands on the common situation whereby the detective's Oedipal discovery of guilt at the top only reduplicates that of the missing *alter ego* with whom he identifies. Like Milton Veitch the fat-cat Patrick expresses his corruption by having a mistress, though to its honour, despite some prurient remarks by Curly ('Like putting your hand between two slices of liver' (p. 56)), the play doesn't duck the social issues by placing a woman's sexuality at the centre of the web. Instead the apparent *femme fatale*, the 'hard, bright, glistening' Jenny, emerges as its central positive character, remaining true to Sarah's vision after Curly himself has abandoned it. The reason for this abandonment constitutes the play's central political point, that the detective project is obsolete because even the excuses of hypocrisy have been abandoned: 'greed and selfishness and cruelty stand exposed in white neon: men are bad because they want to be. No excuses left' (p. 71).

Hare's attempt to reverse the form is not, then, a postmodernist game with notions of reality and meaning, but a thought-out political statement. It is not in any case completely out of key with the hardboiled project, since as we have seen it only pushes the standard cover-up motif a step or two further: just far enough to show the limits of our standard identification of the impulse to detect with an overriding desire for justice. The formula is useful in other ways, notably in the parallel between its declarative first-person mode and the kind of non-naturalistic self-and-world-defining soliloquy recent political theatre has retrieved as a powerful stage convention. Hare's choice of Guildford as his main setting is also nicely placed by the hardboiled convention: rather than the more expected metropolis, Guildford echoes the dream of wealth embodied in the Californian playgrounds of Chandler and Macdonald while retaining connotations of faint absurdity for English ears, which then themselves prove worth examining. The geographically negligible journeys by which the plot finally connects Guildford to places like London and Eastbourne parody the freeway odysseys of a Lew Archer but also really do invoke the poetic sense of connection encapsulated in the Macdonald quote which prefaces the play's published version:

> I had to admit that I lived for nights like these, moving across the city's great broken body making connections among its millions of cells. I had a crazy wish or fantasy that some day before I died, if I had all the right neural connections, the city would come all the way alive.

By turning Macdonald's nightmare city into the puny Guildford, Hare underscores the parodic microcosm of America England has become, but also redefines the whole wealthy semi-rural South-East as an extension of London's genuinely powerful 'mean square mile' (p. 88).

The element of parody is also important for understanding the way in which Hare bestows such dramatic and extended treatment on what is, in the annals of detective writing, a very minor incident: some routinely vicious sharp practice in the property market and the alienation of a drop-out daughter. The space left by what ought to be a murder at least enables Hare to suggest that the pettier savageries we take for granted, including Curly's own profession of arms-selling, are the real evils we need to address ourselves to. A final piece of adroitness on Hare's part is that the sense of having touched a great many social bases generated by the fairly complex plot allows the social spectrum actually portrayed to be quite small. Unlike Brenton, Hare rarely includes many working-class characters in his plays, which doubtless implies a sensibly frank admission of his own public-school background, but sometimes makes his pictures of the state of the nation seem comparatively bloodless. Here the connotations of the form, the sense that somehow the mean streets have been walked whether we actually see them or not, help to resolve the problem: it is in the hinted rather than visible connections between 'millions of cells' (as well as the classic sleaze of the Shadow of the Moon Club, with the constant crooning of Michael Lomax and his Freshman Three) that Hare's Guildford seems, at least, to come 'all the way alive'.

In a more recent play, Caryl Churchill's biting satire of the stock market, *Serious Money*, a quest very similar to Curly's is also used as a means of focusing a range of broader issues. Here the detective-figure is Scilla Todd, whose inquiry into her brother Jake's death peters out in much the same way as Curly's and for similar reasons: in a world of general corruption, the question of whether he was murdered or committed suicide after being found with his hands in the till is irrelevant. In a play which works to exclude any glimmer of idealism, her quest is in any case motivated chiefly by resentment that her brother was making 'serious money' without letting her in on it, so that her final sell-out to the multinational firm on whose behalf the British Establishment may have killed him is hardly a great shock. Similarly, the corruption of the wealthy father which is virtually *de rigeur* for this formula gets virtually lost amidst the even more rapacious behaviour of his juniors, rather as the detective plot itself gets lost among the play's more urgently exciting scenes of trading and money-making. The play's central theme of a kind of exponential acceleration of callousness is well demonstrated in its throwaway treatment not only of detection but even of the kind of politicised undercutting of detection exploited by *Knuckle*. *

My concluding discussion of two television drama serials – Brenton's *Dead Head* and Dennis Potter's *The Singing Detective* – should perhaps be prefaced by an apology for not having first explored more generally the film and television treatments of detection which provide them with much of their vocabulary.

Clearly, modern images not only of the classical private eye but also of man-on-the-run paranoia and police procedure derive as much from the visual media as from books, and a fuller study would talk about the iconic qualities of Bogart in *The Maltese Falcon* and *The Big Sleep*, the importance of Hitchcock, and the groundbreaking impact of *Z Cars* and *Hill Street Blues*. But I am chiefly concerned with the uses to which detective images have been put for particular ends; it has therefore seemed easier to pick off particular filmic or televisual points as they arise, rather than trying to establish the whole context in which these two serials really ought to be 'read'.

One filmic element I shall try to remain aware of is that of the active movement through fragmented bits of reality which can be called 'metonymy' and which I earlier suggested receives a great deal of priority in the detective form as a whole. Lacking many techniques of non-temporal cross-reference, film and television seem in some ways to be made for the active piecing-together work of detection, and such piecing-together is very much the subject of the two serials to be discussed. None the less, the element that makes them most clearly 'art', compared to most television, is that the piecing-together is precisely meditated on *as* a subject, and therefore also as a metaphor for something else: political under-standing in Brenton's case and psychological understanding in Potter's. This preoccupation then breeds a recourse to whatever cross-referring techniques television does possess in order to establish metaphorical connection. These are probably greater than those of film in that the viewer is less caught up in the immediate action and more able to compare events coolly; and also in that, in the serial, the repetitive/cumulative effect of the separate episodes permits a habit of recapitulating images in different contexts.

Hare's and Churchill's motif of detection ending in sell-out also provides the core of Howard Brenton's 1986 television serial *Dead Head* in which the quest to identify a highly placed sex-murderer is combined with the conventions of the man-on-the-run thriller. Eddie Cass, a petty crook, is framed for murder by being paid to take charge of a package containing a woman's severed head; he is then alternately hounded and bribed by various shadowy authority-figures, whose inconsistent behaviour is partly clarified by the discovery that his estranged wife Dana has become the well-placed killer's current mistress. Working largely to save himself, but perhaps also Dana, Eddie traverses a range of locations from the seedy to the aristocratic in his quest to identify the maniac and the powerful forces protecting him. At the end, however, informed of the killer's identity by one of these protectors, Eddie abandons the quest totally and is seen, in a deliberately bathetic conclusion, smoking a cigar in the Bahamas with Dana, whom we had previously imagined to have been decapitated in her turn. Although we never discover the killer's name ourselves, heavy hints such as Eddie's servile references to Queen and Country and the theme-song's sinister version of the nursery rhyme 'Pussycat, Pussycat' imply that he is a member of the immediate royal family.

While perhaps mischieviously prompting further speculation, the play's aim is clearly not to make any such charge in reality, but to draw attention to the powers at the state's disposal when it does have something to cover up. (The possible references range from the long-standing legend that Jack the Ripper was really the Duke of Clarence to the much-publicised behaviour of Prince Andrew before his sedate marriage; and, on a more serious level, the beginning of Peter Wright's leakages about MI5 plans to bring down the Wilson government. Brenton himself cites the Stalker, Ponting and Tisdall affairs.) The other side of the coin is the inadequacy or treachery of the various apparent helpers Eddie encounters on his path – an alienated secret-serviceman finally shot by the SAS, an upper-class woman who has sex with the handcuffed Eddie without releasing him, a Black Power leader turned and then killed by the police, another upper-class woman and her junkie ex-Falklands soldier-boyfriend who end up chasing Eddie round Glasgow in a tank – followed finally by Eddie's own self-betrayal. The nightmarish crumbling away of any possible opposition is a recurrent theme of Brenton's, but may have owed some specific gravity to the year of writing, 1984.

In his introduction to the published script, Brenton remarks that 'I was accused by some of paranoia, ludicrously because Eddie's predicament is obviously a deliberate reworking of the old joke: "You're not paranoid. People *are* trying to kill you" ' (Breton, p. 5). Through its very crudity of attack, *Dead Head* tries to force us to see modern Britain through the black-and-white lens of John Buchan (there are many cinematic references to Hitchcock's film of *39 Steps*, particularly in the train-and-handcuff imagery of Episode 2) and Cornell Woolrich, the 'Why me?' motifs of whose 'Black Series' are a staple of the *film noir* style proclaimed by the producer Robert Walker in his sub-introduction (p. 6). But while these models, along with Chandler and Orwell, provide valid images for powerful fears, they carry with them some trappings which Brenton simply does not bother to rework. The time-honoured motif of the *femme fatale* crops up repeatedly: Dana, the Black Power leader's girlfriend Jill, and the two clearly signposted rich bitches Sandra and Angela all routinely offer sex and betrayal as two versions of the same thing. The general theme of the common man's 'traducement' by the Establishment could have been conveyed without this programmatic treatment of women, and earlier stage plays such as *Weapons of Happiness* and *Sore Throats* don't suggest that Brenton is expressing a personal phobia here. (In these plays a disappointed view of sex as an image of political frustration is most often voiced by women.) The presentation of the upper classes as united in their enjoyment of active sadism also has a useful condensing effect but also, in its actual presentation, cuts a great many corners.

Unlike Brenton's stage plays, which sometimes shock us with the unexpected, *Dead Head* shocks by giving us our expectations but then exceeding them: hence the generic expectation that the mystery should revolve around the psychodrama of a rich family is simply trumped in spades by the revelation that the family in question is the royal one. This technique of excess may be the only way to make the television thriller say something 'different' from what it usually seems to say, but here it doesn't always come off. The dramatically laid trail through a whole society is well attended to as far as geography is concerned (Peckham, Regent's Park, Herefordshire, Birmingham, Bristol, Glasgow and all the other locations are lovingly detailed by name, as in Chandler's chapter openings), but socially consists of a binary ping-pong between sleaze and high-life which seems chiefly determined by the need to repeat the same moment of transition until it becomes a kind of fixed metaphor. As a way of insisting that class has not gone away as the determining element in British life this is honourable, but as a use of paranoid detection to initiate us into a much more fragmented reality it wastes a lot of opportunities.

Dennis Potter's more renowned television serial, *The Singing Detective*, deploys hardboiled conventions far more knowingly. The hero, a thriller-writer significantly named Philip Marlow without the 'e', adopts his namesake as an *alter ego*, using the very conventionality of the rituals surrounding him as a source of strength in his own struggle to return to the real world. Marlowe's trenchcoat, hat and gun, together with a distorted version of his wisecracking style, function as so many layers of protection against painful contact: a function closely related to the fact that, outside his fantasies, Marlow is laid up in hospital with psoriasis, a skin disease which indeed makes physical contact unbearably painful. The 'plot' is relatively simple: with the help of the Marlowe persona, who helps him to recall and overcome a classically Oedipal childhood trauma, Marlow is partially cured and restored to the wife on to whom he had previously projected his sexual disgust. The presentation of his many different layers of consciousness is, however, extremely complex and constitutes the virtuoso excitement of the serial, to the extent that it is only by clinging on to realistic conventions which are constantly being undermined that we are able to give the psychological narrative any final precedence over the others.

What the Marlowe persona offers to Marlow is primarily a way of moving inwards while seeming to move outwards. His threatening world of seedy bars, indecipherable connections, hoods and highlife conspiracy is deliberately never reducible to a single plot: characters, motives and settings change without rhyme or reason except in so far as we can relate them to the bedridden Marlow's circling obsessions with his wife, his mother and the partly fantasised figure of Binney, a negative *alter ego* who combines the roles of Oedipal rival and injured victim. In the first few episodes this 'plot' seems to be that of one of Marlow's thrillers, set in 1945, in which the trench-coated detective (played by the same actor as Marlow) is drawn by the dubious Binney into an intrigue concerning prostitutes who may be Russian agents, escaping Nazis, and two hit-men whose role is never fully explained. Later, all this becomes confused with a paranoid fantasy in which Binney and Marlow's wife Nicola plot to sell the film rights of the original story, but both plots are entwined with each other and with the hospitalised Marlow's obsessions, and neither has any coherent outcome.

The lack of closure in the two 'detective' plots allows us to focus instead on the *idea* of plot, as something drawing us forward into the unknown. The unruffled figure of the detective moves outwards into danger and darkness while Marlow moves inward and, in particular, back into the traumatic childhood where, it emerges, his witnessing of a sexual encounter between his mother and the original Binney led to his mother's suicide and the beginning of his psoriasis and lifelong sexual paranoia. The Chandler/Macdonald pattern of an outer plot surrounding an inner family psychodrama is thus reproduced, and it is appropriately only when the detective enters the hospital ward, the scene of the inner drama, and cures his *alter ego* Marlow by 'killing' him, that the serial comes to an end.

Potter is not only playing with the idea of the corny plot but also with that of 'corniness' in general. This theme is amplified by the inclusion of popular songs from the 1940s as a way of linking all the disparate contexts together. The fact that the 'singing detective' is among other things a dance-hall crooner who mimes to old hits confirms his role as a kind of arch-priest of corn. Another 1940s association, with the end of the war, is caught up by the substitution of a shattered Graham-Greenesque London for Chandler's Los Angeles: the detective's Americanese delivery in this context only confirms the sense of a deeply British fantasy contained in protective layers of cliché. But the clichés all finally relate to the period of Marlow's childhood: the popular songs are strongly associated with his parents, particularly his tragic father; the postwar euphoria is linked with the sadistic schoolteacher who dominates the middle stage of his recollections; a detective is what the young Marlow decides to become, for appropriately Freudian reasons, on witnessing the primal Oedipal scene between his mother and Binney in the woods. (A deconstructionist might argue that the very corniness of this scene – the epicentre both of the serial and of all the subsequent fuss in *Radio Times* – as an explanation of all the subsequent misery is also the centre from which all the other layers of corniness radiate.)

At one point Marlow contrasts the conventional novel of 'all solutions and no clues' ('He said, she said, and descriptions of the sky') with an ideal work of 'All clues. No solutions' (Potter, p. 140). This can be seen as the programme of *The Singing Detective* itself, where the various clues provided by the songs, the duplication of actors in various roles, and the recurrence of various dislocated images such as the scarecrow, seem to lead endlessly and tantalisingly from one level of the narrative to another. At the same time it is arguable that the old Chandler/Macdonald form, which leads from a sense of something being wrong with the world to the discovery of a kind of solution in the behaviour of a single family, is faithfully observed. But unlike those in the other texts discussed it is not a privileged family, except in so far as it is enshrined in

Potter's other work and in so far as the intense concentration on Marlow himself makes it hover over the whole plot. It differs even more, perhaps, in that Potter's portrayal of it does not seem to have any 'subversive' intention, despite his convincingly realistic depiction of its cramped misery. Whereas most of the other texts discussed present the power of the father as a symbol of the corrupting nature of power more generally, here there is just a yearning to see his traditional authority restored. Marlow's father becomes an inarticulate King Hamlet, unconsciously dooming his son to avenge his slighted authority against usurpers (the fantasy Binney) and women, particularly Marlow's own wife Nicola. Marlow's fantasy of the 'Singing Detective' is among other things his tribute to this wronged and musically gifted father.

Potter's serial doesn't claim the political sanctity of the other works discussed (unlike its 1989 successor *Blackeyes*), and so we are not forced to make up our minds about Marlow's generally condescending behaviour as an intellectual white male. Leaving aside his admittedly pathological behaviour towards his wife, his adoration of Nurse Mills depends on her task of greasing his penis without making personal demands; he is matey with Ali as long as his heavy-handed spoofing of racist attitudes is accepted as a cosy joke; and we are allowed to sympathise with his indirect murder of the vulgarly Cockney George. But overall, the enormous complexity of the serial (including the different 'realisms' of the hospital, marital and childhood scenes, the absurdist musings of the two 'mysterious men', the metafictional issues raised by the thriller-reading Reginald, the ardently resisted but inevitable psychoanalytical conclusions of Dr Gibbon) boils down to something quite simple: the state of mind of a gifted but insufficiently acknowledged individual, cut off from but cleverly responding to the surrounding world. A generation older than most of the other writers considered in this section, and powerfully presenting his literary generation's frequent experience of trauma on moving from working-class roots into a new kind of middle class, Potter ruthlessly targets a particular kind of social stuffiness to which defensive individual revolt seems the only answer. But it is also arguable that, though he uses some powerful new techniques for shuffling the representational pack, he finally deals us some very familiar cards.

Postscript

Julian Symons's announcement of the demise of the classical whodunnit, as he gazed into 'the crystal ball' in 1972, now seems somewhat premature, in the light of its recent emergence into a new kind of literary respectability.[1] A continuing spate of texts from Umberto Eco to Dennis Potter confirms the claims of critics such as Holquist and Tani that much 'postmodernist' literature either emulates or parodies the form, which has also demonstrated at least a workaday usefulness to feminism and a range of other socially critical positions. But there has also (1989) been a massive renaissance of interest in the British 'Golden Age', greatly assisted by an unending spate of television serialisations: by a kind of Through-the-Looking-Glass reversal, the reader's acceptance of a stereotyped milieu for the sake of the plot is rapidly being replaced by the viewer's acceptance of the automatic pleasures of the plot for the sake of the lovingly visualised milieu.

Although P. D. James and Ruth Rendell have become national treasures and the covers of serious novels routinely display reviews claiming that they are first-rate detective stories as well as significant literature, no one, clearly, wants the distinction to disappear altogether. Literature needs detective fiction as its other, the thing it is being innovatory by constantly approaching. Sometimes it is the face of the people, if not as substance then as imagined audience; sometimes the tabooed return to the womb of storytelling and/or the Home Counties proprieties.

Looking into the 1989 'crystal ball', at the immediate future at any rate, it is hard not to see a steady re-advance of 'plot' on all fronts, in serious as well as detective fiction, if only because of its usefulness as a well-tried clothes-horse for so many other kinds of writing. In the heartlands of postmodernism, every attempt to deconstruct the closures of plot enhances its mystique and makes it more indispensable to the next effort. At less rarified levels, it has a proven ability to make literary social work sell. In its own native land of Green Penguins (now 'Penguin Classic Crime') and bloodstained Fontanas (now re-done in pastoral pastels, in the case of Christie) the renovators and fireplace-restorers are at work, and few TV arts presenters have not put a willing hand to the brush.

It seems reasonable to speculate on the special significance of plot to an increasingly property-conscious age. Remembering Aristotle's dictum that the best plots concern a handful of families, it is easy to see plot as a special kind of property, to be nurtured, 'stored for years' before 'sale', as Zangwill puts it, and even then eked out to the last drop. It has an assessable rarity value, hard edges, and remarkably little odour; and it is ruthlessly competitive in that each model must always at least claim to improve on the last. Even, or especially, in 'serious' works, the sense of an eking – what Barthes called the Delay in the Hermeneutic Sentence – is reverting once more from being a source of shame to one of pride.

In this book as a whole, I hope to have provided some kind of longer perspectives for this sort of half-polarity, half-collaboration between the literatures. If the crystal ball suggests an increasingly conservative configuration, a short while ago – and at several staging posts before that – it didn't. The space for change implied in the 'missing *Wunderkind*' motif was at least a genuinely liberal space, bespeaking the possibly unrepeatable postwar faith in the regenerative if abused potential of youth. While such a faith is hard to kill completely, new social and educational emphases on vocational savvy are rapidly rendering the motif passé or else (as in the case of Ian McEwan's recent *The Child in Time*)[2] the spark of new potential is pushed so early into childhood as to make the cause of its disappearance undetectable. Literary plots sometimes do have the serious job of uncovering political ones – Sidney's ulcers covered with tissue – as well as the sinecure of self-conservation. Where the tissue is seen as transparent the 'unroofing' aspect of detection is largely a formality – as, notably, in the Golden Age which, as we have seen, still rumbles on. Where the tissue is more problematic, as for writers as various as Sophocles, Webster, Gaboriau, Zangwill and Hammett, the re-plotting of plot itself becomes a kind of necessity.

Notes

Publication details of works referred to significantly in the text are given in full in the Bibliography: hence these notes only give full details of works mentioned in passing or referred to chiefly in the notes themselves. Citations in brackets in the text refer to the name of the author/editor and page. Abbreviated titles are given only when more than one work appears in the Bibliography under that author's name.

Notes to the Preface

1. See Poe, p. 326; and Jameson, in Most and Stowe, p. 125. (N.B. Since most subsequent references in this Preface are taken up later, I have not annotated it in detail.)
2. See Karl Marx and Friedrich Engels, *The Holy Family* (Moscow, 1956); and Bertold Brecht, '*Über die Popularität des Kriminalromans*', in Jochen Vogt, *Der Kriminalroman* (Munich, 1971).
3. See Raymond Williams, *Keywords* (London, 1983) pp. 183–8.

Notes to Chapter 1: Detective Fiction and Scandal

1. See especially Knight, ch. 1; Ousby, ch. 1; Porter, ch. 8; and Foucault, chs 1 and 2.
2. As suggested by Fielding's full title, *The History of the Life of the Late Mr Jonathan Wild the Great*. Wild flourished from 1714 to 1725, when he operated simultaneously as a thief-taker, gang-leader and 'recoverer' of stolen property. Ambivalently celebrated by Defoe ('An Account of the Life of Jonathan Wild', 1725) and Gay (as Peachum in *The Beggar's Opera*, 1727), Wild's businesslike approach to corruption was seen by contemporaries as paralleling Walpole's, and he went on to provide a more distant model for Fagin and Moriarty (see Ousby, pp. 13–18, and p. 102 in this volume). His activities prepared the way for Henry and John Fielding's establishment of the Bow Street Runners in 1753, both as an example of the type of crime to be combated, and of the level of organisation needed to combat it. See *'An Enquiry into Causes of the Late Increase of Robbers' and Related Writings*, ed. Malvin R. Zirker (Oxford, 1988) for some of Fielding's further attempts to foster a 'detective' consciousness through his writings.
3. Capote's *In Cold Blood* was published London in 1966. De Quincey's essay and Postscript are conveniently published together in *The English Mail-Coach and Other Essays* (London, 1961).
4. The birth of police detection as a literary subject can be dated to the Parisian thief-turned-*chef de Sûreté* Vidocq, whose 1828–9 *Memoirs* are ritually derided in Poe's 'Murders in the Rue Morgue' (see pp. 46–7), and best analysed by Knight (pp. 28–37). For the accuracy or otherwise

of Poe/Dupin's deductions in the Mary Rogers case, see p. 51 and n. 9 to Chapter 3.

5. See Edwards, p. 115. The story dates from the period of *The Memoirs of Sherlock Holmes*, but was not published in book-form until *His Last Bow*, 1917. The thought-reading passage was transferred to 'The Resident Patient' in *The Memoirs*.

6. See Georg Büchner, *Dantons Tod* and *Woyzeck*, ed. Margaret Jacobs (Manchester, 1971) pp. xxiii–xxiv.

7. See Edwards, p. 204. Recounting the incident to the *Pall Mall Gazette* as an example of his infallibility, Bell remarked that it 'struck me as funny at the time'.

8. See pp. 10 and 84. The story not named on p. 10 is 'The Boscombe Valley Mystery'.

9. See p. 154.

10. Much more could be said about the continuity from such pictures of the malcontented factotum as displaced professional (soldier in Bosola's case) to the ex-DA officer Philip Marlowe and the ex-military spies of Deighton and Le Carré.

11. See *The Tragedy of Master Arden of Feversham* (1592), ed. M. L. Wine (London, 1973); and *A Warning for Fair Women* (1599), Tudor Facsimile Texts (Amersham, Bucks., 1912). The latter is particularly interesting for its rough soldering of classical Senecan horror on to close documentary-style reportage of a real-life petty-bourgeois *crime passionel*.

12. Clement Scott, quoted in Raymond Williams, *Drama from Ibsen to Brecht* (Harmondsworth, Middx, 1973) p. 17.

13. See Knight, pp. 20–8, for an excellent analysis of proto-detective elements in *Caleb*; see also Ousby, ch. 2, for a useful account of Godwin's negative attitude to spying.

14. See p. 55 and n. 12 to Chapter 3.

15. See pp. 63 and 70.

16. See Charles Dickens, 'The Detective Police', 'Three "Detective" Anecdotes' and 'On Duty with Inspector Field', in *The Uncommercial Traveller and Reprinted Pieces, Etc.* (London, 1958) pp. 485–526. The articles set up some of the key images of the British 'bobby', at least up to Dixon of Dock Green: salt-of-the-earth but Olympian, strict-but-kindly, street-credible but incorruptible – ultimately the pre-eminent ally in the struggle to transcend class-divisions attempted in the panoptic structures of Dickens's own novels.

Notes to Chapter 2: *Oedipus* and Aristotle

1. See Dorothy L. Sayers, 'Aristotle and Detective Fiction' (1946), in Winks, pp. 25–34. Sayers's article does not refer specifically to *Oedipus*, but shows, point for point, how closely Artistotle's detailed prescriptions for effective plotting are adhered to by 'Golden Age' detective writing like Sayers's own. The carapace of humour within which this piece of genuine scholarship is enwrapped is a good example of the serious/frivolous schizophrenia long prescribed for discussion of the genre.

2. See Todorov, p. 45; and Aristotle, in Dorsch, p. 39: 'the representation of the action is the plot of the tragedy', or as John Jones half retranslates it in *On Aristotle and Greek Tragedy* (London, 1962) p. 24, 'the *muthos* is the *mimesis* of the *praxis*'.

3. See, somewhat in general, Northrop Frye, *Anatomy of Criticism* (Princeton, N.J., 1971) p. 66; Roland Barthes, *Image, Music, Text*, ed. and trs. Stephen Heath (London, 1977) pp. 87–91; Pierre Macherey, *A Theory of Literary Production* (London, 1978) throughout; William V. Spanos, 'The Detective and the Boundary', in *Casebook on Existentialism, 2* (New York, 1976) pp. 163–89. For postmodernist uses of detection to make negative points about closure, see pp. 151–2 and 178 in this book and also Alain Robbe-Grillet, *Les Gommes* (Paris, 1953); Leonardo Sciascia, *Todo Modo* (Turin, 1974); Thomas Pynchon, *The Crying of Lot 49* (London, 1967); and Paul Auster, *The New York Trilogy* (London, 1987).

4. See Augusto Boal, *Theatre of the Oppressed*, trs. C. A. and M. O. Leal McBride (London, 1979) pp. 1–50.

5. See Freud, pp. 261–4.

6. John R. Reed, 'English Imperialism and the Unacknowledged Crime of *The Moonstone*', *CLIO*, vol. 2 (1973) pp. 281–90.

7. See Eliot's Introduction to the World's Classics edition of *The Moonstone* (London, 1928) pp. v–viii.

Notes to 3: Poe

1. See Richard Wilbur, 'Edgar Allan Poe' in his *Responses* (New York and London, 1976) p. 59.

2. See Symons, pp. 36–40; and Dorothy Sayers, 'The Omnibus of Crime', in Winks, p. 60.

3. See Jacques Lacan, 'Seminar on "The Purloined Letter"', in Most and Stowe, p. 30.

4. See, for example, Poe, p. 328, where Dupin's solution of the case is accompanied with a reminder of 'his abstract manner at such times'.

5. See ch. 13 of Samuel Taylor Coleridge, *Biographia Literaria* (Princeton, N.J., 1983) vol. 1, pp. 295–306, for his classic distinction between 'Fancy' and 'Imagination'.

6. See n. 4 to Chapter 1.

7. See John Locke, *An Essay Concerning Human Understanding* (Oxford, 1975) Book II, ch. xi, para. 2, p. 156. 'Wit lying most in the assemblage of Ideas, . . . Judgement, on the contrary, lies quite on the other side, in separating carefully . . . a way of proceeding quite contrary to Metaphor and Allusion.'

8. See Roman Jakobson, 'Two Aspects of Language and Two Types of Aphasic Disturbance', in Roman Jakobson and Morris Halle, *Fundamentals of Language* (The Hague and Paris, 1956 and 1971) pp. 90–6.

9. See John Walsh, *Poe the Detective: The Curious Circumstances Behind 'The Mystery of Marie Rogêt'* (New Brunswick, 1968).

10. See Holquist, in Most and Stowe, pp. 164–74; and Tani, *passim*.

11. See Lacan; and Jacques Derrida, 'The Purveyor of Truth', *Yale French Studies*, no. 52 (1975) pp. 31–113. The latter is more a deconstruction of the former than of Poe's story, but usefully points out Lacan's unacknowledged reliance on Bonaparte, and gives a valuable account of the 'frame' of the three stories as a sequence.

12. ' – Un dessein si funeste,/ S'il n'est digne d'Atrée, est digne de Thyeste'. In this quote from Crébillon's tragedy *Atrée*, Atreus muses that his macabre revenge on his brother Thyestes is beneath his own dignity, but well suited to his victim's. Thyestes had run off with Atreus's wife, in return for which Atreus killed Thyestes's children and served them up to him in a banquet. The irony of the quote is, hence, that while Atreus attempts to preserve his dignity on a higher plane than his brother's, he has in fact sunk below it.

Notes to Chapter 4: Gaboriau

1. Thus Murch states (p. 126) that the end of *L'Affaire Lerouge* focuses 'interest on Monsieur Lecoq', whereas, apart from a glancing late mention, he only features at all for a brief page near the beginning. Similarly Edwards (pp. 352–3) misattributes Tabaret's ur-Holmesian behaviour when hot on the scent to Lecoq, in a detailed comparison of passages which does not disguise the author's unfamiliarity with *Lerouge*. Less heinously, Tani refers (p. 16) to a 'gratuitous flashback' near the end of *Lerouge*: a charge more applicable to *Monsieur Lecoq* and, indeed, the two other Lecoq novels, than to a book where such flashbacks have been fed to us more briefly throughout. At a more theoretical level, the standard teleological stricture is expressed pithily in Boileau and Narcejac's *Le Roman policier*, p. 37: 'Nous sommes, cette fois, en plein mélodrame. Mais justement le "mélo" est le corps étranger qu'il faudra extirper du roman policier' [*translation*: 'With Gaboriau, we are in the presence of full melodrama. But melodrama is precisely the foreign body that the detective novel needed to reject']. This carpeting of the melodrama from which the form sprung as a body foreign to it is an entirely retrospective operation.

2. Translated anonymously as *The Widow Lerouge* (New York, Charles Scribner's Sons, 1902). All page references to Gaboriau are to the relevant volume of the uniform Scribner's series.

3. Walter Benjamin, 'Paris, die Haupstadt des XIX Jahrhunderts', in his *Illuminationen, Ausgewählte Schriften* (Frankfurt am Main, 1961) pp. 193–4. Quoted by Tani, p. 21, whose translation this is.

4. The Scribner's series published them separately, as *Monsieur Lecoq* (New York, 1902) and *The Honor of the Name* (New York, 1902). E. F. Bleiler's reprint of the (New York, 1908) W. R. Caldwell edition (Emile Gaboriau, *Monsieur Lecoq*, New York, Dover Publications, 1975) omits all of the second part except the indispensible ending on the grounds that it is 'one extended yawn' (p. 255).

5. Freud's alternative term for the Oedipus complex (see n. 5 to Chapter 2) accurately describes the content of much 'prose' or 'domestic'

romance.

6. Marie-Anne', or 'Marianne', has indeed been the standard name for the idea of Republican France from the Revolution on. I quote from Ian Jeffrey's introductory notes to a recent art exhibition exploring precisely this kind of issue: *La France: Images of Women and Ideas of Nation, 1789–1989* (catalogue published London, 1989). 'A political Marianne appeared first of all in 1637, as a patriotic Jewish princess in revolt against Roman invaders, in a play *La Mariane*, by Tristan l'Hermite. . . . The name "Marianno" also came up in the Midi with reference to opposition to the Jacobin Republic of 1792. It was the name given to the Republic of 1848, and after Louis Napoleon's coup it was taken up by a secret society, 'La Marianne'. After 1850 it was a name applied derisively to the Republic. Paul Trouillas, in *Le Complexe de Marianne*, thinks over the name itself with its references to the Virgin Mary, to St Anne, her mother, and to its familiar use as a diminutive for Mary. It chimes too with the Champ-de-Mars and *La Marseillaise*, with *mariage* and even with the battle of the Marne. It is at once respectworthy and familiar, warlike and comfortable, virginal and connubial. Trouillas concludes that her name alone answers to a variety of often conflicting desires, from the transcendental to the transgressive' (p. 27).

7. See especially Christopher Marlowe, *The Jew of Malta*, ed. T. W. Craik (London, 1966) II.iii and III.ii, pp. 38–57, where Barabas, a thrifty outsider spurned, like Lacheneur, after surrendering his wealth to an ungrateful overlord, uses the charms of his daughter Abigail to foment discord among his oppressors before turning to an armed insurrection leading to his death. As well as this plot-echo, the name 'Lacheneur', especially as it descends to the more sinister Jean, perhaps echoes that of the self-publicising criminal Lacenaire, hanged 1836, whom Foucault links specifically with the aestheticising and embourgeoisement of crime represented in fiction by Gaboriau.

8. In *L'Argent des autres* (Paris, 1874), Gaboriau treats the Commune contemptuously in passing, but his main fire is still reserved for the financial corruption seen as specifically characterising the Second Empire.

Notes to Chapter 5: Sherlock Holmes – The Series

1. For a magisterial introduction to the 'Holmesian' world, see William S. Baring-Gould's two-volume *The Annotated Sherlock Holmes* (London, 1968), which rearranges the canon in 'biographical' sequence and then scrutinises it for inconsistencies and cross-references, adducing a barrage of 'scholarship' in the process. One thing this does inform us about very clearly is a certain – indeed a Sherlockian – confidence that such researches will finally yield some indivisible objective truth. For the 'formulaic' approach, see most of the more seriously critical studies.

2. See Gaboriau, *Monsieur Lecoq*, p. 345: 'The race of great criminals is

dying out'.
3. See, for instance only, Dorothy Sayers, 'The Omnibus of Crime', in Winks, pp. 69–71.
4. George Lillo's 'bourgeois tragedy' *George Barnwell, or, The London Merchant* (1731), in John Hampden (ed.), *Eighteenth-Century Plays* (London, 1928), was still well remembered in 1861, being a favourite of Mr Wopsle's in *Great Expectations*.
5. See Doyle's autobiography *Memories and Adventures*, p. 95, for the drily prophetic reasons behind the invention: 'considering these various journals with their disconnected stories, it had struck me that a single character running through a series, if it only engaged the attention of the reader, would bind that reader to that particular magazine'.
6. See Umberto Eco and Thomas A. Sebeok (eds), *The Sign of Three: Dupin, Holmes, Pierce* (Bloomington, Ind., 1983), particularly the articles by Eco and Sebeok themselves, on Holmes's relation to the logician Charles S. Pierce's theories of deduction, induction and abduction, each dependent on a different type of syllogism.

Notes to Chapter 6: Sherlock Holmes – The Valleys of Fear

1. In *Naked is the Best Disguise: The Death and Resurrection of Sherlock Holmes* (Indianapolis and New York, 1974), Samuel Rosenberg establishes some useful links between Holmes and the wider throught of the time, but unbalances them with repeated exclamations of astonishment at their novelty, and with special pleading for a number of 'image clusters' not always clearly supported by the texts.
2. See Doyle, *Complete Adventures*, p. 161: 'His rooms were brilliantly lit, and, even as I looked up, I saw his tall, spare figure pass twice in a dark silhouette against the blind.'
3. See Doyle, *Memories and Adventures*, p. 81: 'I believe that if I had never touched Holmes, who has tended to obscure my higher work, my position in literature would at the present moment be a more commanding one.'
4. See Edwards, p. 353.
5. See Diane Johnson, *The Life of Dashiell Hammett* (London, 1985) pp. 20–1. The case of the 'Wobbly' Frank Little, murdered with the approval of the local Montana mine-owner and, perhaps, the help of Hammett's fellow Pinkerton agents, made a particular impression on Hammett, who had himself been offered money to do the job.
6. See Arthur H. Lewis, *Lament for the Molly Maguires* (London, 1965), and Wayne G. Broehl Jr, *The Molly Maguires* (Cambridge, Mass., 1965). While not exonerating the Mollies, both books show how Gowen fomented the conflict in order to destroy union power in the coalfields: his skilful manipulation of the situation, including McParlan himself, is described by Lewis, pp. 242–6.

Notes to Chapter 7: Detective Fiction and Ideas

1. See Porter, ch. 8, pp. 146–89; and George Grella, 'The Formal Detective Novel' and 'The Hard-Boiled Detective Novel', in Winks, esp. pp. 101 and 105.

2. For Israel Zangwill's career as a social writer and leading – later disillusioned – Zionist, see pp. xiv–xv of E. F. Bleiler's Introduction to his Dover Press edition of *Three Victorian Detective Novels* (New York, 1978) from which all subsequent references to Zangwill's *Big Bow Mystery* are taken. For Arthur Morrison's career as a very significant social writer – he was born in the East End docks and educated at the People's Palace (a forerunner of the WEA), for which he also worked – see Bleiler's Introduction to another invaluable Dover publication: Arthur Morrison, *Best Martin Hewitt Detective Stories*, pp. vii–xi. For a tiny segment of G. K. Chesterton's encyclopaedic cultural/political concerns, see n. 7 below. E. C. Bentley was a journalist who wrote leaders for the *Daily Telegraph*: otherwise his main claim to fame, apart from *Trent*, is his schoolboy invention of the haikuesque verse-form whose memorability depends chiefly on his typically British-eccentric middle name, Clerihew. (In parenthesis, Doyle, along with his literary aspirations – see n. 3 to Chapter 6 – often intervened courageously on behalf of victims of British law, from the obscure Oscar Slater to the dangerously notorious Oscar Wilde and Roger Casement.)

3. Winwood Reade's book *The Martyrdom of Man* (London, 1872) is a fascinating compendium of progressive atheism and bloodcurdling Social Darwinism, denouncing the Indian Mutiny despite the 'sickly school of politicians who declare that all countries belong to their inhabitants, and that to take them is a crime' (p. 504); and equally denouncing a Christianity which maintains that 'the soul of the poorest creature in the streets and the soul of the greatest philosopher or poet [the next page names Goethe as a supreme instance] are equal' (p. 517: the references are to the London, 1877 edition). *The Sign of Four* clearly imports a great deal of its mental equipment from such passages, from its description of the devilish Mutiny and its doubts about artisans' souls to Holmes's closing Goethean musings on his own potential superhumanity.

4. The original collections concerning these two figures, Arthur Morrison's *The Dorrington Deed-Box* (London, 1897) and R. Austin Freeman/Clifford Ashdown's *The Adventures of Romney Pringle* (London, 1902) are now hard to come by, but examples from each can be found in Hugh Greene (ed.), *The Rivals of Sherlock Holmes* (Harmondsworth, Middx, 1971), from which my references to Morrison's 'The Affair of the "Avalanche Bicycle and Tyre Co., Limited"' are taken. Further Dorrington and Pringle adventures can be found in Greene's continuations of the *Rivals* series (*More Rivals, Further Rivals*, etc.). The frame of the *Deed-Box* stories is that Dorrington has been forced to flee after attempting to murder the rich but naïve Australian who narrates the first adventure: the remaining stories are reconstruc-

ted from Dorrington's abandoned papers, but his eventual fate is left open.

5. Written in 1910–11, E. C. Bentley's *Trent's Last Case* was finally published successfully in New York (1913), after the very significant alteration of the hero's name from that of a vulnerable engine-part, 'Gasket' (with its *Genevieve*esque British-as-good-losers connotations) to the more 'trenchant' and upper-class-geographical 'Trent'. My references – including those to Sayers's Introduction – are to the Perennial Library edition (New York, 1978)

6. See 'The Mystery of Marie Rogêt', Poe, p. 417; and p. 52 above.

7. For a useful account of 'Distributism', with its Cobbett-inspired appeals to the notion of a yeomanry, see Dudley Barker, *G. K. Chesterton: A Biography* (London, 1973) pp. 258–9.

8. G. K. Chesterton, 'The Yellow Bird', in *The Poet and the Lunatics* (London, 1929).

Notes to Chapter 8: 'A Little Art Jargon'

1. See, for instance, Malcolm Bradbury and James McFarlane (eds), *Modernism, 1890–1930* (Hassocks, Sussex, and Atlantic Highlands, N.J., 1978) pp. 30–5, where Cyril Connolly is cited as dating modernism from 1880, Richard Ellman from 1900, Graham Hough from 1910, and Harry Levin from 1922.

2. See Frank Kermode, *Romantic Image* (London, 1957), esp. ch. 3, p. 46.

3. See, e.g., Henry James, 'The Beast in the Jungle' and 'The Aspern Papers'.

4. See Jerry Palmer, *Thrillers* (London, 1978) *passim*; Cawelti, pp. 95–6; Knight, esp. ch. 3 and 4; and Ernst Kaemmel, 'Literature Under the Table', in Most and Stowe, esp. p. 58.

5. See Raymond Williams, *Culture and Society, 1780–1950* (London, 1958) ch. 2, esp. pp. 32–6.

6. See Doyle's *Memories and Adventures*, p. 75, on one publisher's rejection of *A Study in Scarlet* as 'both too short and too long'.

Notes to Chapter 9: A Version of Pastoral

1. See W. H. Auden, 'The Guilty Vicarage' (1948), in Winks, p. 19; C. Day Lewis writing as Nicholas Blake, 'The Detective Story – Why?' (1942), in Haycraft, p. 402; George Orwell, 'Raffles and Miss Blandish' (1944), in *Critical Essays* (London, 1946) p. 143; William Empson, *Some Versions of Pastoral* (London, 1935) ch. 1. Orwell's 'cricket' image is actually applied to Raffles the thief, but in another 1944 essay, '*Grandeur et décadence du roman policier anglais*' (*Fontaine*, Algiers, 1944), the world of Holmes is regarded with an identical pastoral nostalgia. (See Patrick Parrinder, 'George Orwell and the Detective Story', in Larry N. Landrum, Pat Browne and Ray B. Browne (eds), *Dimensions of Detective Fiction* (Bowling Green, Ky, 1976) pp. 64–7.) It may be noted that apart from Empson the 1930s writers mentioned actually

crystallised their vision of the genre in the 1940s; and whenever they precisely date its 'grandeur' (only Orwell draws the line at 1918), they all contrast its past glories to the present rise of the thriller, which wins ambiguous admiration for being more realistic and/or more working-class, but is also viewed with deep unease for blurring moral boundaries which a greater familiarity with Dorrington and Pringle might have shown to be blurred already.

Though of an older generation and different political views, T. S. Eliot was equally fascinated by the detective form.

See Peter Ackroyd, *T. S. Eliot* (London, 1984): 'Detective fiction was his passion' (p. 67). Eliot reviewed (anonymously) some twenty-four detective novels in *Criterion* in 1927 alone; could quote Sherlock Holmes from memory (and borrowed significantly from 'The Musgrave Ritual' and *The Hound of the Baskervilles* in *Murder in the Cathedral* and *Four Quartets*); wrote an important introduction to Collins's *The Moonstone* (London, 1928; pp. v–xii); and was an avid reader of Chandler and Simenon.

2. See, for example, Porter, ch. 7; Knight, pp. 112–3; Roger Caillois, 'The Detective Novel as a Game', in Most and Stowe, pp. 8–9.
3. See particularly the current (1989) stream of television adaptations of Holmes, Wimsey, Marple, Poirot, Campion, Dalgleish and Wexford, all neatly ready to slot into such prepared overseas niches as the American PSB 'culture' channel's *Mystery*. The country houses also featured in the even more cultural *Masterpiece Theatre* (introduced by Alistair Cooke rather than Vincent Price) are the key part of the package; though of the series mentioned the excellent *Poirot* has honourably gone for Thirties Art Deco throughout.
4. See Knight, pp. 107–13.
5. See ibid., p. 116.
6. See Christie, *Agatha Christie: An Autobiography*, especially pp. 112–22, 359–66, 447–50.
7. This is often done: see Watson, ch. 13, 'The Little World of Mayhem Parva'; and David I. Grossvogel, 'Agatha Christie: Containment of the Unknown', in Most and Stowe, pp. 252–65.
8. *Ten Little Indians* became *And Then There Were None* in the USA. The vicissitudes of this most embarrassing of titles are somehow of a piece with the enormous lapse of taste around which the novel itself is constructed.
9. See R. W. Chapman (ed.), *Jane Austen's Letters* (Oxford, 1932) letter 100, vol. II, p. 401; and Jane Austen, *Northanger Abbey* (Oxford, 1923) p. 198.
10. This only applies in full to Wimsey and Campion: Innes's Appleby and Marsh's Alleyn are officially policemen, but much of their authors' stylistic energy is spent on differentiating their breeding from the simpler qualities of sidekicks such as Alleyn's indicatively named 'Brer Fox'. The American Carr does not enmesh his amateurs Fell and Merrivale so deeply in the English caste system, relying chiefly on rudeness and bluster to establish their social credentials.
11. The story appears in Margery Allingham, *Mr Campion and Others*

(London, 1939).
12. See Winks, p. 18.
13. See pp. 60–1 and n. 3 to Chapter 4.
14. See, for example, Sarah Paretsky, *Indemnity Only* (London, 1982) and *Deadlock* (London, 1984); and Gillian Slovo, *Morbid Symptoms* (London, 1984), *Death by Analysis* (London, 1985) and *Death Comes Staccato* (London, 1987), discussed on pp. 181–4.
15. See Michele B. Slung (ed.), *Crime On Her Mind: Fifteen Stories and Female Sleuths from the Victorian Era to the Forties* (Harmondsworth, Middx, 1977) pp. 14–17. Slung discusses the relative claims to priority of Mrs Paschal (1861?) and Andrew Forrester's Female Detective (1864), and points out that from then to 1901 'no fewer than twenty women detectives made their appearance'. (Though as Slung's subtitle indicates things didn't stop there, her earlier heroines are both more memorable and more active.)
16. See Christie, *Agatha Christie: An Autobiography*, pp. 448–9.

Notes to Chapter 10: The Hardboiled Heritage

1. See Porter, ch. 6. 2. See E. F. Bleiler's Introduction to his Dover edition of Gaboriau's *Monsieur Lecoq* (New York, 1975) p. xix, for the early reception and wholesale pirating of Gaboriau in America.
3. See Empson, p. 23.
4. See Winks, p. 19.
5. Both in Raymond Chandler, *Killer in the Rain* (Harmondsworth, Middx, 1966).
6. In Haycraft, p. 237.
7. Compare Knight, *Form and Ideology*, ch. 5, with his essay 'A Hard Cheerfulness', in Brian Docherty (ed.), *American Crime Fiction: Studies in the Genre* (London, 1988) pp. 71–87.
8. See Ross Macdonald, 'The Writer as Detective Hero' (1973), in Winks, pp. 179–87.
9. See Symons, ch. 14, 'Crime Novel and Police Novel', pp. 162–7.
10. For Highsmith's amoralism, see her remark that 'Criminals are dramatically interesting, because for a time at least they are active, free in spirit, and they do not knuckle down to anyone. . . . I find the public passion for justice quite boring and artificial, for neither life nor nature cares if justice is ever done or not' (quoted in Symons, p. 167). In fact, however, most of her novels are terrifying studies of the impossibility of such 'freedom'.
11. Added for Hare, *The History Plays*, to which my citations refer.

Notes to the Postscript

1. See the 1972 edition of *Bloody Murder* which predicts a declining market for 'the detective story' as a whole, though Symons consistently limits the phrase to the old-fashioned end of the genre. The concluding chapter called 'The Crystal Ball Revisited' in the 1985 revision regards

the prediction as largely confirmed (see p. 235).

2. Ian McEwan, *The Child in Time* (London, 1987). It is not a detective story, but the motif of the impossible quest for the missing child constitutes a similar (though less hopeful) indictment of the world depicted to the *Wunderkind*-quests discussed in the last chapter.

Bibliography

N.B.: This bibliography should be seen only as the first point of reference for anything quoted directly in the text. For other works mentioned, see the index and/or notes.

Aristotle, *On the Art of Poetry*, in Dorsch (ed.), below.

Auden, W. H., 'The Guilty Vicarage' (1948), in Winks (ed.), below.

Austen, Jane, *Emma* (Oxford, 1923).

Auster, Paul, *The New York Trilogy* (London, 1987).

Benjamin, Walter, *Illuminationen, Ausgewählte Schriften* (Frankfurt am Main, (1961).

Bentley, E. C., *Trent's Last Case* (New York, 1978).

Blake, Nicholas, 'The Detective Story – Why?' (1942), in Haycraft (ed.), below.

Bleiler, E. F. (ed.), *Three Victorian Detective Novels* (New York, 1978).

Boileau, Pierre, and Thomas Narcejac, *Le Roman policier* (Vendôme, 1975).

Bonaparte, Marie, *The Life and Works of Edgar Allan Poe: A Psycho-Analytic Interpretation*, trs. J. Rodker (London, 1971).

Bradbury, Malcolm, *The Social Context of Modern English Literature* (Oxford, 1971).

Brenton, Howard, *Dead Head* (London, 1987).

Carlson, Eric W. (ed.), *Critical Essays on Edgar Allan Poe* (Boston, Mass., 1987).

Carr, John Dickson, *The Hollow Man* (Harmondsworth, Middx, 1951).

Cawelti, John G., *Adventure, Mystery and Romance: Formula Stories as Art and Popular Culture* (Chicago, Ill., 1976).

Chandler, Raymond, *The Big Sleep* (London, 1979).

——, *Farewell, My Lovely* (Harmondsworth, Middx, 1949).

——, *Killer in the Rain* (Harmondsworth, Middx, 1966), including 'Killer in the Rain', 'The Curtain' and 'The Man Who Liked Dogs'.

——, *The Little Sister* (Harmondsworth, Middx, 1955).

——, *Raymond Chandler Speaking*, ed. Dorothy Gardiner and Kathrine Sorley Walker (London, 1984).

——, 'The Simple Art of Murder', in Haycraft (ed.), below.

Chesterton, G. K., *The Defendant* (London, 1914).

——, *The Penguin Complete Father Brown* (Harmondsworth, Middx, 1981).

Christie, Agatha, *Agatha Christie: An Autobiography* (Glasgow, 1978).

——, *Death on the Nile* (Harmondsworth, Middx, 1953).

——, *The Murder at the Vicarage* (Glasgow, 1961).

——, *The Mysterious Affair at Styles* (London, 1954).

——, *Peril at End House* (Glasgow, 1961).

——, *Towards Zero* (Glasgow, 1959).

Churchill, Caryl, *Serious Money* (London, 1987).

Collins, William Wilkie, *The Moonstone* (Harmondsworth, Middx, 1966).

Conrad, Joseph, *Heart of Darkness* (Harmondsworth, Middx, 1983).

Dorsch, T. D. (ed. and trs.), *Classical Literary Criticism* (Harmondsworth, Middx, 1965).

Doyle, Sir Arthur Conan, *Memories and Adventures* (London, 1924).

——, *The Penguin Complete Adventures of Sherlock Holmes* (London, 1981).

Draper, R. P. (ed.), *Tragedy: Developments in Criticism* (London, 1980).

Edwards, Owen Dudley, *The Quest for Sherlock Holmes: A Biographical Study of Arthur Conan Doyle* (Edinburgh, 1983).

Empson, William, *Some Versions of Pastoral* (London, 1935).

Foucault, Michel, *Discipline and Punish*, trs. Alan Sheridan (New York, 1977).

Freud, Sigmund, *The Interpretation of Dreams*, ed. and trs. James Strachey (London, 1954).

Gaboriau, Emile, *The Honor of the Name* (New York, 1902).

——, *Monsieur Lecoq* (New York, 1902).

——, *The Widow Lerouge* (New York, 1902).

Godwin, William, *Caleb Williams* (Oxford, 1977).

Greene, Hugh (ed.), *The Rivals of Sherlock Holmes* (Harmondsworth, Middx, 1971).

Hammett, Dashiell, *Red Harvest* (London, 1975).

Hare, David, *The History Plays* (London, 1984).

Haycraft, Howard (ed.), *The Art of the Mystery Story: A Collection of Critical Essays* (New York, 1983).

Holquist, David, 'Whodunnit and Other Questions: Metaphysical Detective Stories in Postwar Fiction' (1971–2), in Most and Stowe (eds), below.

James, Henry, *The Lesson of the Master and Other Stories* (London, 1984).

James, P. D. *Shroud for a Nightingale* (London, 1973).

——, *A Taste for Death* (London, 1987).

——, *An Unsuitable Job for a Woman* (London, 1974).

Jameson, F. R., 'On Raymond Chandler' (1970), in Most and Stowe (eds), below.

Jones, John, *On Aristotle and Greek Tragedy* (London, 1962).

Kermode, Frank, 'Novel and Narrative' (1974), in Most and Stowe (eds), below.

Knight, Stephen, *Form and Ideology in Crime Fiction* (London, 1980).

Knox, Ronald, 'A Detective Story Decalogue' (1929), in Winks (ed.), below.

Lacan, Jacques, 'Seminar on "The Purloined Letter"' (1956, trs. Jeffrey Mehlman, 1972), in Most and Stowe (eds), below.

McIlvanney, William, *The Papers of Tony Veitch* (London, 1984).

Mandel, Ernest, *Delightful Murder: A Social History of the Crime Story* (London and Sydney, 1984).

Morrison, Arthur, 'The Affair of the "Avalanche Bicycle and Tyre Co., Ltd"' (1897), in Greene (ed.), above.

Most, Glenn W., and William W. Stowe (eds), *The Poetics of Murder: Detective Fiction and Literary Theory* (San Diego, New York and London, 1983).

Murch, A. E., *The Development of the Detective Novel* (London, 1958).

Nicolson, Marjorie, 'The Professor and the Detective' (1929), in Haycraft (ed.), above.

Orwell, George, 'Raffles and Miss Blandish', in *Critical Essays* (London, 1946).

Ousby, Ian, *Bloodhounds of Heaven: The Detective in English Fiction from Godwin to Doyle* (Cambridge, Mass., and London, 1976).

Pederson-Krag, Geraldine, 'Detective Stories and the Primal Scene' (1949), in Most and Stowe (eds), above.

Pinkerton, Allan J., *The Molly Maguires and the Detectives* (New York, 1905).

Poe, Edgar Allan, *The Complete Poems and Stories of Edgar Allan Poe, with Selections from his Critical Writings*, ed. Arthur Hobson Quinn and Edward H. O'Neill, 2 vols (New York, 1946).

Porter, Dennis, *The Pursuit of Crime: Art and Ideology in Detective Fiction* (New Haven, Conn. and London, 1981).

Potter, Dennis, *The Singing Detective* (London, 1986).

Reade, Winwood, *The Martyrdom of Man* (London, 1877).

Rosenberg, Samuel, *Naked is the Best Disguise: The Death and Resurrection of Sherlock Holmes* (Indianapolis and New York, 1974).

Rycroft, Charles, 'The Analysis of a Detective Story' (1957), reprinted in *Imagination and Reality: Psycho-Analytical Essays, 1951–1961* (London, 1968).

Sayers, Dorothy L., 'Aristotle and Detective Fiction' (1946), and Introduction to *The Omnibus of Crime* (1929), both in Winks (ed.), below

——, Introduction to *Trent's Last Case* (undated), in Bentley, above.

Sidney, Sir Philip, *An Apologie for Poetrie*, quoted in Draper (ed.), above.

Slovo, Gillian, *Death Comes Staccato* (London, 1987).

Sophocles, *The Three Theban Plays*, trs. Robert Fagles (Harmondsworth, Middx, 1984).

Symons, Julian, *Bloody Murder: From the Detective Story to the Crime Novel*, rev. edn (Harmondsworth, Middx, 1985).

Tani, Stefano, *The Doomed Detective: The Contribution of the Detective Novel to Postmodern American and Italian Fiction* (Carbondale, Ill., and Edwardsville, Ill., 1984).

Todorov, Tsvetan, *The Poetics of Prose*, trs. Richard Howard (Oxford, 1977).

Watson, Colin, *Snobbery with Violence: English Crime Stories and their Audience* (London, 1987).

Wilbur, Richard, 'Poe and the Art of Suggestion', in Carlson (ed.), above.

——, *Responses* (New York and London, 1986).

Wilde, Oscar, *The Complete Works of Oscar Wilde* (London and Glasgow, 1966).

Williams, Raymond, *The Country and the City* (St Albans, Herts., 1985).

Winks, Robin W. (ed.), *Detective Fiction: A Collection of Critical Essays* (Englewood Cliffs, N.J., 1980).

Zangwill, Israel, *The Big Bow Mystery* (1891), in Bleiler (ed.), above.

Index